American Fiction, American Myth

American Fiction, American Myth

Essays by Philip Young

With a Foreword by David Morrell
and Introduction by Sandra Spanier

The Pennsylvania State University Press
University Park, Pennsylvania

Library of Congress Cataloging-in-Publication Data

Young, Philip, 1918–1991
American Fiction, American Myth : Essays by Philip Young; edited by David Morrell and Sandra Spanier.
With a Foreword by David Morrell and Introduction by Sandra Spanier.
p. cm.
Includes bibliographical references and index.
ISBN 0-271-02036-9 (cloth : alk. paper)
1. American literature—History and criticism. 2. Hemingway, Ernest, 1899–1961—Criticism and Interpretation. I. Morrell, David.
II. Spanier, Sandra Whipple
III. Title.
PS121.Y64 2000
810.9—dc21
99-053719

Printed in the United States of America
Published by The Pennsylvania State University Press,
University Park, PA 16802-1003

It is the policy of The Pennsylvania State University Press to use acid-free paper for the first printing of all clothbound books. Publications on uncoated stock satisfy the minimum requirements of American National Standard for Information Sciences—Permanence of Paper for Printed Library Materials, ANSI Z39.48-1992.

To Katherine Young:

his closest reader

Contents

Foreword

Scholars do make a difference. Back in the fall of 1965, I was a fourth-year English major at a small college in Ontario, Canada. My wife, Donna, a beginning high school history teacher, used her slim salary to pay our rent and put food on the table while I supplemented her income by working weekends at Sears in the heating and air-conditioning department (about which I knew nothing). Life decisions had to be made. For a long time, my ambition had been to write fiction, but the reality that few earn a living at it had begun to sink in. Moreover, Donna had recently discovered that she was pregnant. With the baby due in the spring, there wasn't much time to figure out how I was going to help support the three of us after I got my B.A. The practical choice would have been to go to work immediately, as Donna had, teaching high school. The trouble was, those delusions about wanting to be a writer kept nagging at me. Plus, I had this thing about Hemingway. I kept reading his work, trying to take a direction from him. I had recently turned to scholarship about him, and thus it happened that on a drizzly November afternoon, ensconced in the college's one-room library, I browsed the meager stacks and came across a critical book called *Ernest Hemingway.* Its author was Philip Young.

This is how it began:

> Jake Barnes, principal character of Hemingway's *The Sun Also Rises,* was reading Turgenev very early one morning while drunk on brandy in Spain, and he speculated that one day, somewhere, he would remember it all, and what he read would seem really to have happened to him.

I came to attention. The directness of Young's language, the feeling that he was sitting across from me, was something that I'd seldom encountered before. In poetry, sure: Walt Whitman. And in novels: *The Catcher in the Rye.* But hardly ever in non-fiction prose, and certainly not in most scholarly books of the time. By the mid-sixties, New Criticism had seized control of English studies. It had developed in reaction to a prejudice that the objective standards of the physical sciences were more valid than the subjectivity of traditional literary analysis. New Critics relied exclusively on an extreme close reading of a text. Nothing wrong there, except for the word "exclusively." To them, an author's background and culture were irrelevant to understanding a text. Indeed, some New Critics even insisted that putting an author's name at the front of a text was beside the point, a distraction. In consequence, the bulk of these critics, trying to be the literary equivalent of objective scientists, wrote in the flat tones that characterize most scientific writing. Their analyses often gave the impression of having been created by a machine.

Not so with Philip Young's *Ernest Hemingway.* Here was a scholar happy to be in the humanities. Unrestrained about showing his own humanity, he understood the importance of tone. The passage I quoted above was from the preface. When I turned to the first chapter, this is what I found:

> On the Place Contrescarpe at the summit of the rue Cardinal Lemoine, Harry remembered, there was a room at the top of a tall hotel, and it was in this room that he had written "the start of all he was to do."

I felt as if I'd been struck by something. Young's almost novelistic approach to criticism—creating a mood, setting a scene, and employing characters—affected me viscerally as much as intellectually. With the shock of recognition that Melville spoke of, I knew that, even with no more evidence than those few sentences, I had happened upon the work of a unique, powerful, and moving writer. How truly unique I eventually discovered, for Young, it turned out, was a specialist in a multi-faceted approach to scholarship called American Studies. The opposite of a New Critic, he believed that an author's background and culture *are* important to understanding a text. Not that Young disdained the rigid close analysis of a text. Not at all. In fact, he'd been trained in that method but had eventually concluded that if you do no more than analyze a text, you haven't gone far enough. There had to be a "so what?" The purpose of studying literature, Young believed, was to make us more aware of ourselves and our world, and anything was fair game if it achieved that purpose. Thus, he applied elements of Hemingway's biography and of American history and culture to his analysis of Hemingway's work. In a controversial move that I thought totally reasonable, he even borrowed from psychoanalytic theories to show how certain traumas in Hemingway's life, notably a bad wounding in World War I, accounted for the core of Hemingway's themes and the way he dramatized them. This was New Critical heresy in the extreme. It was also as lively as can be, and I couldn't wait to read more.

Too soon, I finished the Hemingway book, which as a bonus had a mind-opening new approach to Twain's *Adventures of Huckleberry Finn* to the effect that this was hardly the jolly kid-on-an-adventure book that most readers believed. There was darkness on that river. The cruel current was deeper than I had imagined. And there was depth in Philip Young. Committing my own New Critical heresy, I wanted to know who he was. Unfortunately the librarian had removed the book's jacket, with whatever biographical note it might have had. I searched the contents of the book, but the only biographical information I found was at the end of the preface, where I was told that the author had finished the book in New York City in November of 1952. Thirteen years prior to my discovery of it. A span of years more than half my then lifetime. Anything could have happened to him by now, I thought. But how to find out?

Surely Young would have written something further about Hemingway, I decided. So I checked the Guide to Periodical Literature, patiently going through the volumes that had been issued since 1952, looking in the subject section under Hemingway. A palpable hit: "The End of Compendium Reviewing," *Kenyon Review,* Fall 1964. My delight soon faded, however. Naively unaware of what the *Kenyon Review* was, I doubted that my small Canadian college would have it. Imagine my surprise when the librarian guided me to a section of the stacks and recent issues of the journal. The odds were so much against it. My life would have been so different. I grabbed the Fall 1964 issue, found an isolated table, and discovered that the essay in question depicted the adventures of a Hemingway scholar who had decided to catch up on his specialty and read all the books about Hemingway that had been published in the previous four years. Although the passages I quoted earlier from the Hemingway book had sung to me, I was in no way prepared for the disarming tone of the essay's first sentence. "Nothing like starting with a confession: this was to have been a whole lot grander."

I blinked. I read on. I started to laugh. "For a while," Young wrote,

> everything was fine. It took many weeks to accumulate the books; so long as they were coming in I felt no need to read them yet; I continually congratulated myself, and with reason, that I had at least been sane enough not to propose reading the torrent of essays and articles. But all of a sudden it dawned on me: maybe the flow, book-wise, was not going to stop. If not, it was the old story: in postponing my fate I was aggravating its severity. . . . An Immoveable Feat.

The librarian peered over her spectacles when I laughed again. I continued laughing as Young described how, on July 4, "despite a painful burn from a sparkler," he counted the books (32), measured the stack they formed (22 and 1/2 inches), then carried them into the bathroom and weighed them (18 pounds), after which he asked himself, "What to do next with this mess?" He spread them across the floor, arranging them in various piles, kicking over three beer cans in the process. "Toward morning I had one pile on one side of a wet rug, eight piles on the other, and went to bed feeling slightly better. On the Sabbath I faced up to them, started reading and (since I have almost no memory) making notes."

An unimagined world opened. You mean you're allowed to write like this? I thought. Criticism can actually be entertaining? But Young's style wasn't all that excited me. So did his attitude. The essay, carefully controlled, gave the illusion of presenting short-hand reviews on three-by-five cards. His praise and condemnation were unadorned. Commenting on an unfortunate volume, he wrote, "Things Taken Out of Context? Cross my heart: in context is worse. Assume no one at Press read this." Obviously, Young wasn't of the genteel academic persuasion. He felt so passionately about the study of literature that he had no patience with those who approached it with foolishness or pretension. In vivid terms, he said what was on his mind, and what was on his mind was common-sensical—or so it seemed until I realized that he had a gift for making the complex seem self-evident and, in contrast with a lot of criticism I had recently read, understandable.

I found a biographical note that told me Young was a professor at The Pennsylvania State University, and a crazy thought entered my mind. At home that night, I asked my wife, "What would you say to quitting your job? I won't be a high school teacher. We'll pack up after I graduate.

We'll go to Penn State. I'll enroll in graduate school and study with this man."

What would any wife in her circumstances have said? With a baby on the way? Facing four years of graduate student poverty? In another country? She agreed.

Dazed, I immediately wrote to Young, telling him how enthused I was by his work and how I wanted to come to study with him. Not rapidly, he sent a letter back, telling me that he couldn't recommend that any student ever go anywhere to study with anybody. Sometimes there were personality conflicts, he warned, or else the professor gets sick, fed up, and dies. Hardly what I had hoped to be told. "Well," I wrote in response, thinking that perhaps he'd been joking, "provided you haven't gotten sick or fed up, I'm going to do my best to come." So it was that in June of 1966, my wife, our recently born daughter, and I set out in a Volkswagen Beetle that contained all the possessions truly important to us: a bag of diapers and our favorite books. Crossing the border at Buffalo, we entered alien territory, journeyed south through New York State, saw our first mountains (the Alleghenies), and finally reached a wooded valley in the center of Pennsylvania: State College, and Penn State.

All because of Philip Young. But he wasn't on campus that summer. Asking around, I was dismayed to learn that what I had suspected was a joke about his getting sick, fed up, or dying, turned out to be somewhat true. When he had responded to my letter, he had been recovering from a heart ailment. Propitiously, though, the first book I saw when I entered a local book store was his *Ernest Hemingway,* handsomely reissued by the Penn State Press, with a new first and last chapter and a subtitle: *A Reconsideration.* Not that I was doing any reconsidering of my own. Reading the new version of his book that sweltering summer (it didn't matter that a faulty thermostat kept the heat on in our small apartment or that the moving van with our meager furniture had failed to arrive), I was captured anew by the magic of his ideas and his prose. I was where I belonged.

Of course, there was the not-so-slight matter of making Young's acquaintance and a good first impression. September came. Having heard that he'd returned to campus, I mustered my resolve, took a deep breath, and knocked on his office door. The spectacled man who opened it was short and sturdy, with a ruggedly appealing face, a sonorous baritone voice, and an amazing presence. In motion, he was graceful. Standing still, he planted himself solidly. Despite his bow tie, he reminded me of a welterweight boxer.

To my surprise, he recalled the letters we had exchanged. To *his* surprise, I had actually come all the way from Canada to study with him. He welcomed me to Penn State, and as we chatted in his office, he looked uncomfortable when I praised his work. His modesty, I realized, was one of the reasons he had tried to discourage me from traveling so far ("merely" in his view) because of him.

Thus began four of the most important years of my life. Hawthorne and Melville. Hemingway and Faulkner. The American Novel after 1900. I attended these and every other course he taught (what rapport he had with his students!). He directed my M.A. thesis on Hemingway. Eventually I became his graduate assistant. After the death of his first wife, Donna and I became involved in his household. "Professor Young" became "Philip," but in a semblance of objectivity, I'll keep referring to him by his last name. It was at his dining room table while he was away for the summer of '68 that I began my first true short story. Later, at that same table, I would start *First Blood.* The Rambo films that resulted from and changed the antiwar point of that novel give no idea of how many American themes learned from Young's classes were incorporated into the book. A cross-cultural myth study that Young recommended also made a difference. Long before Joseph Campbell's *The Hero with a Thousand Faces* was widely familiar, Young had discovered it.

He directed my doctoral dissertation on John Barth. He helped me get my first teaching job at the University of Iowa, where he had written a version of his Hemingway book as his doctoral dissertation. One of the first things I did when I got there was to go to the library and hold that dissertation in my hand. He changed my life. When he died in 1991 from complications of treatment for lung cancer, I felt as if my father more than my mentor had died.

Fortunately, he survives in his remarkable prose. A painstaking writer, he completed only five books: *Ernest Hemingway* (1952) and its revised version *A Reconsideration* (1966); *Three Bags Full: Essays in American Fiction* (1973); *Revolutionary Ladies,* a study of high-born Loyalist women during the American Revolution (1977); *Hawthorne's Secret: An Un-Told Tale* (1984), more about that secret later; and *The Private Melville,* about other secrets, these in Melville's life and work (1993).

He left a wealth of uncollected essays, however, enough for this further book. They illustrate the freshness of his ideas and the delight of his style. His prose resonates with his distinctly American voice. It has the feel of everyday speech (he once labeled an unsavory character in an early American novel "a jerk"), but at the same time, it is sophisticated: literary although never pompous, always playful. In a compendium review of scholarship about Hawthorne, he amused himself by gently ringing allusive bells. "Thus," he said, "thirty-one poetical quotations, twenty of them from *The Waste Land,* were stuck in the text like plums in the pudding. How many, O gentle reader (Wordsworth), can you pluck?"

He used a similar device in the evocative opening to "Hemingway and Me: A Rather Long Story."

> 2 July 1961 it was, late of a hot bright Sunday morning, when dark amid a blaze of noon the phone rang with the news of Hemingway's sudden departure from the living. All the instruments agreed: the day of his death was a hot bright day, and the shock of it ran the whole world round.

The most obvious literary antecedents are from Milton's *Samson Agonistes,* which Arthur Koestler echoed in his *Darkness at Noon:* "O dark, dark, dark, amid the blaze of noon, / Irrecoverably dark, total eclipse, /Without all hope of day." From Auden's "In Memory of W.B. Yeats": "What instruments we have agree / The day of his death was a dark cold day." And from Melville's famous statement about Hawthorne: "For genius, all over the world, stands hand in hand, and one shock of recognition runs the whole circle round."

At the same time, the passage is reminiscent of verse, its strong irregular rhythm comparable to the "sprung rhythm" that Gerard Manley Hopkins is known for. The beats we anticipate are postponed. The ones we don't anticipate hurry us along. There is an order to the irregularity similar to the effects of jazz (which Hopkins didn't know but which Young certainly did). The effect is sometimes achieved by punctuation—few other writers have so enjoyed using semicolons and colons, which for Young act almost as bars in a musical passage. Other times, the effect depends on inverted sentences and dropped words: " 'To T.S. Eliot, the master of us all'. Thus Fitzgerald in the front of his *Great Gatsby* when first it appeared in 1925." Or else Young employs the reverse—an absolutely correct, grammatically inclusive sentence, as in his reminiscence about his mentor, Austin Warren: "I can only tell how it was with me then, hoping that since Austin was so large a part of how it was, a little will emerge of how *he* was."

Those are both first sentences, by the way. Young was a master of them. "People who think about New England tend to get gloomy." "There never has been much doubt that something was very much the matter with Edgar Allen Poe." "Great ages of practically everything decline and fall, but it takes time." "It is a coincidence of uncertain import that the American Novel got off to its shaky start in the same year, 1789, as the American Republic." "Peter Rugg, the missing man, is nearly everywhere missing." To begin reading a Philip Young essay is to embark on a stylistic adventure.

For convenience (how he loved that kind of transition), my coeditor, Sandra Spanier, and I, with advice from Young's second wife, Katherine, have divided these essays into three groups that best represent his areas of interest: American Myth, Our Hemingway Man, and Scholar at Large. From his graduate-school days in the forties, long before hardly anyone else was exploring the topic, Young was fascinated with certain American stories and situations that can be loosely (for a new country) called American myths. He took these stories and situations, examined, analyzed, dug, and probed, using Jung, Freud, Campbell, and any other myth scholar that was of use to reach complex conclusions that seemed the last word until he went even deeper and found astonishing further significances about America and ourselves. The first of these essays, and his favorite of everything that he wrote, was "Fallen from Time: Rip Van Winkle." In the autumn of 1959, a few months after he joined Penn State's English department, he unveiled this essay at a colloquium he was asked to deliver to his colleagues. As Robert Frank, one of those colleagues, remembers, Young

> explored the tunnels and underbrush of the human psyche. The intellectual experience was itself a great gift. But the greater gift was to department morale. Gone was any sense of nobodiness. Here was a winner, someone any department, however ivy-walled or Gothic-windowed, would be proud to claim. And he was one of ours! In time Phil would be joined by other stars. . . . But he was the first to make us feel that we were, in my man Chaucer's words, "stellified."

"Fallen from Time" is here paired with "The Mother of Us All: Pocahontas" and a hitherto-uncollected myth study, "The Story of the Missing Man," providing a sense of the book about this powerful material that Young had ambitions to complete.

From the missing man to Our Hemingway Man. Young was one of those rare academics whose talents and interests projected him onto a larger stage: a public intellectual who was interviewed by Mike Wallace, appeared several times on the *Today* show, and had his essays published in such public forums as the *Atlantic Monthly* and the *New York Times Book Review.* This larger recognition was mostly because of his work on Hemingway. Young's theory was that Hemingway had been so traumatized by his severe wounding in World War I that the writer's fiction was to a great degree unwitting self-psychoanalysis. The theory so disturbed Hemingway that a long drama through the mail and through lawyers ensued as Hemingway tried unsuccessfully to stop publication of Young's book. Young supplied a narrative of the controversy in "Hemingway and Me: A Rather Long Story," one of the few previously reprinted essays included here: essential because it supplies information that Young takes for granted in his later and until now ungrouped Hemingway material. From being an involuntary adversary of Hemingway, Young eventually became an ally of the writer's widow, Mary, in her contest against A. E. Hotchner's bogus biography of Hemingway and in her need to have her late-husband's manuscripts catalogued. Relatively unknown versions of those scholarly adventures are included here, as are Young's analyses of Hemingway's *To Have and Have Not* and the pattern of the Nick Adams stories.

Young's pantheon place in Hemingway studies is described in Kelli A. Larson's 1992 review of Hemingway research, "Stepping into the Labyrinth."

> The repetition found in Hemingway scholarship over the past decade and a half is both astounding and disturbing. Admittedly, the sheer volume of criticism produced annually creates difficulties in keeping abreast of all the latest advancements in the area. However, a number of purported new studies point to, rest squarely upon, or steal shamelessly from classic explorations by authors such as Carlos Baker and Philip Young—without so much as a passing footnote, let alone the coauthor designation they deserve. Perhaps the Hemingway code and wound theory have pervaded our culture to the extent that they now fall under the realm of public domain, so that contemporary scholars are no longer obligated to acknowledge or even recognize their origins.

In "The Assumptions of Literature," Young thought of himself more as a scholar than a critic (he was equally skilled in both roles), and this book's final section, Scholar at Large, illustrates how far and wide and deep his research of American literature took him. Limits of space prevent us from including all the essays that have not been collected (footnotes will refer to other essays by him). But those that *have* been included are representative. His first published academic article—on Edgar Allen Poe—does not on its own contain the "so what?" that Young insisted the best criticism and scholarship provided. Still, when juxtaposed with "Fathers and Sons and Lovers" (a typically allusive Young title and an abridged chapter from the out-of-print *Hawthorne's Secret*), the essay shows how early in his career a psychoanalytic approach to literature had occupied him. "In Search of a Lost Generation" is a masterly discussion of writers in Paris in the twenties. After "Scott Fitzgerald's *Waste Land*," two poignant autobiographical essays alternate with two overviews of literary forms: "American Poetry" and "American Fiction, American Life." The poetry essay is of note because it doesn't strain to make discoveries or invent new interpretations. Instead it surveys American poetry in the first half of the twentieth century and orders this complex subject so that anyone coming new to it (an undergraduate, say, or the students in India to whom it was directed) will have a sound basis of understanding from which to proceed. When with a Ph.D. fresh in hand I was hired by the University of Iowa in 1970, the first course I taught was American poetry. "Not my field," I objected. "Too bad," my chairman replied. I wish I had known about Young's poetry essay (one of the few I somehow missed) because it would have been the basis for my syllabus and would have made my first year of teaching so much easier.

In matters of American literature, there have been few critics and scholars whose work transcends the academy. Van Wyck Brooks, Edmund Wilson, and Malcolm Cowley come to mind. Not many. Although each had different approaches, they were linked by a joy in the humanities, by a sensibility and a style that allowed them to communicate to the world at large. Once, at a faculty Christmas party, I asked an expert in an arcane branch of literary investigation to explain it to me. In a casual social setting, he found the task impossible, and I don't think it was because of the punch. Silently, I gave thanks for Philip Young and the example he provides to young scholars. There has to be a "so what?" "I get paid for saying the obvious," he used to tell me. Of course, what was obvious to him wasn't to the rest of us. And the way he spoke, like the way he wrote, would have left everybody at that Christmas party enraptured.

David Morrell

Introduction

The resemblance is uncanny. Three fresh-faced boys in the great American outdoors: one smiling straight at you, gripping the barrel of a shotgun in one hand and the hind legs of a dangling rabbit in the other, one showing off a string of shining trout, the third standing by a lake holding a tin cup, his other hand on his hip, grinning up into the sun. All three boys wear battered straw hats. The first is Huck Finn as rendered by E. W. Kemble in the 1884 illustration that was the frontispiece to the first edition of Twain's novel. The boy with the fish is Ernest Hemingway up in Michigan, circa 1913, who would write in *Green Hills of Africa* (1935) that "All modern American literature comes from one book by Mark Twain called *Huckleberry Finn*." The third is a teenaged Philip Young in upstate New York, who in his 1952 book that would be the first word in Hemingway studies, not only linked Hemingway's recurring protagonist to Hemingway himself but claimed that "the adventures of the generic Nick Adams are the adventures of Huckleberry Finn in our time." Young also illuminated the darker lower layer of the myth of carefree American boyhood and unfettered manhood that Twain and Hemingway were widely thought to celebrate.

Philip Young used the "goose-pimpling snapshot" of the young Hemingway as an illustration in his book when it was republished as *A Reconsideration* in 1966. (No other photograph of Hemingway is as revealing, he wrote: "It looks more like our image of Huck than any painting Norman Rockwell or Thomas Hart Benton has done or will do.") Young liked quirky coincidence and was keenly attuned to resonance. Of his own studies in what he called "American myth," he wrote in his preface to *Three Bags Full:* "In the traditional tales of Pocahontas and Rip Van Winkle I heard at the start faint gongs announcing no one knew what, subliminal murmurs in an unintelligible tongue." He must have relished his own youthful resemblance to Huck and the young Hemingway, for he displayed the framed images in his home as a triptych.

Unlike those Midwestern boys, Philip Young was an Easterner: born

May 26, 1918, in Boston to Katharine Pratt and Roswell Philip Young and raised in nearby Brookline and Wellesley Hills. Yet Young's affinity for the work of Ernest Hemingway may have been more natural than he realized. They had a lot in common. Both grew up in well-educated, well-to-do families in prospering suburbs of great cities, with access to urban excitement and bucolic escape. These were not stifled Main Street American lives. Hemingway reputedly called his hometown of Oak Park, Illinois, a city of "broad lawns and narrow minds" and left it happily and for good at the age of twenty. But from the playground of the Oliver Wendell Holmes Elementary School, the young Hemingway could look across the street to the architectural studio and home of Frank Lloyd Wright, who had made the city of Oak Park a showplace of his Prairie School modernism. Hemingway's father was a doctor, his mother a talented musician who designed and built with her inheritance the family's home, including a music wing for lessons and performances.

The mothers of Philip Young and John F. Kennedy (born a year earlier, in 1917) wheeled their sons in baby carriages to the same Brookline grocery. Young attended a private high school while living at home, frequenting the city for everything from haircuts to his hated dancing lessons. For the rest of his life Greater Boston was his favorite haunt—from Salem, where he found the documentation of Hawthorne's Secret in the archives of the Essex Institute, to Fenway Park. Young described his paternal ancestors as yeomen. (His great-grandfather's great-grandfather "as a Young Man Went West, reached Ohio, got the picture, and returned to upstate New York, where he ran an inn all through the Revolution"—"my kind of ancestor," he said.) But his mother's people were "gentry, no question." Her father was a Pratt, her mother a Loring. Young grew up with the impression that the Pratts were brains, the Lorings class. It was his genealogical research into the Loring line, traceable back to pre-Revolutionary Boston—they were Tories—that led to his award-winning 1978 book *Revolutionary Ladies* ("Being the surprising true histories of some forgotten American women—all beautiful, rich, and Loyalist—whose lives were shaped by scandal and turned upside down by the War for Independence"). Young's mother was a graduate of Wellesley College; Philip would follow his father's footsteps to Amherst College, where in 1940 he received an A.B. in English with honors in creative writing and philosophy. (His great-uncle James Bissett Pratt was a philosopher and friend of William James.) Before the United States entered World War II, Young briefly engaged in graduate study at Harvard and the University of Iowa.

Both the Hemingways and the Youngs were affluent enough to be "summer people" in unspoiled places where the American wilderness of Huck's day still could be easily imagined. Ernest Hemingway spent every summer of his youth but one (when he was at the war in Italy) at the family's cottage on Walloon Lake in northern Michigan near Petosky. Philip Young's family regularly summered, and summers still, at the cottage his grandfather built at Keuka Lake in upstate New York. (He even calculated that he had been conceived there.) Another resonance: Keuka is not far from Elmira, New York, where both of Young's parents were born and raised—and where Mark Twain retreated from his red-brick Victorian mansion in Hartford to spend *his* summers in the hills just outside town at his sister-in-law's Quarry Farm. It was in the breezy octagonal study built for him on a hill beyond the house, overlooking Elmira and the pastoral river valley, that Twain finished the manuscript of his *Adventures of Huckleberry Finn* in the summer of 1883.

A precocious boy who could read by the time he got to kindergarten, Philip Young likely made Huck's acquaintance early on. When asked once what drew him to Hemingway, Young recalled: "My first contact with Hemingway came as a kid when I found one of his books my father had hidden so I wouldn't read it. Naturally, I read it and that's partly how it started." Perhaps it was the war experience that later enabled him to read Hemingway so astutely and led him to see such significance in the wounding the author incurred as an eighteen-year-old Red Cross volunteer in Italy in July 1918. As soon as the U.S. declared war in 1941, Young enlisted in the Army and served for the duration as a first lieutenant in the 170th Field Artillery Battalion. In the winter of 1944–45 both Hemingway and Young were in the European Theater—Hemingway in the thick of the Battle of the Bulge as a war correspondent, Young in the Battle of the Rhine at Remagen, where the Allies finally established a bridgehead into Germany. As a forward observer, Young's job was to direct ground fire toward the enemy using complex trigonometric calculations from his vantage point in the rear of a flimsy three-man plane. Forward observers were reputed to have the shortest life span of any troops, and the work did not come naturally to Young, having once scored 17 percent on an open-book geometry test in high school and having been admitted to Amherst on the condition that he never take math. He did not have to be physically wounded to know about the traumas of war. For distinguished service he was awarded the Air Medal and two battle stars. After the war he returned to the University of Iowa, where he completed his Ph.D. in English in 1948. His dissertation was a study of Huckleberry Finn and Hemingway's Nick Adams, the prototypical "Hemingway hero" (Young invented the term that is now as generic as jello): "a twentieth-century American, born, raised, and hurt in the Middle West, who like all of us has been going through life with the marks his experiences have made on him."

The rest, as they say, is history, and I cannot improve on Young's telling of it. His classic piece "Hemingway and Me: A Rather Long Story," originally published as the preface to the 1966 *Reconsideration* of his landmark study, details the tragi-comic saga of his dealings with his reluctant subject. Thanks to the phenomenal success of his Hemingway book, in 1953 Young moved straight from the rank of adjunct assistant professor at New York University's Heights campus in upper Manhattan to associate professor at Kansas State University in Manhattan, Kansas, "without ever having achieved genuine assistant professorhood," as he tells us in his autobiographical "One Man's Apple." He spent good years at Kansas State, with stints as visiting associate professor at the University of Minnesota in 1955–56 and State Department-sponsored lecturer in India in 1957, but he later confessed that the Midwest ultimately remained "a section of the country that is to me alien and underprivileged." He was glad when a job offer appeared from the East.

Young accepted a full professorship at The Pennsylvania State University in 1959, was appointed Research Professor and Fellow of the Institute of Arts and Humanistic Studies in 1966, and in 1981 was named Evan Pugh Professor. He was the first professor of English to receive that distinction, the highest awarded by the University. He stayed for the rest of his life. His second growth roots were here, he wrote in 1985: "You can only do so much transplanting." In another of those quirks of fate he loved, it seems only natural that he should have found the central Pennsylvania climate congenial. Penn State's tradition in American Literature is long and distinguished. A plaque erected by the Alumni Association in front of the building housing the English Department and just down from the main steps of the library reads: "With the arrival in 1894 of Fred Lewis Pattee, for whom Pattee Library is named, Penn State became one of the earliest centers for American literary studies—at the time a controversial departure from English literature. A pioneering scholar in American literary history, Pattee was the first in the nation to hold the title of Professor of American Literature." Even after he officially retired in 1988, Philip Young continued to walk the half mile to his office on campus every day, intently at work on a book-length study of Herman Melville. "Two days before he entered the hospital for cancer surgery from which he never recovered my husband completed the manuscript for *The Private Melville*," writes Katherine Young in her Editor's Note to Philip Young's last book. He died on October 4, 1991, knowing it had been accepted by the Penn State Press. Katherine edited the book and saw it through to publication in 1993.

Philip Young was lively company and a gifted jazz pianist. An informal jazz group collected almost as soon as he arrived at Penn State, his colleague Robert W. Frank, Jr. (Chaucerian and trombonist) noted in his eulogy: "Not every English department could supply five choruses of 'Hello, Dolly.' " But Young was also a true scholar, whose greatest notion of fun was poking around in a library. Years before the Hemingway Collection was magnificently housed at the John F. Kennedy Library, a building of white marble and glass expanses designed by I. M. Pei and overlooking Boston Bay at Dorchester Point, Philip Young collaborated with Rare Books Librarian Charles W. Mann to inventory Hemingway's manuscripts at the invitation of the author's widow. On being locked in the vault of a Manhattan bank with over 19,000 sheets of Hemingway's papers, interspersed with plenty of disintegrating rusty paperclips and a few Key West mouse skeletons, Young claimed, "I could never be happier working than I was in that vault if I lived to be a hundred."

Young knew the value of a well-kept archive and maintained neat scrapbooks of notices and reviews of each of his published books. The collection is extraordinary. Tucked into one black pebbled portfolio cover is a letter (the original) from Malcolm Cowley to Philip Young dated April 20, 1951—a "private and interim report" responding to the manuscript that Rinehart had sent him to review. Cowley tells Young he is "brilliantly on the right track," but offers a number of qualifications and suggestions and additional deep-background-only information. A carbon of Young's letter of response is filed with it, as well as Cowley's full official reader's report—six single-spaced pages, with Young's responses to the critique penciled in the margins. The reactions of the then-unemployed former $200-a-year English instructor to the words of the great critic and man of letters range from the acquiescent and humble "OK: fix it" and "overstated by me" to the combatively self-confident "No can do." (I select for a general audience one of the more polite examples.)

Pasted on the brittle, yellowed, foot-square pages of a dark blue scrapbook are the announcements and reviews of *Ernest Hemingway.* The earliest prepublication notice predates publication by three years, for all the complicated reasons Young inimitably recounts in "Hemingway and Me." This first book by a young unknown was to be among the first three published in a new series of Rinehart Critical Studies alongside *Robert Burns* and *John Donne* by the distinguished scholars David Daiches, then Chairman of the Literary Division at Cornell University, and Austin Warren, Young's mentor at the University of Iowa. A note scrawled in ink across the bottom of that announcement from the February 1950 Rinehart catalog, signed "T." (presumably Young's editor Thomas Bledsoe) reads: "You're in good company, Moe."

An allusion to the Three Stooges is not the only extraliterary delight the scrapbook has to offer. The whole collection adds up to a vivid chronicle of the mid-century literary and cultural scene and places Philip Young's critical study of Hemingway squarely in the midst of it. His was one of the first two books on the author, published within a few months of each other. (Carlos Baker's *Hemingway: The Writer as Artist,* the other classic in the field, appeared in October 1952.) In its September 1, 1952, issue, *Life* magazine published complete and for the first time Hemingway's new novel: *The Old Man and the Sea.* Rinehart held up publication while Young wrote a new final chapter, making his the first book to take into account Hemingway's latest. This was News. Along with tidbits about Mamie Eisenhower, the Duchess of Windsor, and Senator Joe McCarthy, notices of the impending publication of Young's book even made it into the syndicated gossip columns of Leonard Lyons and Hy Gardner. When the book finally did come out on February 26, 1953, Charles Poore immediately panned it in the *New York Times.* "And," Young tells us with characteristic understatement, "that was the last bad review I saw."

By all measures—quantity, quality, visibility, geographical range, prestige of publication venue, noteworthiness of reviewer (Granville Hicks, Saul Bellow)—the reviews are astounding. The word "brilliant" echoes throughout the lot. I count seventy-eight reviews in publications ranging from *The New Yorker* and the *New Criterion,* the *Partisan Review* and the *Saturday Review of Literature,* to the Wichita *Beacon* and Elmira *Star-*

Gazette. Those are the domestic reviews. The international response fills another volume with another two dozen reviews clipped from the London *Times Literary Supplement,* the Belfast *News-Letter,* the *Litterair Paspoort* of Amsterdam, *Dagens Nyheter* of Stockholm, and a paper called *Sydsvenska Dagbladet Snällposten,* provenance undetermined. Around the globe, reviewers remarked on Young's refreshing style. "It is rare and exhilarating to come upon a work of literary criticism as penetrating and at the same time as lucidly written as this one" (Yorkshire *Post*). His book is "like a perfect dinner from champagne to brandy" (Houston *Post*). "Mr. Young is an exciting combination of efficient, thorough critic and enjoyable compere" (Calcutta *Sunday Statesman*).

It is arguable whether any single study of a contemporary writer could ever again match the magnitude of Philip Young's impact on Hemingway studies, on the way he is taught as well as read. Whether in agreement with Young or not, every scholar since has had to reckon with him. Beyond the soundness and brilliance of his argument, the timing of his book was perfect. In a unique convergence of circumstances Young could not have foreseen or hoped for, his book would ride the crest of public attention from the 1952 publication of *The Old Man and the Sea* through the 1953 Pulitzer Prize through the awarding of the 1954 Nobel Prize for Literature.

But if Young's study had not been the real thing, it would not have lasted as it has. And Philip Young was hardly a one-note musician. His subsequent books also got amazing press. All were profoundly original contributions to their fields. Published by Harcourt Brace Jovanovich, Godine, and Knopf, as well as the Penn State Press, the books of Philip Young continued to be reviewed (in addition to all the scholarly journals) in places like the *New York Times,* the *New York Review of Books, The New Republic,* and the London *Times Literary Supplement* by the likes of Herbert Mitgang, Leo Marx, and Malcolm Cowley. *Hawthorne's Secret* (1984), the last book published in his lifetime, attracted notice in *Newsweek* and *The Village Voice,* was praised by Doris Grumbach on National Public Radio, sparked a medical debate in *Scientific American,* and prompted an editorial in the *Los Angeles Times* headlined: "Hidden Meanings, or Just Cigars?" Young's friend "Jack" Barth wrote in a letter of September 28, 1984, "Good show, Phil. You write awfully well, handle massive homework lightly, and make your case w'out overstatement or prurience." Eight years after the book's publication and a year after Young's death, John Updike acknowledged Young's important and startling discoveries in a piece on Hawthorne called "Man of Secrets," published in the September 1992 *New Yorker.*

Ernest Hemingway wrote to Young's editor Thomas Bledsoe in his first letter, dated December 9, 1951: "I am a very serious but not a solemn writer." Philip Young could have said the same of himself. As the blurb on the dust jacket of *Three Bags Full* puts it: "Philip Young is an academic and suitably distinguished, but his professorship comes with a small *p*, as small as the *d* in democracy. His style is strong, his authority relaxed. . . . He knows a lot but is so utterly unimpressed with his own learning (to be professional is not necessarily to be cowed) that he can give it away to readers and entertain them at the same time." The *Boston Globe* review of *Three Bags Full* is headlined "A Breezy Scholar." Young knew that his breeziness sometimes could arouse suspicion. (And occasional irritation: "While undergraduates and other lay readers, for whom this book was apparently written, may enjoy Young's search for biographical scandal, specialists will find little here worthy of their attention," sniffed one academic reviewer of *Hawthorne's Secret.*) In "Iowa City, and After," Young remembered that even when he returned to graduate school following World War II, his mentor Austin Warren wondered if he were "truly *serieux.*" "I suspect that question dogged him, though he never spoke it; twenty years later he wrote me—apropos of something sassy I had written—'you are as serious "underneath" as anyone need be.' "

Philip Young's most memorable advice to me as a student writing a doctoral dissertation was to "keep the Ph.D. stink off it." He wore his learning lightly. His erudition was both broad and deep, encompassing Hawthorne and Hemingway, Brockden Brown and Barth. He was a scholar's scholar. But he also envisioned audiences beyond academe. Scholar at large, he addressed not only expert specialists but high school English teachers, Peace Corps volunteers, American literature students in New Delhi, readers of the *New York Times* and State College, Pennsylvania's *Town and Gown.* His is scholarship with a voice—scholarship that delights as well as instructs.

In editing this volume, David Morrell and I have aimed to keep intrusions to a minimum, annotating the essays only to refer the reader at relevant points to other works by Young or to identify the occasions for which various essays were written. At the end of each essay we have indicated the date of its original publication. A bibliography of the Essential Philip Young can be found at the back of the volume. Knowing that he was an inveterate reviser, if elements of one essay were repeated elsewhere, we have trimmed a few paragraphs for the sake of avoiding redundancy. In these and other matters we have consulted with Katherine Young, who in her Editor's Note to *The Private Melville* described herself as having been, in their twenty-five years together, her husband's "first reader and his most demanding critic." We are grateful to Katherine Young for her enthusiasm and help in all aspects of this project.

We wish to thank Beth Widmaier for preparing the index and helping with proofreading. We also thank Don Bialostosky, head of the English Department, as well as Dean Susan Welch and the College of Liberal Arts at Penn State University for their support of this project.

Sandra Spanier

I.

American Myth

1.

Fallen from Time: Rip Van Winkle

Black wing, brown wing, hover over;
Twenty years and the spring is over;
To-day grieves, to-morrow grieves,
Cover me over, light-in-leaves . . .
—T. S. Eliot, *Landscapes*

Washington Irving is reported to have spent a June evening in 1818 talking with his brother-in-law about the old days in Sleepy Hollow. Melancholy of late, the writer was pleased to find himself laughing. Suddenly he got up and went to his room. By morning he had the manuscript of the first and most famous American short story, and his best single claim to a permanent reputation.

Nearly a century and a half have elapsed, and the name of Rip Van Winkle, one of the oldest in our fiction, is as alive as ever. The subject of innumerable representations—among them some of the country's finest paintings—America's archetypal sleeper is almost equally well known abroad. Nor is his fame simply popular, or commercial. The most complex of poets, as well as the least sophisticated of children, are attracted to him.

But there is something ironic here, for at its center Rip's story is every bit as enigmatic as it is renowned, and the usual understanding of

Rip himself, spread so wide, is shallow. Very few of the millions of people who have enjoyed his tale would be comfortable for long if pressed to say exactly what "happened" to him, or if asked to explain what there is about the "poor, simple fellow" that has exerted so general and deep a fascination. Thanks to Irving, the thunder Rip heard is still rolling out of the Catskills. And it is pregnant thunder, charged with meaning. Perhaps it is time someone tried to make out what it has to say.

Irving's story may not be an easy one, but it can easily be told in such a way as to refresh the memories of those who have not encountered it of late. The hero of the tale was a good-natured, middle-aged fellow, and a henpecked husband, who lived with his Dutch neighbors in a peaceful village in the Catskill mountains along the Hudson River in the period immediately preceding the American Revolution. The trouble with Rip was that although he would hunt and fish all day, or even do odd jobs for the neighborhood women, and entertain their children, he was "insuperably averse" to exerting himself for his own practical benefit. He had lost an inheritance, his farm was in the worst condition of any in the vicinity and, worst of all, his termagant wife was always upbraiding him about these things. He had only one "domestic adherent," his dog Wolf, and one comfortable retreat, a bench outside the local inn, where under the sign of His Majesty George the Third met a kind of "perpetual club." But he was driven eventually even from this refuge, and forced to the woods for peace. On a fine fall day it happened.

Rip was shooting squirrels in a high part of the mountains. Tiring in the late afternoon, he rested on a green knoll beside a deep glen, with a sleepy view of miles of forest and the Hudson moving drowsily through it. Suddenly he heard the distant sound of his name. He saw a crow winging its way across the mountain, and Wolf bristling, and then he made out an odd figure, a short old fellow in antique Dutch clothes, coming up from the ravine with a heavy keg on his back. Rip quickly gave him a hand, and as they labored he heard distant thunder coming from a cleft in the rocks. They passed through this crevice, and came into a kind of amphitheatre, walled by precipices. Stunned with awe, Rip saw in the middle of the space a group of odd-looking men playing at ninepins. They had peculiar, long-nosed faces; all wore beads; one man, stout and old, appeared to be their commander. "What seemed particularly odd," however, was that "although these folk were evidently amusing themselves, yet they maintained the gravest faces, the most mysterious silence, and were, withal, the most melancholy party of pleasure he had ever witnessed." The only sound was the thunder of the balls as they rolled.

When the men saw Rip they stopped their play and stared at him as if they were statues. His heart turned within him; trembling, he obeyed his guide and waited on the company. They drank from the keg in silence, and then went on with their game. Soon Rip was trying the liquor, but he drank more than he could hold, and passed into a profound sleep.

When he woke he was back on the green knoll. It was morning and an eagle wheeled aloft. His gun was rusted away, Wolf was gone, and there was no sign of the opening in the cliffs. He called his dog, but the cawing of crows high in the air was the only answer, and he headed lamely for home. As he approached his village he saw no one he knew. People kept stroking their chins when they looked at him, and when he picked up the gesture from them he discovered that his beard was now gray and a foot long. As he entered town he saw that the village itself had grown. But his own house was in ruins, and a half-starved dog that looked like Wolf skulked about the wreckage and snarled at him. In town the inn was gone, replaced by an ugly building called Jonathan Doolittle's Union Hotel, and on the old sign King George's portrait had new clothes, and beneath it a new legend: George Washington. Even the nature of the people seemed changed: their drowsy ways had become disputatious. Rudely challenged to state his affiliations, "Federal or Democrat," Rip can only protest that he is loyal to his king, whereupon he is taken by some for a spy. No one knows him, the friends he asks for are dead, and he comes to doubt his own identity, until his daughter Judith's recognition confirms it. Now he is welcomed home, learns that his wife is dead ("in a fit of passion at a New England peddler"), and that he has unaccountably been gone for twenty years. The oldest and most learned member of the community is able to throw a little light on the story he tells: it is every twenty years that Hendrik Hudson, the river's discoverer, keeps a sort of vigil in the Catskills with the crew of the *Half-Moon,* and playing at nine-pins they make the mountains ring with the distant peals of thunder. And so Rip—idle, revered and happy—retires to his place on the bench at the door of the inn.

To be sure this story, though a fine one, is not perfect. For one thing, although Irving's Federalism enables him to jab in mildly amusing fashion at the shabby and pretentious republicanism of Rip's new village, such pleasantries come at the expense of our being wholly convinced of what he is trying to tell us—that Rip at the end is in clover. But the village is no longer entirely the place for him, and the fine old inn where he sits is just not there any more.

That this is, however, the rare sort of story that both satisfies and stimulates is shown by the fact that it has been so often retold, chiefly for the stage. There have been at least five plays—beginning with John Kerr's, which first appeared in Washington in 1829—and three operas, and several children's versions. But none has added anything important to our understanding of the story. Joseph Jefferson, who played the role of Rip for forty-five years in his own extraordinarily popular interpretation, had a few sensible ideas about the material, but he also failed to throw out much of the nineteenth-century baggage handed down from Kerr.

Though Joyce and Dylan Thomas have punned elaborately on Rip's name, most of the poets who have invoked him have done nothing much either to interpret the story or the character, and only Hart Crane has given him serious and extended attention. *The Bridge* (1930) has a section called "Van Winkle," whom Crane thought of as "the muse of memory"—or, as he put it to his sponsor, Otto Kahn, "the guardian angel of the trip to the past." Here Rip is a figure evoked from recollection of the poet's childhood and the nation's; since this is to introduce Rip in a thoughtful and promising way, it is too bad that very little is really done with him in the poem.

This is unfortunate partly for the reason that Rip is, potentially, a truly mythic figure. He is conceivably even more: *ur*-mythic. At any rate a primal, primeval myth has been postulated (by Joseph Campbell in his *Hero with a Thousand Faces*), and has been described—as "a separation from the world, a penetration to some source of power, and a life-enhancing return." And this is a most excellent description of what happens in "Rip Van Winkle." But no one has elevated the story to this status. As Constance Rourke wrote of it twenty-five years ago, the tale "has never been finished, and still awaits a final imaginative re-creation." If, then, we are to be helped to understand the story more deeply by considering what has been done with it, we had better consider what had been done with it before Irving wrote it.

II

In 1912 an eminent Dutch historian, Tieman De Vries by name, published under the title of *Dutch History, Art and Literature for Americans* a series of lectures he had delivered at The University of Chicago. A large part of this book is devoted to a monumentally inept attack on Washington Irving for having, in "Rip Van Winkle," characterized the Dutch people as stupid, lazy, and credulous. For his overwhelming blow the author, protesting great reluctance and sadness, brings forth the revelation that "Rip" is not the "original" story that Irving is "generally given credit for," anyway. The bitter truth, he discloses, is that the tale had been told before: its embryo is a myth about an ancient Greek named Epimenides, and this germ was "fully developed" by Erasmus (a citizen of Rotterdam) in 1496. In the myth Epimenides was sent to look for a sheep, lay down in a cave, slept for fifty-seven years and waked to find everything changed and himself unrecognized until a brother identified him. Erasmus used this story, then, to attack the Scotist theologians of his day (whom he thought asleep) as Irving used it on the Dutch. The fact that Irving never admitted knowing Erasmus's story, says De Vries, "touches too much the character of our beloved young author to be decided in a few words," and thus, having written the words, he drops the subject.

Quite aside from the foolishness about the Dutch, who are fondly treated in the story, there are two real blunders here. First, Irving's indebtedness was so widely recognized when the story first appeared as to be a subject for newspaper comment and, second, his source was not Erasmus, whose tale is in no sense "fully developed," but an old German tale published by Otmar, the Grimm of his period, in his *Volke-Sagen* of 1800. Actually Irving was on this occasion very noisily accused of plagiarism. At the end of his story he had appended a note in which he hinted that Rip's origin was "a little German superstition about Frederick *der Rothbart* and the Kypphauser mountain," but this has always been regarded as a red herring—so freely had he borrowed from another, and adjacent, story in Otmar: the folk tale of Peter Klaus. About the only thing Irving could do when this was pointed out he did: threw up his hands and said that of course he knew the tale of Peter Klaus; he had seen it in *three* collections of German legends.

There were probably still other sources for "Rip Van Winkle." We know, for instance, that in 1817 Sir Walter Scott told Irving the story of Thomas of Erceldoune ("Thomas the Rhymer"), who was bewitched by the Queen of the Fairies for seven years. "Doldrum"—a farce about a man's surprise at the changes he found after waking from a seven-year slumber—was played in New York when Irving was fourteen. It is almost certain, moreover, that Irving knew at least a couple of the other versions of the old tradition.

The idea of persons sleeping for long periods is, of course, very common in myth, legend, and folklore. So sleep Arthur and Merlin and John the Divine, and Charlemagne and Frederick Barbarossa (or Rothbart, or Redbeard) and Wilhelm Tell, and Odin (or Woden), the Norse (or Teutonic) god, and Endymion the shepherd, and Siegfried and Oisin and several dozen other heroes of many lands, as well as Sleeping Beauty and Bruennhilde and other mythical ladies—and also the protagonists of many novels, who wake to their author's vision of utopia, or hell. And there are several myths and legends about these sleepers which come pretty close to the story Irving told. Probably the best known of these concerns the Seven Sleepers. These men, natives of Ephesus, were early Christians persecuted by the Emperor Decius. They hid in a mountain and fell asleep. On waking they assumed that a night had passed, and one of them slipped into town to buy bread. When he got there he was stunned to see a cross over the gate, and then to hear the Lord's name spoken freely. When he paid for the bread his coins, now archaic, gave him away, and he discovered he had slept for 360 years.

This myth has spread widely, and found its way into books so different as the Koran, where Muhammed adapted it and introduced a dog who sleeps with the seven men, and Mark Twain's *Innocents Abroad,* where Twain tells the story at considerable length (and says he knows it to be a true story, as he personally has visited the cave). Somewhat similar myths are also known in the religious literature of the Jews. In a section on fasting in the Babylonian Talmud, to choose a single instance, appears one of several stories about Honi the Circle Drawer, lately thrust into prominence as a candidate for identification with the Tender of Righteousness of the Dead Sea Scrolls. One day Honi sat down to eat, the story goes, and sleep came; a rocky formation enclosed him, and he slept for seventy years. When he went home nobody would believe he was Honi; greatly hurt, he prayed for death and died.

The thing that is really vital to "Rip Van Winkle," but missing from all these other stories, is a revelation—some kind of mysterious activity witnessed by the sleeper. But such tales also exist—for instance, the Chinese story of Wang Chih, who comes upon some aged men playing chess in a mountain grotto, is given a date-stone to put in his mouth, and sleeps for centuries, finally waking to return home to practice Taoist rites and attain immortality.

More akin to Rip's is the misadventure of Herla, King of the Britons. He is approached by an ugly dwarf, somewhat resembling Pan, who tells him that he will grace Herla's wedding to the daughter of the King of France, and that Herla will in turn attend the wedding of the dwarf-king. At the Briton's marriage ceremony, the dwarf-guests serve food and drink from precious vessels. A year later, at the wedding of the dwarf-king in a mountain cavern, Herla takes a bloodhound in his arms, and he and his men are enjoined not to dismount until the bloodhound jumps. Some who try are turned to dust, but the hound never jumps and Herla thus wanders hopelessly and "maketh mad marches" with his army for the space of two hundred years. At last he reaches the sunlight and meets a shepherd who can scarcely understand the language the king speaks.*

Closer still, in one way, is the story of a blacksmith recorded in the Grimms' *Teutonic Mythology*. While trying to find wood to make a handle for his hammer, he gets lost; there are the familiar rift in the mountains, some mysterious bowlers, and a magic gift—this time a bowling ball that turns to gold. (Others who have entered this cliff have seen an old man with a long white beard holding a goblet.)

The most detailed precedent for Irving, however, and beyond a doubt his principal source, is the tale of Peter Klaus, which appeared in Otmar's collection.† This is a story of a goatherd from Sittendorf who used to pasture his sheep on the Kyfhauser mountain in Thuringia. One day he discovered that a goat had disappeared into a crack in a cliff and, following her, he came to a cave where he found her eating oats that fell from a ceiling which shook with the stamping of horses. While Peter stood there in astonishment a groom appeared and beckoned him to follow; soon they came to a hollow, surrounded by high walls into which, through the thick overhanging branches, a dim light fell. Here there was a rich, well-graded lawn, where twelve serious knights were bowling. None of them said a word. Peter was put to work setting pins.

*This is the only story of its kind, except for "Rip," that can be attributed to anyone—in this case to Walter Map, author of the early thirteenth century *De Nugis Curialium* ("Courtier's Trifles"), in which it appears. An intolerant but witty feudal aristocrat, probably Welsh, Map is best known for his "Dissuasion from Matrimony," long attributed to a Latin writer of a thousand years before him. In this essay he counsels young men that women are monsters and vipers (do not look for exceptions, he says: "Friend, fear all the sex"). Thus Map provides a precedent both for Rip's adventure and for Irving's whimsical antifeminism. It is very doubtful, however, if not impossible, that Irving knew of him; Herla's story has been cited as the true source of "Rip Van Winkle," but Map's book was not available to Irving until some three decades after the Irving story had been published.

†Otmar's book is very hard to come by, but Henry A. Pochmann's "Irving's German Sources in *The Sketch Book*," *Studies in Philology* XXVII (July 1930), 489–94, prints the most relevant portions of it.

At first his knees shook as he stole glimpses of the silent, long-bearded knights, but gradually his fear left him, and finally he took a drink from a tankard. This was rejuvenating, and as often as he felt tired he drank from the vessel, which never emptied. This gave him strength, but sleep overcame him nonetheless, and when he woke he was back at the green spot where he grazed his goats. The goats, however, were gone, and so was his dog. There were trees and bushes he couldn't remember, and in bewilderment he went into Sittendorf, below him, to ask about his herd.

Outside the village the people were unfamiliar, differently dressed and strange-spoken. They stared at him and stroked their chins as he asked for his sheep; when involuntarily he stroked his own chin he found that his beard had grown a foot long. He went to his house, which was in decay, and there he saw an emaciated dog which snarled at him. He staggered off, calling vainly for his wife and children. The villagers crowded around him, demanding to know what he was looking for, and when he asked about old friends he learned that they were dead. Then he saw a pretty young woman, who exactly resembled his wife, and when he asked her father's name she answered, "Peter Klaus, God rest his soul. It is more than twenty years since . . . his sheep came back without him." Then he shouted, "I am Peter Klaus, and no other," and was warmly welcomed home.

Since this elaborate parallel with Irving epitomizes the process whereby a national literature adapted foreign materials and began to function, it is somewhat appropriate that our first short story should owe so large a debt to a European source. But it is not at all clear why this *particular* story should have come down to us across a span of some twenty-five centuries—from the time, say, of Epimenides. Some of its charm is obvious; the idea of falling clean out of time, for instance, must be universally fascinating. But the very heart of "Rip Van Winkle," and of "Peter Klaus"—the strange pageant in the mountain—is still, from whatever version of it may be the earliest on down to the present time, enigmatic.

In the scene with the "dwarfs"—to focus again on Irving—it is not even clear what is going on. When the silent men of outlandish appearance and their leader go through their motions, the feeling is very strong that their actions are intended to convey something. But what? They are bowling, of course, and producing the sound of thunder, but why are they doing this? Why are they so sad and silent as they do it? Why so odd-looking? And why does Rip's participation cost him a generation of his life? The action is fairly pulsing with overtones: the men are speaking in signs; their motions cry out for translation as vigorously as if this were, as it seems, some strangely solemn charade. The question, which seems never even to have been asked, is what are we to make of this thundering pantomine? What have the gods to impart?

The notion that somewhere in the story lurks a secondary, or symbolic, meaning is by no means new. Walter Map, for instance, intended the latter part of his story about Herla to be a satire on the court of King Henry II, which he thought unstable. Erasmus, as already noted, attacked the Scotists through his; and the Talmud draws a moral from Honi's lonely end: "Either companionship or death." More interesting, however, is Arnold Toynbee's interpretation of "Rip Van Winkle" in the third volume of his *Study of History.* There is likely to be, he feels, something "old-fashioned" about any given colonial ethos, and his theory comes to a generalization: "Geographical expansion [of a civilization] produces social retardation." Toynbee thinks Rip an expression of his principle, the long sleep symbolizing the slumber of social progress in a newly settled place. Irving "was really expressing in mythological imagery the essence of the overseas experience. . . ."

The trouble with the interpretations of Map, Erasmus, and the Talmud is that they are forced and arbitrary, and the trouble with Toynbee's is that the story doesn't fit the theory it is supposed to express. If we ever had a period during which social progress was not retarded then it was exactly the period Rip slept through. In that generation we were transformed from a group of loosely bound and often provincial colonies into a cocky and independent republic with a new kind of government and—as the story itself makes clear enough—a whole new and new-fashioned spirit. In order to fit the thesis Irving must have had Rip return to a village where nothing much had happened or changed, and thus he must have written a different story. But he chose instead to write a story on the order of the myth about Honi the Circle Drawer who, according to one tradition, slept through the destruction of the First Temple and the building of the second, or like the one about the Seven Sleepers, who slept through the Christian revolution.* In all these tales the startling de-

*Indeed Irving may have got some specific ideas from the Seven Sleepers myth, for there the surprising changes in the speech of the people, and the prominent new sign over the gate of the town, are precedents for two of the very few important details to be found in "Rip" but not in "Peter Klaus." Elsewhere there is an exact precedent for the form Irving's change of signs took. In the famous *New England Primer,* with its alphabetical rimes ("In Adam's fall we sinned all"), a

velopments that have taken place during the sleep are a large part of the "point." And even if to Toynbee nationalism is—and was even in eighteenth-century America—a thoroughly deplorable thing, it was not a sign of social retardation.

Since such explanations as these will not help much more than the poets and playwrights have done to show us what is going on in "Rip Van Winkle," and since there is nowhere else to look, we are forced at long last to squint for ourselves through that crevice in the mountain. There, in the shadows, lurk figures and images which take us back, along a chronological line, to a time before the beginnings of recorded history. And if we could identify and understand these figures and images we should have, finally, the answers to most of our questions.

Many editions of Irving's story carry as an epigraph some lines he took from the seventeenth-century poet William Cartwright:

> By Woden, God of Saxons,
> From whence comes Wensday, that is Wodensday,
> Truth is a thing that ever I will keep
> Until thylke day in which I creep into
> My sepulchre—.

The most plausible reading of these lines is: "By God it's a true story I'm telling." But this makes Irving's two notes—in which he calls this a true tale—redundant. Less simply read, it might be the story itself saying, "By God, I'll keep to myself the truth about this thing as long as I live." At any rate, it is either a curious coincidence or an obscure clue that, in swearing by Woden, Irving has pointed to the remotest origins of his story that can be uncovered. To bare these origins would be to force the story, at last, to give up its secrets.

Here is a grab bag of traditional elements—folk, legendary, and mythic. The green knoll on which Rip sits when he hears his name has behind it the Green Mounds of Irish fairy tales—often prehistoric burial mounds. It is an appropriate spot for his bewitching and approximate to the "buried men" he is about to visit. Magic potions and sacred drinks are so standard in mythology, folklore, and religion as to suggest parallels

woodcut of King George that appeared in early editions eventually became very smudged; when this happened the portrait began to carry the name of our first President ("By Washington, great deeds were done").

automatically as Rip plays Ganymede, wine-pourer to the gods. A less familiar little tradition lies behind those dogs, which Rip and Peter find barely and implausibly alive after so many years—this takes us all the way back to Odysseus, returning after a generation's absence to find his dog Argos in Ithaca, still half-alive and lying on a heap of dung.

But the most important recognition in Irving's story concerns the identity of the men Rip meets in the mountain, and of their leader. These are "Hendrik Hudson" and his crew.* The blacksmith and Peter Klaus never identify their strange mountain men, and the unnamed leaders never appear. Nevertheless, it is not hard to guess with considerable assurance of being right both who they are and by whom they are led. It was the Odensberg that the blacksmith entered, and the Kyfhauser that Peter wormed his way into; it is in the Odensberg, according to legend, that Charlemagne and his knights are sleeping, and the Kyfhauser where sleep Frederick Barbarossa and his.† Hudson, then, is playing the role of the great kings of European countries, as Arthur plays it in England, and is a survival of this tradition. This recognition opens the door.

Part of the Barbarossa legend, which is better known and more detailed than the one of Charlemagne, concerns the conditions under which he can return to active life. Around the Kyfhauser a flock of ravens is said to fly, and each time the king wakes he asks if they are still there (they are, and this means the time has not come). Another important detail of the story is his beard: it is extraordinarily long already, and when it has grown three times around the table where he sits, his time will have come. It is very likely, then, that the black wings hovering over Rip just before he enters the mountain, and just after he emerges into consciousness, are the ravens of Barbarossa—just as the beards which are prominent in his story and Peter's (although the natural enough consequences of not shaving for twenty years) come down to us from this legend.

But the most important detail of all is a game, common to so many

*It should, of course, be "Henry": Hudson sailed from Holland but was English. Of all the people Irving could have put in the Catskills, however, Hudson was a fine choice, not only because the river below him was named for him and discovered by him, but because he was (in 1611 on another trip) the victim of a mutiny near Hudson Bay, was abandoned there, and disappeared for good. Thus he is like the heroes of myth and legend who sleep in mountains; no one knows where, or if, he was buried, and it is easier to think of him as not entirely dead.

†This is clear in the story that lies, in Otmar's collection, adjacent to the one of Peter Klaus—the "little German Superstition about Frederick *der Rothbart*" that Irving claimed as the origin of "Rip." It is almost certain, then, that Irving knew who led the knights Peter saw, and who Hudson's most immediately ancestor was. How much more he may have known about the origins of the materials he was borrowing is very difficult to say.

of these stories—the Chinese and Japanese versions, and Peter Klaus and the blacksmith and Rip. And the fact that the game in the stories that primarily concern us here is always bowling, which makes the sound of thunder, gives the whole show away: we are dealing, ultimately, with the gods, and in the farthest recess of this cave the figure with the red beard (to represent lightning), that helped to identify him with Frederick the Redbeard, is the god of thunder—Thor, God of Saxons, whence comes Thorsday, that is, Thursday.

More clearly the prototype of all these sleeping heroes, however, is the magnificently white-bearded Woden, or Odin, the god of the dead whom Cartwright swore by. In the legend about Charlemagne, the people who saw the king described him as a man with a white beard, and the name of the mountain Charlemagne inhabits, the Odensberg, suggests all by itself his ancestor. But the fact that the blacksmith on the Odensberg is in search of wood for a handle to an instrument of power which was the very emblem of the god of thunder, a hammer, suggests Thor just as strongly. So thoroughly have the two gods been confused in these myths that the king who is buried in Odin's mountain has in some stories the red coloring and the red horse that are really appropriate to Thor. On this horse the god issues from the mountain with his men, every so-many years, and in this activity he is again Odin, the leader of the Wild Hunt.

These confusions between Thor and Odin are not surprising, since the two figures are confused in Norse mythology itself. Although Thor was the son of Odin, he was also sometimes an older god than Odin; often he was a god superior to Odin, and sometimes they were thought of as exactly the same god. The direct ancestor of the Hudson Rip saw, then, was a Thor who has many of the attributes of Odin, and recognizing this takes us to the source of the traditions out of which Irving's scene is principally compounded. Recognizing these traditions, in turn, enables us to understand the subliminal richness of its materials, buried under the detritus of centuries.

The ravens which fly about the Kyfhauser, and the crows and eagle of the Catskills, are lineal descendants of the ravens Thought and Memory who sat on Odin's shoulder and kept him informed, or of the eagle that hovered over Odin's own retreat, or of the flight of ravens, "Odin's messengers" (without whose message Frederick cannot emerge)—or of all three. The dogs in the stories, mixing Greek myth with Teutonic, are progeny of the wolves Geri and Freki who sat at Odin's feet, or of the totem wolf which hung over the west door of his residence—in honor of which ancestry Rip's dog gets his name, Wolf. The drink which both invigorated and overpowered Rip is the same drink Barbarossa's knights gave Peter; it belongs also in the goblet Charlemagne was seen holding, and, despite all the magic drinks of folklore and myth, it is ultimately "Odin's mead," from which Odin got wisdom, and inspired poets; it was a magic draft related to the drink always available in the Abode of the Blest, the drink that rejuvenates, and obliterates all sorrow.

In a like manner, the odd appearance of Hudson's crew, those ugly, drab, short and curious creatures (one fellow's face is comprised entirely of his nose) are echoes of the dwarfs Herla met—although those dwarfs also looked like Pan, mixing Greek and Teutonic (and probably Welsh) mythology again. But Hudson's men get their appearance from the Night-Elves who made Thor's hammer—those ugly little long-nosed people, dirty-brown in color, who lived in caves and clefts. Beneath this effective disguise the crewmen of the *Half-Moon* are really the knights of Barbarossa and Charlemagne, who are the brave dead warriors brought back from the battlefields by the Valkyries to Odin's hall of the dead: Rip has really been in Valhalla and seen the slain collected around their god, who by the old confusion is now Thor, whose men they have become. The reason for the oddness of their behavior—their melancholy and their lacklustre stares—has become completely obvious, if indeed it was not before: they are dead. And one of Odin's chief characteristics, his extreme aloofness, accounts for the fact that Rip got but a glimpse of their leader, while neither Peter nor the blacksmith ever saw him at all.

Why such pagan gods should have been imagined as sleeping in mountains can be plausibly explained. When converted to Christianity, the people who had worshipped these figures could not quickly and completely reject the faith of their fathers. To them the outmoded gods lingered on, wandering, sleeping, and appearing infrequently. Later, vanished but actual heroes like Charlemagne, Frederick, Sir Francis Drake, Prince Sebastian of Portugal, and Arthur, were given attributes of the earlier gods. It was most common as well to place them in a mountain, where they were in earth, like the dead, but not under it—not under level ground, that is—like the really dead. Here they are sequestered in their slumbers, but the gods can be thought of as not entirely departed, and the heroes as in a position to return.

Occasionally mortals get to visit the legendary heroes who have taken over the attributes of vanished gods. When this happens, the visitor suffers a magic sleep and a long lacuna in his life: he has lapsed into a pagan world, got himself bewitched, and trafficked with a forbidden god. The punishment is severe. Thus Herla lost everything and Peter lost his flock, wife, home, and twenty years of life—though Rip, to be sure, in Irving's half-convincing happy ending, doesn't suffer so badly. The reason for the punishment is nevertheless clear: it is Christianity's dire objection to traffic with such cults as attached to those gods, as with any intercourse with fairies. This centuries-old element of the story is an historical, symbolic, and didactic expression of the church's long struggle with paganism—and has nothing to do with any social retardation of progress in colonies. Look what happened to Herla and Peter, Christian instruction could say. They were kind and ingenuous men. What then could happen to you? And then because the story is compelling in its own right it survives past the need for it, even after the knowledge of its purpose is centuries forgotten.

Is there any other connection between the visit and the great changes that follow in the life of the man who made it? And what are these visitors doing where they are not supposed to be? The sleeping gods and heroes could be described, and have been, without any mortal to intrude on them, and it doesn't look as though the mortals had just happened in: most of them appear to have been approached and led. And Rip was called by name.

Almost all of the protagonists of these stories, if they witnessed anything within the mountain, saw some kind of game. The fact that the origins of many games fade into ritual and ritual dance suggests that the games in these legends and myths might have their origin in some rite. And some authorities (Jane Harrison and Lord Raglan are notable examples) believe that all myths have their origin in ritual—that a myth is never a folk-explanation of natural phenomena, or anything of the sort, but a narrative that was once linked with a ritual—is the story, in other words, which has outlived the ritual, that the ritual once enacted. Frazer had a more moderate view, and felt that there is a *class* of myths which have been dramatized in ritual, and that these myths were enacted as magical ceremonies in order to produce the natural effects which they describe in figurative language. This hypothesis has it further that the core of such a myth traces back, finally, to the divinity who is imagined to have founded the rite. The actors are simply impersonating an activity of the originator and worshipping him in this way, his acts being the prototype of the rite. Gradually, then, the rite may be performed more out of piety than from any belief in its efficacy, and finally may be forgotten while the myth endures.

Whatever the merits of this theory one thing seems fairly sure: if it explains the origins of any myths, Rip descends from one of them. The bowlers of the Catskills are impersonating a disguised Thor, in a figurative or symbolic way, in his principal role as God of Thunder, and the actions of these resurrected men are the means of their worship. The solemnity Rip and Peter felt, in the presence of a mystery, is entirely appropriate to so sacred and secret an occasion. "Rip Van Winkle," then, is our version of a myth that survives as a description of a nearly forgotten ceremony in the worship of Thor for the production of rain. It proceeds by a symbolic imitation of how rain is made. The ritual is of the magical sort, and is intended to influence nature through the physical sympathy, or resemblance, between the ceremony and the effect it is supposed to produce.* Indeed the story is an example of what Robert Graves has called "true myth": it is an instance of "the reduction to narrative shorthand of ritual mime."

Exactly *why* Rip was allowed to witness this mystery is a secret which, since he was ignorant of the reason himself, he has been able to keep for many generations. So, in all likelihood, was Irving unaware of the original reason for the outsider's presence at the ceremony: even by Peter Klaus's time the myth had so badly deteriorated into folklore that only the fragments we are deciphering remained. But the secret is out by now: Rip and Peter were initiates. Rip goes right through the steps. While he sits dreamily and alone on the green knoll the period of preliminary isolation passes; then he is summoned by name. Helping to carry the heavy keg up the side of the ravine, which he may have had to volunteer to do, is a sort of test. There followed a kind of procession, and something like a vigil, and finally the experience of communication with the divinity and his disciples. Rip is even given a magic drink, which as a novice he is first required to serve, and after this he is plunged into the magic sleep. When he wakes he is in a new phase of life, and on this level the great changes he finds about him are symbols of the changes in him, and of the differences in his situation, now that he is initiate.

Rip has also been reborn in another, reinforcing way, for the imagery

*The thunder that Thor made came ordinarily from the roar of his chariot, of course, but the method described in the myth Irving drew on is by no means unknown. Grimm reported that on hearing thunder North Germans were likely to remark, "the angels are playing at bowls"; and in our own country there is a close parallel in the mythology of the Zuni Indians of New Mexico, whose warriors when they die go off to make lightning in the sky, where rainmakers cause thunder with great "gaming stones."

of his emergence into a new life inevitably and unavoidably suggests an issue "from the womb." This concept, which is often thrown about gratuitously, really urges itself here, for Irving's description of the entrance to the mountain, taken from "Peter Klaus," is extremely arresting—almost as pointed, say, as accounts anthropologists have given of pits dug in the ground by primitive tribesmen, and trimmed about the edges with overhanging shrubbery (which ditches the men dance about in the spring, while brandishing their spears and chanting that these are no ditches, but what they were built to represent). The imagery is the same when Rip is led eerily through the ravine till he comes to the bottom of a hollow, surrounded by perpendicular precipices, over the brinks of which hang the branches of trees.

From this setting he is delivered into his old age. Ripe for escape before, he has experienced an escape only one step short of death. Apparently well into middle age, and saddled with a wife who had completely lost her desirability, he laid down his gun and entered the mountain. Here he witnessed some symbolical activity—which, in the severely censored form of the pins and bowling balls, has overtones of human, as well as vegetable, fertility—and he saw it all as joyless and melancholy. Magically confirmed in his own feeling about the matter, he drank, slept like a baby, and was released into the world he had longed for—into an all-male society, the perpetual men's club that used to meet at the inn, which his wife can no longer violate as, unforgivably, she had done before. His gun is ruined and useless, and his wife is gone. But it makes no difference now; he has slept painlessly through his "change of life."

The trouble with this story as some kind of "male-menopause myth" is that the reading is partly based on a misinterpretation attributed, perhaps unfairly, to Rip. Lacking the information we have, he made a mistake: the men were lifeless and unhappy at their bowling because they were dead. More than that, they were still the followers of Thor, whose sign was lightning and whose emblem was a hammer. Thor was god of power, and of human as well as vegetable fertility. He was god of the vital moistures in general, an ithyphallic, not a detumescent, god. Even dead, his worshippers made a great deal of noise in his service. In short, the bowling which sends thunder across the Catskills is violently masculine symbolic activity in a very feminine mountain. And in this last vague but massive symbol is a final irony, for the mystery revealed to Rip had thus two aspects, animal or human, and vegetable—one for each of Thor's two fertility powers.

Of what pertinence were all these revelations to Rip? What does it mean to him that the strange men he saw have come down to us from the men of Thor, or that he was initiated into an ancient mystery and shown the sacred secrets of all life? No relevance at all to him and no meaning whatever. And that is the ironical point. Befuddled, unwitting, and likeable old Rip: no man in the valley, luxuriantly green already, thought less or as little about the crops, and no man he knew could have been chosen to witness the secrets of human fertility and found them more sleep-provoking.

III

What would have interested him, and what did he want? Concentrating somewhat anthropologically on the story's central scene in an attempt to get at the bottom of it, we have not got to the bottom of the character. But if for a moment we will think more as psychologists, and consider the story as a sort of dream—as a product of the unconscious, itself a kind of anthropologist—we open a whole new and remarkable area of meaning. Suddenly everything seems illusive, unreal; time goes into abeyance and the sense of history is lost; the very identity of the central figure is shaken, and reason dissolves.

The easiest entry to the dream level of "Rip Van Winkle" passes through that inn where Rip once sat with his friends—the inn which was "gone," and replaced by a hotel straight out of nightmare: "a large rickety wooden building . . . with great gaping windows . . . mended with old hats and petticoats"—and in front a sign with a familiar face all out of place in its setting. Soon, however, "idle with impunity" and "reverenced as one of the patriarchs of the village," Rip "took his place once more on the bench at the inn door." A conflict in Irving explains the confusion. He wanted to show the great changes a revolution had brought, but wished more deeply to feel, and wanted us to feel, that aside from the happy loss of his wife nothing had really happened to Rip. Toynbee, responding fully to this ab-sense of time and change, made what amounts to the same mistake. But it is a meaningful slip, and on one level they are both right. For Rip, time and history *have* ceased operation. Nothing *has* happened, and the inn is there to signal the fact.

What, then, are we to think when we come to the start of the very next paragraph and are told (in a kind of preliminary postscript at the end of the tale proper) that Rip is now telling his story "to every stranger that arrived at Mr. Doolittle's hotel"? The inn is there, is gone and replaced, is there again, is gone again. Reality is slithering away; and so it must eventually do, for this is not ultimately its world. Nor is this truly the world of fiction, unless of Kafka's. It is the world of the unconscious, where time and history are not suspended, exactly, but do not exist—where everything exists at once. It is the region where people and things are always appearing in unreasonable places, and everything is passing strange: but distorted toward some hard-to-recognize truth. The recurring transformation of Irving's hostelry belongs in this night world. It represents a "willful accident," and as such makes its own kind of sense. Irving was groping very darkly in a world of symbol, myth, and dream for meanings beyond awareness.

In this strange new world Rip's identity is harder to establish than the identity of that shifting meeting place. Removed as he is from time, the confusion of generations is appalling, and he is hard pressed to know in which of at least three generations he really "belongs." It will be next to impossible to know for sure, for the truth is he had almost as little part in his own generation as the one he slept through. This was entirely clear, had we the wit to see it, when we first met him. He was not an adult, but a child playing with children, a kid with a dog. He lived with his wife, to be sure, but only in a manner of speaking, for he accepted instead his "only alternative": "to take gun in hand and stroll away into the wood." Or, more striking, he would escape her by sitting on a wet rock with a rod in his hand "as long and heavy as a Tartar's lance, and fish all day . . . even though he should not be encouraged by a single nibble." "A great favorite among all the good wives of the village," he ran their errands and did "such little jobs as their less obliging husbands would not do for them"—not, by pointed implication, what their husbands would do: "As to doing family duty . . . he found it impossible."

At the inn with the menfolk, Rip shows that he wants to be a father. But at home he is a son, and not up to it: he is the son who wants to be the father but his mother won't let him. He represents, to be technical for a moment, the ego arrested at the infantile level in an Oedipal situation; under pressure he reverts all the way back to the sleep of the womb.

The scene in the mountain now takes on a new and different suggestiveness. It is at once the dream of a child and an adult dream reflecting Rip's own predicament. The great noses of the mountain men give the next phallic clue, as they must likewise have done in the ancient Teutonic mythology. (The psychoanalytic and the anthropological mix well: they are both—the first personally, the second culturally—"regressive.") From this viewpoint the dwarfs are really disguised little boys with pins and balls practicing, in highly activated silence, a forbidden rite; Rip is not invited to play, too, and they make him work, so he sneaks their drink and goes off to sleep. On the other hand the dwarfs are also so many mirrors to the "adult" Rip, held up as revelations which his consciousness is not likely to read: they are aged little men playing games, who have grown old but not up. Our protagonist, then, is both gerontion and child—or is neither, precisely. He has nor youth nor age, but as it were an after-dinner's sleep, dreaming on both.

On his return to the village, the sense of the decomposition of his "self" becomes even more awesome. His wife-mother is gone, but he is still a child as much as he is anything, and as such he must find his role in a relationship to someone else. But now it is completely bewildering. He is soon confronted with the very "ditto of himself," a negligent loafer named Rip—actually his son. Worse, he faces a woman who seems both strange and, as his poor mind struggles into recollection, hauntingly familiar. She had, she says, a father named Rip, and she carries in her arms a child of that name. Who, then, is our protagonist? His own unaccepted and "impossible" self, or the son of his wife that he used to be and emotionally remains? Or his own son, the loafer leaning there against the tree and, after the ravages of twenty years that passed as a night, looking more like the man Rip impersonated than he suddenly does himself? Or perhaps another Rip, the child of his daughter, now surrogate for his departed wife, and the sign of his true emotional state? Or even, conceivably, the husband of this replacement wife-mother, and the father of this son—or of that one, or of himself? The sense of generation is shattered; his daughter's house, in which he lives, is a whole house of mirrors, and everywhere he looks he sees a different distortion. He has one moment of panicked insight: "God knows . . . I'm not myself—I'm somebody else—that's me yonder—no—that's somebody else got into my shoes. . . ." Small wonder he takes his leave of all these people for the security of the role he can play at Mr. Doolittle's.

It is clear now that Rip escaped no change of life, but his very manhood—went from childhood to second childhood with next to nothing in between. It is not just his wife he has dodged, either, but all the obligations of maturity: occupation, domestic and financial responsibility, a political position, duty to society in a time of war. His relation to history is so ambiguous that—ridiculous suspicion—he is thought a spy. Charming and infantile, he narcissistically prefers himself; he will tell his tale of twenty years' sleep at Mr. Do-little's, where Irving leaves him for the last time. It has become a symbol for the sleep that has been his life.

Considering the universality of his fame, it is a wonder that no European, say, has pointed gleefully to this figure as a symbol of America, for he presents a near-perfect image of the way a large part of the world looks at us: likeable enough, up to a point and at times, but essentially immature, self-centered, careless, and above all—and perhaps dangerously—innocent. Even more pointedly, Rip is a stereotype of the American male as seen from abroad, or in some jaundiced quarters at home: he is perfectly the jolly overgrown child, abysmally ignorant of his own wife and the whole world of adult men—perpetually "one of the boys," hanging around what they are pleased to think of as a "perpetual men's club"; a disguised Rotarian who simply will not and cannot grow up. In moments of candor we will probably admit that a stereotype with no germ of truth in it could not exist: some such mythic America, some such mythic American, exist both actually and in the consciousness of the world. Rip will do very well as their prototype.

"Rip Van Winkle" is then, and finally, a wonderfully rich tale—the richest in our literature—and an astonishingly complex experience arising from a struggle among many kinds of meaning. On the "prehistoric" level we are dimly aware of immemorial ritual significance, on the psychological of an extraordinary picture of the self arrested in a timeless infancy—rich appeals, both, to the child and primitive in everyone that never grow up and never die in anyone. These awarenesses conflict in the story, as they do in life, with the adult and rational perception that we do indeed grow old, that time and history never stop. In much the same way, our affection for Rip himself must oppose our reluctant discovery that as a man we cannot fully respect him.

But in addition to all his other sides, this remarkable Van Winkle also, of course, projects and personifies our sense of the flight—and more: the ravages—of time. And this is what wins us ultimately to his side. We know perfectly well that as an adult this darling of generations of Americans will not entirely do. But if he does seem, finally, meek, blessed, pure in heart, and if we mock him for what he has missed we do it tenderly—partly because it is something hidden in ourselves we mock. And this is not just our own hidden childishness. It is all our own lost lives and roles, the lives and roles that once seemed possible and are possible no more. In twenty years all springs are over; without mockery it might be too sad to bear. Today would grieve, and tomorrow would grieve; best cover it over lightly.

And so here is Rip at the end: Lazarus come from the dead, come back to tell us all. He will tell us all, and badgering any who will listen, he tries: Well now—have you heard what happened to *me?* But it won't do; he doesn't know. And that is a pity, truly. Here is a man in whom rest complexities and deficiencies a lifetime might contemplate, as the world has done; a man who has peered toward the dawn of civilization, witnessed ancient mysteries, and stared at his essential nature; a man who now in town is looking at the future and realizing a dream of the ages. And he cannot communicate his visions.

But supposing that he could, that he could tell us all: would it have been worthwhile? Visions, revelations like these are private. To translate what the thunder meant, to confront the meaning of life and the future of all our childish selves, we all have to go up into our own mountains.

1960

2.

The Mother of Us All: Pocahontas

Were there two sides to Pocahontas?
Did she have a fourth dimension?
—Ernest Hemingway

> . . . having feasted him after their best barbarous manner they could, a long consultation was held, but the conclusion was, two great stones were brought before *Powhatan*: then as many as could layd hands on him, dragged him to them, and thereon laid his head, and being ready with their clubs, to beate out his braines, *Pocahontas* the Kings dearest daughter, when no intreaty could prevail, got his head in her arms, and laid her owne upon his to save him from death: whereat the Emperour was contented he should live to make him hatchets, and her bells, beads, and copper. . . .

Of course it may never have happened at all, and even if it did we think we may be a little tired of it. Yet three and a half centuries have elapsed, and this interminable sentence about an incident from the travels of Captain John Smith still lives. Americans, their literature swarming with its offspring, still without revulsion can summon up the old image: Smith pinned down by savages, his head on a rock, all those clubs about to smash it; and the lovely Indian princess, curiously moved out from the crowd and across all the allegiances of her family, home, and land, her religion and her race, lowering her head to his. Why can this commonplace, even banal, picture absorb us yet?

Shopworn by sentimentality, Pocahontas endures and stands with the most appealing of our saints. She has passed subtly into our folklore, where she lives as a popular fable—a parable taught children, who carry some vague memory of her through their lives. She is an American legend, a woman whose actual story has blended with imaginary elements in time become traditional. Finally, she is one of our few, true native myths, for with our poets she has successfully attained the status of goddess, has been beatified, made holy, and offered as a magical and moving explanation of our national origins. What has happened to her story, why did it happen—and in fact what really was her story? It may be that our very familiarity with Pocahontas has kept us from looking at her closely enough to see what is there.

I

Even in the sketchiest of outlines, the story from which all the folklore and legends take off is a good one. As every schoolboy knows, the English arrived in Jamestown in 1607. During December of that year, while exploring the Chickahominy River, Smith—who had worked his way up from prisoner to leader of the expedition—was captured by men of Chief Powhatan, and two of his companions were killed. It was at this time that he reputedly was rescued from death by the chief's favorite child, a young girl—no more than twelve or thirteen—called Pocahontas. Then, after what struck him as some very odd behavior on the part of the Indians, he was allowed to return to Jamestown, a place where—the great majority of its members dying within a year of their arrival—one of the most appalling casualty rates in history was being established. By placating the Indians and planting corn, and with the help again of Pocahontas, who is said often to have brought supplies, and once to have come through the forest on a dark night to warn of an attack by her father, Smith is usually credited with having temporarily saved the colony. He gave the credit to her, however, as having done most, "next under God," to preserve the settlers.

The Captain returned to England in 1609, and in that year ships under Sir Thomas Gates brought relief to a group of people so desperate that one man had eaten his wife. The *Sea Venture,* flagship of the fleet, was wrecked in Bermuda, but its survivors somehow built a new vessel, and with it made Jamestown. One of its passengers was an Englishman named John Rolfe. Some time elapsed before he saw Pocahontas, because for a while she had no connection with the vicissitudes of the colonists. But in 1613, while visiting the chief of the Potomacs, she was tricked into captivity by an Indian bribed with a copper kettle, and taken as security for English men and equipment held by Powhatan. Now she met Rolfe, whose first wife had died in Virginia, and soon they expressed a desire to marry. Powhatan gave his approval, but Rolfe had to get permission from his own superiors and wrote Sir Thomas Dale a passionate, tedious letter protesting that he wished to marry Pocahontas despite, as he put it, her "rude education, manners barbarous and cursed generation," for the good of the plantation, the honor of England, the glory of God, and his own salvation—not "to gorge myself with incontinency" but, according to God's wish, to convert the girl. Even Smith had said that conversion was the first duty of the settlers; permission was granted. Dale gave the girl a good deal of religious instruction, christened her Rebecca—it was the first such conversion by the colonists—and in April of 1614 she and Rolfe were married.

Rolfe, it is generally believed, was primarily responsible for the production of the tobacco—detested by both King James and Smith—which made the colony permanent, and in 1616 he and his wife and their son Thomas were taken abroad by Dale to publicize the success of Jamestown. Thus it was that Pocahontas, less than six weeks after the death of William Shakespeare, arrived in England. In the party, too, was an Indian named Tomocomo, whom a thoughtful Powhatan had sent as a scout. He had a sheaf of sticks in which he was to place a notch for each white person he encountered, and some equally troublesome instruction to see this "God" about whom the English talked so much.

Pocahontas fared better, for a time. She was honored by the church and feted by the King and Queen, to whom Smith in glowing terms had commended her as his savior. James Stuart demanded to know if her commoner husband had not committed a treasonable act in marrying a princess. The Lady Rebecca became the toast of London, where alert pubs changed their names to "La Belle Sauvage." But not everything went well. She saw Smith again and was mysteriously displeased. Then while preparing for her return to Jamestown she was taken sick, very likely with smallpox, and died. She made a godly end, according to Smith, at the age of perhaps twenty-two, and was buried on the 21st of March, 1617, at Gravesend, on the banks of the Thames.

Her father survived her by only a year. Her husband returned to Virginia alone, married once again, and was killed four years later by Indians led by her uncle. Her son Thomas grew up in England, and then came back to this country to start the line of proud Virginians—of Jeffersons and Lees, of Randolphs, Marshalls, and an estimated two million other people—who to this day trace their ancestry back to the Indian girl. Smith transferred his affections to New England, which he named, but was never able to get the colonial job he wanted and died in bed in 1631. As for Pocahontas, the exact place of her burial is unknown, and the only tangible remains of her are a pair of earrings and a portrait, done in 1616, showing a dark and handsome if uncomfortable young lady, incongruously overdressed in English clothes.

There are other details of a more or less factual nature that have been added to this story by people who knew Pocahontas, or who wrote of her during her lifetime. Smith himself supplies some of them. It is he who describes that day in England when he somehow so upset her, and she "turned about, obscured her face," on seeing him—an event which, since Smith either could not explain it or did not wish to, has tantalized generations of romantics.

There is also the testimony of Samuel Purchas, who was present when Pocahontas was received by the Lord Bishop of London with even more pomp than was accorded other great ladies of the time, and who records in *Hakluytus Posthumus* or *Purchas his Pilgrimes* (1625) the impressive dignity with which the young lady received her honors. And in his *True Discourse of the Present Estate of Virginia* (1615) Ralph Hamor put down the pious details of her conversion and marriage.

But not all these additions conform to the somewhat stuffy reputation that has been built for her. Smith, for instance, coldly comments that he might have married the girl himself—or "done what he listed" with her. He also supplies a colorful but usually neglected incident relating how she and "her women" came one day "naked out of the woods, only covered behind and before with a few green leaves . . . singing and dauncing with most excellent ill varietie, oft falling into their infernall passions"; and also tells how, later, "all these Nymphes more tormented him than ever, with crowding, pressing and hanging about him, most tediously crying, Love you not me?"

In addition, William Strachey, in his *Historie of Travaile into Virginia Britannia,* written about 1615, supplies information which does not appear in Sunday School versions of the story. The first secretary of America's oldest colony and the friend of great poets, including Donne, Jonson, and probably Shakespeare, Strachey disturbs the tenderhearted by noting that Rolfe's future bride is already married, to a "private captaine, called Kocoum." Even worse is his description of Pocahontas in earlier days as a "well-featured but wanton yong girle" who used to come to the fort and "get the boyese forth with her into the markett place, and make them wheele, falling on their hands, turning their heels upwards, whome she would followe and wheele so herself, naked as she was, all the fort over."

These are all the important sources of the Pocahontas story. Strachey's intelligence was not published until some 234 years after he wrote. Smith's swashbuckling accounts of his own adventures were taken as gospel for even longer, though for quite a while the story of Pocahontas had very little circulation, and was seldom repeated outside a couple of books on Virginia. But when about the start of the nineteenth century Americans began to search intensely for their history, the romance was resurrected, and Pocahontas began to loom large as the guardian angel of our oldest colony. Exaggerating even Smith's accounts of her, historians entered into a quaint struggle to outdo each other with praise, concentrating, of course, on the rescue story. Considering the flimsiness of the evidence, it is odd that for a long time no one seems to have entertained the slightest doubt of its authenticity. On all sides, instead, sprung up the most assiduous and vigilant defense of the lady. Here the case of the Honorable Waddy Thompson is instructive. Poor Thompson, who had been our minister to Mexico, published in 1846 his "Recollections" of that place, and in his desire to praise a girl named Marina, "the *chère amie* and interpreter of Cortez," he let slip a remark he must have regretted the rest of his days. He said that Pocahontas was "thrown into the shade" by her.

The response to these imprudent words was dreadful; an anonymous Kentuckian rushed into print a whole pamphlet Vindicating her Memory. He appealed to all Virginians, to all Americans, and finally "to the admirers of virtue, humanity, and nobleness of soul, wherever to be found," against this Erroneous Judgment. Pocahontas had every gift Marina possessed, and—no *chère amie*—she had also, he added, her "good name." Indeed, it is not possible to improve on her, and to demonstrate either this or his scholarship the gentleman from Kentucky appended long accounts of her from the work of twenty-six historians, including French, German, and Italian representatives. Her character is "not surpassed by any in the whole range of history" is one estimate.

The author of this pamphlet also spoke of "proof" that Pocahontas rescued Smith, which he called "one of the most incontestable facts in history": "The proof is, the account of it given by Captain Smith, a man incapable of falsehood or exaggeration . . . hundreds of eye-witnesses . . . and to this may be added tradition." Here the gentleman defends, somewhat ineptly, what no man is known to have attacked, despite the fact that there have always been excellent reasons for contesting the rescue. For one thing, the Captain had a real inclination toward this sort of tale. His *Generall Historie* of 1624, which tells the full story for the first time, reveals a peculiar talent for being "offered rescue and protection in my greatest dangers" by various "honorable and vertuous Ladies." Most striking of these is the Lady Tragabigzanda, who fell in love with him when he was in bondage, not this time to her father but to her husband, the powerful Bashaw Bogall of Constantinople. She delivered him from this slavery, and sent him to her brother, "till time made her Master of her selfe"—before which, however, Smith made a fantastic escape.

Then, much worse and apparent from the beginning, there is the well-known fact that Smith's *True Relation* of 1608, which tells of his capture by Powhatan, and speaks also of the chief's kindness and assurances of early release, contains no mention at all of any rescue. He had plenty of other opportunities to tell the story, too, but neither he nor anyone else who wrote on Jamestown is known to have referred to the event until 1622, when he remarked in his *New England Trials,* which includes his third version of his capture: "God made Pocahontas the King's daughter the means to deliver me." Then in 1624, when his *General Historie* was published, he told the story as we know it, and also printed for the first time his letter of eight years before to Queen Anne.

The obvious inference here is that if the rescue was actually performed Smith would have said so in the first place or, if he had not, would have told the story to others who would have repeated it. His *Historie* is boastful; it is hard to know how much of it he may have made up or borrowed from other travelers of the period. And there was a historical precedent for the Pocahontas tale: the story of a soldier, Juan Ortiz, who was lost on an expedition to Florida in 1528 and was found there by De Soto about twelve years later. Ortiz said he had been captured by Indians, and saved at the last second from burning at the stake by the chief's daughter, who later came at night in peril of her life to warn him of her father's plot to kill him. This story had appeared in London, in an English translation by Richard Hakluyt, in 1609, the year of Smith's return to that city.

Despite all grounds for suspicion, however, Smith's tale went unchallenged for well over two centuries—until about 1860, that is, when two historians, Edward D. Neill (who became known as the scavenger of Virginia history) and Charles Deane, began to make what now seem the obvious objections. These men were quickly joined by others, and in order to publicize Deane's case there entered the cause no less an intellect than that of Henry Adams. Writing anonymously in the *North American Review* in 1867, Adams lowered his biggest guns and patiently blasted what he called "the most romantic episode" in our history into what must have seemed to him and his crushed readers total oblivion. Henry Cabot Lodge concurred that the rescue belongs to fiction. Many other great men expressed themselves on the question, and quickly it became the custom to speak of the Pocahontas "legend."

Other historians, however, rushed to the defense. Chief among these were John Fiske, the philosopher and historian, and William Wirt Henry. Fiske in 1879 flatly dismissed the dismissals, and went on to champion the story. Why is it not in the *True Relation* of 1608? Because the editor of that work had obeyed an injunction against printing anything that might discourage potential colonists, and in a preface had explained that Smith had written "somewhat more" than was being published. Certainly the Captain was not allowed simply to go free, after having killed two Indians. The rescue by Pocahontas was quite in accordance with Indian custom. Any member of a tribe had a right to claim a prisoner as son or lover—but how could Smith have known enough about this to invent the tale? That scene in which he describes the weird behavior of his captors following his rescue was clearly a ceremony of adoption into the tribe, the natural consequence of Pocahontas' act. Why didn't Smith tell the story to his compatriots? Because he feared that if they knew the favor of an Indian woman was possible they would desert.

And so the battle, which continues to the present day, was on. There is a rebuttal. Why, for example, censor from Smith's first book a charming rescue story (which might cause desertions) and include, as the editor did, an excessively discouraging description of one of Smith's companions, "John Robinson slaine, with 20 or 30 arrowes" in him? There is no easy answer to that. But, after the short period of the story's disrepute (conveniently passed in time for the Jamestown Tercentenary of 1907), wide acceptance ruled again—especially with proudly celebrating Virginians, who appeared to have forgotten that by their rules the girl was colored. Credence in the story, however, is of course not limited to the South. Indeed by 1957, when the 350th anniversary of the founding was elaborately solemnized, most Americans, including a majority of the published authorities, seemed to subscribe to the tale as fact. For the celebrations Paul Green wrote a "Symphonic Outdoor Drama" called *The Founders,* in which the key events of the young lady's life took on the force of ritual observance in performances at Williamsburg. Since the evidence is not decisive, perhaps everybody has a right to believe as he wishes.

II

Exactly what happened would not seem to make any enormous difference anyway. What counts more is the truly extraordinary way in which the story—despite the profound awkwardness of a climax that comes in the very opening scene—pervades our culture. Pocahontas is represented in countless paintings and monuments; she gives her name to ships, motels, coal mines, towns, counties, and pseudonymous writers, to secret orders and business firms. There are histories of her and Smith by everyone from poet (John Gould Fletcher) to politician ("Alfalfa Bill" Murray, a descendant). But all other signs of her fade before the plays, poems, novels, and children's books which for the last 150 years have flooded our literature. Dramatizing the story from the alleged facts, and filling gaps or inadequacies with invented material usually presented as fact, there are so many different treatments, ranging from the serious to the absurd, that they begin to look numberless.

But they fall into patterns. The first person to make literary use of Pocahontas was no less a writer than the rare Ben Jonson, who included an obscure reference to her in his *Staple of News* of 1625. Then, much later, she was treated at length in a little novel called *The Female American* (1767). Here the story as we know it is, however, simply a rehearsal for far greater events, and the really memorable thing about the book is that its author was an English lady known as Unca Eliza Winkfield, who changed Pocahontas' name to Unca, and Smith's to Winkfield, and gave her a daughter called, once more, Unca.

The writer who really started things, by first romanticizing the story in a proper way, was still another Englishman—an adventuresome fellow named John Davis, a sailor who came to this country in 1798 and spent nearly five years traveling about on foot. Very young and romantic, hyperthyroid, chronically tumescent, and rather charming, Davis wrote a book about his journey called *Travels of Four Years and a Half in the United States of America*. As a part of this work he "delivered to the world" the history of Pocahontas which, he announced, was reserved for his pen. Possessed of a lively and libidinous imagination, which he seemed unable to distinguish from his written sources, Davis tore into the story with hearty masculine appetite.

He begins with Smith in the hands of Powhatan, who keeps offering his prisoner a woman. The squaws fight fiercely for the honor, but to Pocahontas' "unspeakable joy" Smith is stern and turns them all down. After she has rescued him she comes to Jamestown, weeping "in all the tumultuous extasy of love." In order to cure her Smith slips off to England, instructing his compatriots to tell the girl he has died. She prostrates herself on his empty grave, beats her bosom, and utters piercing cries. One night while she is strewing flowers about his resting place she is come upon by Rolfe, secretly in love with her and of late much given to taking moonlight walks while composing love poems. ("Of these effusions I have three in my possession," says Davis, and he prints them.) Surprised by Rolfe's appearance, Pocahontas inadvertently falls in his arms, whereupon he seizes his opportunity and drinks from her lips "the poison of delight." A woman is "never more susceptible of a new passion than when agitated by the remains of a former one," is Davis' dark but profitable explanation, and thus it is that hours later, come dawn, Rolfe "still rioted in the draught of intoxication from her lips." Eventually they marry ("nor did satiety necessarily follow from fruition," the author adds anxiously). They go to England, and Pocahontas dies there.

Davis made it clear that he wrote as a historian: "I have adhered inviolably to facts; rejecting every circumstance that had not evidence to support it," he insisted, speaking of "recourse to records and original papers." The man was too modest, for of course these were, like Rolfe's poems, original enough but with him. And he should be given credit, too, for having seen the possibilities of uniting richly embroidered history with a mammary fixation (habitually the bosoms of his Indian women are either "throbbing" or "in convulsive throes"). That he did see the promise of this combination, and in advance of his time, is indicated by the fact that he himself soon wrote what he called a "historical novel" on "Pokahontas." The book is formally titled *First Settlers of Virginia* (1806), but it simply pads the previous account of the girl's adventures to novel length. Dropping Rolfe's claim to the poetry, Davis managed to add a couple of mildly pornographic native scenes, to use Smith's story of the enamored Indian girls ("Love you not me?") twice, and to present Pocahontas as "unrobed" in her first scene with Rolfe. He also prefaced a second edition with a letter from Thomas Jefferson to the effect that the President of the United States "subscribed with pleasure" to this Indian Tale.

After Davis, the deluge. This began with a vast number of plays now mostly lost, but including four prominent and commercially successful ones which are preserved. To James Nelson Barker, ex-mayor of Philadelphia and future first controller of the Treasury in Van Buren's cabinet, goes a series of firsts: his *Indian Princess* of 1808 (although anticipated in 1784 by the little-known German *Pocahontas* of Johann Wilhelm Rose) was the first important Pocahontas play and the first to be produced of the Indian plays which soon threatened to take over our stage completely; it is generally cited also as the first American play to appear in London after opening in this country. Hugely popular, and rather deservedly so, Barker's success was followed by that of George Washington Parke Custis, step-grandson of our first president, with his *Pocahontas* of 1830, and by Robert Dale Owen. The latter, son of the more famous Robert Owen, founder of the radical Owenite communities, and himself a very early advocate of birth control, the free discussion of sex, and the rights of women, made his Pocahontas (1837) an anachronistic feminist. His play, though over-long, is not incompetent and reads very well beside *The Forest Princess* (1844) of Charlotte Barnes Conner. Mrs. Conner, an actress, stuck close to the worst nineteenth-century concepts of theater and produced a series of unlikely postures which are epitomized in her final scene, where a pious Rebecca dying in England, hand stretched heavenward, speaks her last iambics:

> I hear my father—Husband, fare thee well.
> We part—but we shall meet—above!

after which the hand drops with the curtain.

John Brougham's *Pocahontas* (1855) was honorably designed to stop this sort of thing, and his travesty did stop the production of "serious" Pocahontas plays for quite a time, greatly diminishing the popularity of the Indian drama to boot. But today his play is, to speak politely, "dated," for the humor depends mainly on puns ("What *iron* fortune *led* you to our shores?" "To now ill-use us would be base *illusion!*") (italics his), line after line for two long acts.

Brougham's burlesque was extremely well received, however, and it performed a service for our drama that nothing has adequately performed for our poetry. Pocahontas poems, produced in the nineteenth century by the carload, are almost uniformly dull, tasteless, and interminable. The efforts of Lydia Huntly Sigourney and William Makepeace Thackeray stand out only a little from the average. Most nineteenth-century Pocahontas poems seem to begin either with some silly sylvan scene or with "Descend O Muse, and this poor pen . . ." Smith always arrives as expected, but the Muse invariably has other things to do.

Equally forbidding are the Pocahontas poems written in the manner of Henry Wadsworth Longfellow. Longfellow neglected to produce any Pocahontas items himself, but there are a great many poems, and several plays in verse, which have sought to rectify his oversight. These pieces are all distinguished by lines of unrhymed trochaic tetrameter ("By the shore of Gitche Gumee / By the shining Big-Sea-Water") which produce a stultifying effect the poets seem to equate with an Indian atmosphere; they suffer from what might properly be known as the Curse of Hiawatha. Of course Longfellow got his famous Hiawatha line from a German translation of a national epic of the Finns, but this is not known to have stopped anyone, and on they go:

> Then the maiden Pocahontas
> Rushes forward, none can stop her,
> Throws her arms about the captive,
> Cries,—"Oh spare him! Spare the Paleface!"

What burlesque and abuse cannot destroy will just have to wear itself out. Although the machinery that mass-produces low-quality Pocahontas literature has long shown signs of collapse, the end is not yet. As recently as 1958 a Pocahontas novel by one Noel B. Gerson, with nothing to recommend it but the story, was smiled on by a very large book club. And so still they come with the story, juggling the climax or devising a new one, and trying to make up somehow for the fact that Smith never married the girl. Both problems can of course be solved at once by ending with the scene from Smith in which he and Pocahontas meet in London. Here Rebecca is overcome at the sight of her lost Captain and dies in his arms, usually of a broken heart; indeed it has become a convention to do it that way. But that has not helped, and it is the plays, particularly, which indicate that an industry really is exhausted. The best written and most interesting parts of their scripts are those that deal with such matters as the construction of campfires with electric fans, logs, and strips of red cloth.

One last sign of the popular Pocahontas drama's waning was the appearance (once Brougham was well-forgotten) of an Everything But the Kitchen Sink School. There exists, for instance, an operetta in which Smith has a "regulation negro" servant, comically named Mahogany, who plays a banjo. A better sample is the *Pocahontas* (1906) of Edwin O. Ropp. Mr. Ropp named three of his Indians Hiawatha, Minnehaha, and Geronimo; and there is a rough spot in the action when a man named simply Roger (Williams?), insisting on the freedom of religious thought, disappears for good in the Virginia forest. As for Pocahontas, she is taken, through her marriage with Rolfe, to England and back again to Virginia, where she lives out her days in the wilderness with her husband, two children, and their Christian grandpapa, Powhatan, singing the praises of home sweet home, as the play ends with lines lifted from the poem of that name. Mr. Ropp dedicated his play, it should be recorded, to a Moral Purpose, to the Jamestown Exposition of 1907, and to Those Who Construct the Panama Canal. The world was ready for another burlesque when, in 1918, Philip Moeller published his *Beautiful Legend of the Amorous Indian.* In this play only one character, the senile mother of Powhatan, speaks Hiawathan, and there is a heart-warming moment in the dialogue when Powhatan's wife says of her aging mother-in-law: "When she talks in that old manner it nearly drives me crazy."

III

It is not hard to find reasons for the low quality of a large part of our Pocahontas literature: the writers had no talent, for instance. A less obvious difficulty has been that most of the poets and playwrights have prided themselves that their works were founded firmly on "historical sources." This impeded the imaginations of most of them, who tried to romanticize history instead of letting the facts act as a stimulus to fiction. As a result of sentimentality and inaccuracy, there is little or no historical value in their products. And because the works are based so solidly on "history," often footnoted, they seldom have any value as fiction, for invariably events are related not because they are dramatic but because they happened—which is aesthetically irrelevant. If the story is to satisfy a modern audience, it must be treated imaginatively.

Properly told it could be a truly epic story. This is indicated by the fact that elements in the relationships of the characters are so like those in other epics of other countries—the *Aeneid,* for instance. Aeneas, we recall, was an adventurer who also sought a westward land and finally anchored at the mouth of a river. The country there was ruled by a king, Latinus, who had a beautiful daughter, Lavinia. Latinus had dreamed that his daughter's husband would come from a foreign land, and that from this union would spring a race destined to rule the world, so he received Aeneas and feasted him. Later tradition goes on to record the marriage, the birth of a son, and the founding of the city in which Romulus and Remus were born. Other parallels—with the stories of Odysseus and Nausicaä, and of Jason and Medea—likewise suggest the epic possibilities of the American tale.

To be sure, a few writers, usually in a far more modest fashion, have tried to make something of Pocahontas. Fewer still have succeeded, but even some of the failures are interesting. Working from the probability that a letter by Strachey, who was on the wrecked *Sea Venture* with Rolfe, provided Shakespeare with material for *The Tempest,* John Esten Cooke wrote a polite novel called *My Lady Pocahontas* (1885) in which he made Shakespeare dependent on the lady and Smith for his characters Miranda and Ferdinand. At the climax, Pocahontas recognizes herself on the stage of the Globe.

Much of this invention has been blithely repeated as history, but such an attempt at legend fails anyway for being too literary. Other attempts have failed for not being literary enough. Mary Virginia Wall in 1908 wrote a book on Pocahontas as *The Daughter of Virginia Dare*—the child, that is, of this first native-born "American," who mysteriously disappeared and Powhatan. Thus it is the spirit of Virginia Dare which accounts for the Indian girl's compassion. Now this could be a fruitful merger, uniting two of our best stories and giving Americans a kind of spiritual genealogy. The fact that to have been Pocahontas' mother Virginia would have had to bear a child at eight does not really matter much. But such scenes as the one in which the daughter comes to her end matter a good deal. On her deathbed, a place that has proved scarcely less fatal for authors than for their heroine, Pocahontas stoutly carols "Hark the Herald Angels Sing" (the Amen "begun on earth and ending in heaven"), and what started with some small promise has backed all the way out of it.

Another, but much better, novel which tries to do something with the story is the *Pocahontas* (1933) of David Garnett. This is a good historical novel with a thesis. In scenes of hideous but authentic brutality, Garnett shows the Indian women torturing their naked prisoners to death in orgies of obscene cruelty. These lead directly to orgies of sexual passion which act as a purge. To this sequence he contrasts the cruelty of the whites, which they sanction with self-righteousness and piety and follow with guilt. Garnett's book is a romantic and primitivistic performance after the manner of D. H. Lawrence which uses Pocahontas, more tender than her compatriots, as a vehicle for a lesson on the superiority of uncivilized peoples. Doctrinaire, and intellectually a little sentimental, this is still probably the best Pocahontas novel.*

Equally good, or maybe better, are two twentieth-century plays, Margaret Ullman's *Pocahontas* (1912) and Virgil Geddes' *Pocahontas and the Elders* (1933). More interesting than the plays themselves, however, are prefatory remarks their authors made about their material. In an introductory quotation Miss Ullman speaks of her heroine as a "Sweet-smelling sacrifice to the good of Western Planting." Geddes writes that his play is a "folkpiece" and his characters "part of the soul's inheritance." Both writers, in other words, were pointing to some pregnant quality of the story which goes beyond its facts. This was a direction which an informal group of modern poets was taking too. The result was the elevation of Pocahontas to myth.

It is Vachel Lindsay who was primarily responsible for this development. In his "Cool Tombs" Carl Sandburg had asked a question:

> Pocahontas' body, lovely as a poplar, sweet
> as a red haw in November or a pawpaw in May—

*It is not nearly so good as John Barth's *The Sot-Weed Factor* (1960), but this unprecedented novel is only incidentally about Pocahontas. Included in it, however, are John Smith's *Secret Historie,* parallel—but far superior—to John Davis' discovery of John Rolfe's poems, and the *Privie Journall* of a rival character. In the course of these extended tours de force a tribal custom is revealed that requires a prospective suitor to take the maidenhead of his bride before marrying her. In the case of Pocahontas no man has been successful in fracturing this membrane (indeed "most had done them selves hurt withal, in there efforts"). But with the aid of a fantastically invigorating vegetable device Smith publicly accomplishes the feat. In its review of the book, entitled "Novelist Libels Pocahontas Story," the *Richmond NewsLeader* demanded to know if, in view of the respectability of the lady's descendants, all this was not "actionable."

did she wonder? does she remember—in the
dust—in the cool tombs?

About 1918 Lindsay quoted this passage, answered yes, she remembers, and went on to explain in a poem which transforms the savior of Jamestown into a symbol of the American spirit. He supplies a magical genealogy whereby the girl becomes, as in his title, "Our Mother Pocahontas." Powhatan is the son of lightning and an oak; his daughter is the lover and bride of the forest. Thus

John Rolfe is not our ancestor.
We rise from out the soul of her
Held in native wonderland,
While the sun's rays kissed her hand,
In the springtime,
In Virginia,
Our mother, Pocahontas.

Though she died in England, Lindsay acknowledges, she returned to Virginia and walked the continent, "Waking / Thrilling, / The midnight land," and blending with it. We in turn are born not of Europe but of her, like a crop, and we are sustained by our inheritance.

One statement does not make a myth, but this concept was passed to other poets, notably to Hart Crane. First, though, came William Carlos Williams. A part of his prose study of the national past, called *In the American Grain* (1925), was devoted to an excoriation of the Puritans, after the fashion of the Twenties, and to praise for the sensual joy of the Indians, who are again taken over as an element of our spiritual ancestry. Williams gave only brief notice to Pocahontas, but he quoted Strachey's description of a naked, wheeling Indian girl.

These are the materials from which Crane, in *The Bridge* (1930), raised Pocahontas to full mythic stature. In some notes he made for the poem, Crane saw her as "the natural body of American fertility," the land that lay before Columbus "like a woman, ripe, waiting to be taken." He followed his notes, and the part of his long poem called "Powhatan's Daughter" develops them. Starting with the quotation from Strachey (which he took from a *transition* review of Williams by Kay Boyle) the poet in a waking dream at the harbor dawn finds someone with him ("Your cool arms murmurously about me lay . . . *a forest shudders in your hair!*"). She disappears, then, from his semiconsciousness to reappear later as the American continent, most familiar to hoboes who "know a body under the wide rain," as the poet himself is familiar with trains that "Wail into distances I knew were hers." The land blooms with her, she becomes a bride (but "virgin to the last of men"), passes herself then to a pioneer mother, a living symbol of the fertility of the land, and makes her last appearance as the earth again—"our native clay . . . red, eternal flesh of Pocahontas. . . ."

Like these four poets, Archibald MacLeish in his *Frescoes for Mr. Rockefeller's City* (1933) was discovering his own land and his faith in its future. Dedicating his book to Sandburg, and deriving a symbol from Crane, MacLeish describes a "Landscape as a Nude"—the American continent as a beautiful naked Indian girl, inviting lovers. With this repetition the concept has taken hold. Thus we have a sort of American Ceres, or Demeter, or Gaea, developed from Pocahontas—a fertility goddess, the mother of us all. We, by our descent from her, become a new race, innocent of both European and all human origins—a race from the earth, as in ancient mythologies of other lands, but an earth that is made of her. We take on a brave, free, mythical past as our alternative to the more prosaic, sordid explanation of history. And the thing is alive, as an image of the beautiful Indian girl is set in perpetual motion, and comes cartwheeling through our veins and down our generations.

IV

For all our concern with Pocahontas, one of the most interesting facts about her seems to have escaped everyone: the story John Smith told, which we have embraced so long, is one of the oldest stories known to man—not just roughly speaking, as in the Odysseus and Aeneas myths, but precisely in all essential parts. The tale of an adventurer, that is, who becomes the captive of the king of another country and another faith, and is rescued by his beautiful daughter, a princess who then gives up her land and her religion for his, is a story known to the popular literatures of many peoples for many centuries. The theme was so common in the Middle Ages that medieval scholars have a name for it: "The Enamoured Moslem Princess." This figure is a woman who characteristically offers herself to a captive Christian knight, the prisoner of her father, rescues him, is converted to Christianity, and goes to his native land—these events usually being followed by combat between his compatriots and hers.*

This is, for instance, the substance of a fifteenth-century French story about *un siegneur de Jagov* who went with a German army to Turkey, was imprisoned and sold as a slave to a *grand seigneur Turk,* whose daughter intervenes in the usual fashion and is converted to Christianity. There is also a medieval story, with roots in the legends of Charlemagne, called *The Sowdone of Babylone*—of Laban, the Sultan, and his daughter Floripas.† In the tenth book of Ordericus Vitalis' *Historia Ecclesiastica,* whose origins are in the twelfth century, the story is the same—this time about a Frenchman, Bohemond, his Turkish captor, Daliman, and his daughter Melaz. It is the same in a romance in which Elie de Saint Gille, a Frank, is carried from Brittany, captive of the amil (prince) Macabré, to the land of the Saracens, where Rosamonde, the amil's daughter, betrays her father, saves Elie, is converted and baptized. There are many other similar old stories: one called "The Turkish Lady and the English Slave"; another, a Balkan ballad, called "Marko Kraljević and the Arab King's Daughter"; still another involving *two* Magyars who are shut in a dungeon by a sultan, then freed by his daughter. The popularity of the tale is further indicated by its inclusion in the *Arabian Nights,* whose origins fade into ancient folklore. Here it appears as an interlude in the longer "Tale of Kamar al-Zaman." Bostán, the beautiful Magian daughter of Bahram, rescues As'ad from her father and is converted to Mohammedanism. Another version, once popular, is in the *Gesta Romanorum,* a collection of "Entertaining Moral Stories" compiled about 1300 from much older but obscure sources. These Latin anecdotes, which contain the germs of plots used by

*See, for instance, F. M. Warren, "The Enamoured Moslem Princess in Orderic Vital and the French Epic," *PMLA* XXIX (1914), 341–58. It is a mistake, however, to speak of this theme as if it were wholly a matter of the distant past. For instance, the Enamoured Moslem Princess figures prominently in the Fourth Canto (1821) of Byron's *Don Juan.* Here she is Haidée, whose mother was a Moor; her father is Lambro, a pirate leader who holds the Christian Juan captive. The chieftain is about to kill his prisoner "When Haidée threw herself her boy before; / . . . 'On me,' she cried, 'let death descend. . . .' " Juan is saved, but is taken off, and Haidée withers away and dies.

†The same story, dramatized, is still performed once a year in Portugal, and has its own historical parallel in Brazilian history. See Vianna Moog, *Bandeirantes e Pioneiros, Parelelo entre Duas Culturas (*Pôrto Alegre: Globo, 1955), 97–103. For that matter, there is an Oriental historical analogue: during the seventeenth-century Hindu-Muslim wars around Delhi, the Muslim princess Zebunnisha saved, in 1664, the rebel Hindu prince Shivaji from her father, Alamgir. They never married. Like the Pocahontas rescue, this incident is frequently used in historical romances of India.

Chaucer and Shakespeare, were widely read in translation in late sixteenth-century England (hence Smith may have known them). Tale V, called "Of Fidelity," is about a youth wasting away as a prisoner of pirates. Their chief has a lovely and virtuous daughter who frees the young man and, being promised marriage, goes to his country. The origins of this version may be in Seneca the Elder, who at the beginning of the Christian era formulated precisely the same situation in his *Controversia* as an imaginary legal case for debate. It is possible that he, in turn, got the story from the Greek Sophists, who had a lively interest in literature and disputation. There is no telling where they may have learned it, but something very like it is in the ancient Greek myth of Ariadne, the daughter of Minos, king of Crete, who rescued an Athenian named Theseus from a labyrinth where her father had imprisoned him to be eaten by the Minotaur, and then went away with him.

It has always been an uncomfortable fact of the Pocahontas story, and an apparently formidable obstacle to its survival, that after appearing to offer herself to Smith, the heroine never married the hero. It is a startling fact, and bewildering, that this curiosity has been an element of the story from the beginning. Though Ariadne had deserted her parents and motherland for Theseus, he for some unknown reason abandoned her by the shore of the sea and sailed away; she later married Dionysus. Orderic's Melaz did not marry Bohemond, but his younger friend Roger. In the tale of Kamar al-Zaman, Bostán marries not As'ad but his brother. Floripas, the Sowdone's daughter, also marries someone other than the man for whom she betrayed her father. Elie de Saint Gille never married Rosamonde; since Szilágyi Niklas says he has a love at home, that Sultan's daughter has to settle for the other Magyar, his companion; though he was later remorseful, Marko neglected the Arab king's daughter after his escape. In a few versions one is left to supply his own denouement, and may presume if he wishes that the hero and heroine marry and live happily ever after. But it is extremely curious that there appear to be no accounts in which we are told specifically that what we might expect invariably to happen actually happens.*

*The widely known and excellent ballad called "Young Beichan" seems an exception, but only because a new element, the motif of promised marriage, has been grafted on. Beichan is London born, and longs strange lands for to see, but is taken by a savage Moor whose daughter, Susan Pye, steals her father's keys and releases him from a prison, after which he goes back to England, having promised to marry the girl in seven years. Later she abandons her country for England, is converted to Christianity, and gets a new name. She arrives in England to discover that

The presence of a disturbing element in a popular story is hard to explain. The notion that melodies unheard are sweetest and cannot fade, that the lover who has not his bliss then can love forever and she be fair does not seem to account for this peculiarity; it was never that way at all. Yet there must be something obscurely "right" about an apparently unsatisfactory ending, or over the many centuries we should have succeeded in changing it. And the durable popularity of the story also urges the presence of some appeal that is not on the surface, some force that has given an advantage in the struggle for survival which we should make out if we can. The notion that the story is symbolic of something is not new. The monks who used it for religious instruction hundreds of years ago sensed this and had their own reading: the young man, they said, represents the human race. Led irresistibly by the force of original sin into the prison of the devil, he is redeemed by Christ, in the form of the girl. But this interpretation incongruously makes Jesus the daughter of Satan, and seems also a little arbitrary. It is too utilitarian—but in that it offers one clue to the story's longevity.

Nothing survives indefinitely without filling some function, and the usefulness of this story is clear: the tale approves and propagates the beliefs of anyone who cares to tell it. An informal survey of the children's sections of two small Midwestern libraries disclosed twenty-six different books on Pocahontas—and no wonder. Quite apart from the opportunity she presents to give children some notion of self-sacrifice, she is, in addition to all her other appeals, perfectly ideal propaganda for both church and state. The story has long been, among other things, a tale of religious conversion, and in its American form is so eloquent a tribute to accepted institutions that there is no need to deflate its power by so much as even mentioning the obvious lesson it teaches. Of course the thing is a little chauvinistic. It is always either indifferent to the attitudes of the betrayed or unconscious of them. Indeed it is a tribute to the high regard we have for ourselves that Pocahontas has never once been cast as a villainess, for she would make an excellent one. From the point of view of her own people her crimes—repeated acts of treason, and cultural and religious

---

Young Beichan has just married. But the ceremony is not yet consummated ("of her body I am free") and Susie Pye, now Lady Jane, is able to marry him after all. F. J. Child prints fourteen versions of this ballad in his *English and Scottish Popular Ballads,* while mentioning many related items in Norse, Spanish, Italian, and German. In its various forms it may have been affected by a fairly well-known legend on more or less the same theme, originating in the thirteenth century and concerning Gilbert Becket, father of St. Thomas à Becket. This also has the happy ending.

apostasy—were serious. But one does not resent a betrayal to his own side, and we can always bear reassuring: love exists, love matters, and we are very eligible, Pocahontas tells us.

The story will work for any culture, informing us, whoever we are, that we are chosen, or preferred. Our own ways, race, religion must be better—so much better that even an Indian (Magian, Moor, Turk), albeit an unusually fine one (witness her recognition of our superiority), perceived our rectitude. But it nicely eases the guilt we have felt since the start of its popularity over the way we had already begun, by 1608, to treat the Indians. Pocahontas is a female Quanto, a "good" Indian, and by taking her to our national bosom we experience a partial absolution. In the lowering of her head we feel a benediction. We are so wonderful she loved us anyway.

And yet the story has an appeal which easily transcends such crude and frequently imperialistic functions—especially in the rescue scene, which implies all the new allegiances that follow from it. There is a picture there, at least in the American rendering, which has compelled us for so long that it must certainly contain meanings that go beyond the illustrations of it in the children's books. It is characteristic of all hallowed images that they cannot adequately be put into words, and no single rendering would articulate all that might be stated anyway. But these are feeble excuses for total silence, and it does not take any great sensitivity to perceive that Pocahontas' gesture—accomplished not by any subterfuge, but by the frank placing of her own body between Smith's and death—is fairly ringing with overtones. This is because we see her act as a rite, a ceremonial sign which bestows life. A surface part of that symbolism has always been clear. The Indians understood it as we do, and immediately Smith was alive and free. But what we have not been conscious of, though the modern poets sensed something like it, is that her candor was that of a bride. That is one thing, buried beneath awareness, that has dimly stirred us. Unable to put it into words, we have let the girl keep her secret, but the ritual that we feel in her action is itself an unorthodox and dramatic ceremony of marriage, and we are touched. We see Pocahontas at the moment of womanhood, coming voluntarily from the assembly to the altar, where she pledges the sacrifice of her own integrity for the giving of life. This is an offering up of innocence to experience, a thing that is always—in our recognition of its necessity—oddly moving. It is an act which bespeaks total renunciation, the giving up of home, land, faith, self, and perhaps even life, that life may go on.

Perhaps this helps to explain why it is that what, in its flattery of him, is at first glance so much a man's story should also be greatly promoted by women. Apparently it is a very pleasant vicarious experience for us all. Yet in the depths of our response to the heart of the story, the rescue, there is something more profoundly wishful than a simple identification with persons in a touching adventure. All myths have an element of wish somewhere in them. But there is something about this one that is also wistful, as though it expressed a wish that did not really expect to be gratified. It is as though something in us says "If only it were true. . . ."

We surely ought to know what it is we wish for. In our fondness for Pocahontas can we make out a longing that is buried somewhere below even the affection we bear for our fair selves and white causes? This yearning might be for another kind of love entirely, a love that has forever been hidden under the differences that set countries, creeds, and colors against each other. From the freedom and noble impracticality of childhood, we as a people have taken this Indian girl to heart. Could we be hinting at a wish for a love that would really cross the barriers of race? When the beautiful brown head comes down, does a whole nation dream this dream?

But it is still only a dream. And that fact helps to explain why it is that from the very beginning the story has had what looks like the wrong ending, why the wedding of the protagonists remains a symbol that was never realized. To be sure the girl eventually married, and the groom was usually the hero's compatriot, but by then the event has lost its joy and its force—seems a substitute for the real thing, and not at all satisfactory. But the story might have died centuries before us, and we would have made much less of Pocahontas, if the substitution were not in some way fit and right. We sense that the adventure has to end the way it does partly because we know the difference between what we dream and what we get. We are not particularly happy with the denouement, but we feel its correctness, and with it we acknowledge that this is all just make-believe.

To understand the rest of our dim and reluctant perception of the propriety of the story's outcome, Americans must see the Indian girl in one last way: as progenitress of all the "Dark Ladies" of our culture—all the erotic and joyous temptresses, the sensual, brunette heroines, whom our civilization (particularly our literature: Hawthorne, Cooper, Melville, and many others) has summoned up only to repress. John Smith is the first man on this continent known to have made this rejection; his refusal to embrace "the wild spirit" embodied in the girl was epic, and a precedent for centuries of denial. Prototypes, too, and just as important, were the arrogantly hypocritical Rolfe and the rest of the colonists, who baptized, christened, commercialized, and ruined the young lady. With censorship and piety as tools, American writers—a few poets, far too late, aside—completed the job, until Pocahontas was domesticated for the whole of our society, where from the very start any healthy, dark happiness in the flesh is supposed to be hidden, or disapproved. Pocahontas is the archetypal sacrifice to respectability in America—a victim of what has been from the beginning our overwhelming anxiety to housebreak all things in nature, until wilderness and wildness be reduced to a few state parks and a few wild oats. Our affection for Pocahontas is the sign of our temptation, and our feeling that her misfortunes in love have a final, awkward fitness comes from our knowing that all that madness is not for us.

1962

3.

The Story of the Missing Man

If Peter Rugg, thought I, has been travelling since the Boston Massacre, there is no reason why he should not travel to the end of time. If the present generation know little of him, the next will know less; and Peter and his child will have no hold on this world.
—Jonathan Dunwell

Peter Rugg, the missing man, is nearly everywhere missing. For every citizen who has heard of him at all, ten thousand, or a hundred thousand, have heard of Rip Van Winkle—to whom, indeed, Peter owes a small and obvious debt. But he was once well known and perhaps should be again, as the dwindling few who remember him all seem to believe. It would be good, in short, if Peter could strengthen his hold on a spinning world that has a place for him.

On the 10th of September in 1824, the New England *Galaxy,* a Boston newspaper, contained many matters of moment. For one thing, Lafayette was in the city at the time, and the paper was full of what he said, and what was said about him. On the communications-to-the-editor page was a fine piece of Johnsonian invective directed against the restrictions placed on the use of carriages in the main streets of the city during the General's visit. And near it was the curious report of a man who signed himself Jonathan Dunwell. This had nothing at all to do with Lafayette. It posed as a reply to a friend who had asked for information on a peculiar subject, and was called "Some Account of Peter Rugg, the Missing Man, Late of Boston, New-England."

Dunwell goes about his business in a straightforward way. He first encountered Rugg, he explains, while travelling in a stage outside Providence, Rhode Island, in the summer of 1820. He saw a man, with a little girl beside him, going in great haste in a weather-beaten carriage that was drawn by a large black horse. The man looked dejected, but anxious and desperate as well; he appeared to be a man in great trouble, and that was all that Dunwell saw. But his driver knew at least this about him—that the man never stops longer than to ask the way to Boston, and to mutter that he must be there by nightfall. The driver also said that in his travels he himself had seen this Peter Rugg on the highways better than a hundred times, and often headed directly *away* from that city. He is always followed by a storm, moreover, which often catches and drenches him and the girl; but when the thunder claps near him the great black horse just increases the frantic pace, and off they go. A peddler submitted to Dunwell that he too had seen this man and his daughter, each time asking the way to Boston, in four states. But he did not wish to see them again: "they do not look to me as though they belonged to this world."

While in Hartford three years later, Dunwell continues, he suddenly heard someone cry out "there goes Peter Rugg and his child! . . . wet and weary, and farther from Boston than ever." The man was already a legend, he learned from a stranger; he had been travelling for more than 20 years to Boston—all the while growing older and wearier while his horse grew stronger. The stranger himself had had a typical exchange with Peter, he said. He told him it was a hundred miles to Boston, and Rugg gave his usual reply: "how can you deceive me so? It is cruel . . . I have lost my way." The man repeated: "one hundred miles." And Rugg objected: "I was told last evening it was but fifty, and I have travelled all night." But, said the man, "you are travelling from Boston. You must turn back." "Alas," said Rugg, "it is all turn back! Boston shifts with the wind . . ." and he was off in a clatter.

Finally Dunwell met Rugg in person, and talked with him. But he learned only that Peter used to live on Middle Street in Boston, and thought he was in Newburyport (it was still Hartford). Then with a cry—

"Ah, that fatal oath!"—he was off again. But Dunwell is soon in Boston himself, and he looks up an aged lady in Middle Street. She reports the surprising news that Rugg had indeed been there one evening a summer ago, and had asked for his wife. On being told that she had been dead for better than twenty years, and on seeing how changed were the streets, the people, the whole town, he had concluded, "Some other Mrs. Rugg, some other Middle Street . . . no home tonight," and had disappeared. At that point Dunwell decided Peter Rugg was losing his hold on this world entirely.

And that evening he got, from a gentleman at the hotel where he was staying, the last pieces of information he was able to gather. Peter, it turns out, had been a good, comfortable man with a wife and daughter and only one flaw, a terrible temper. One morning he took the little girl on a trip to Concord, and on his way back he was overtaken by a violent storm. In what is now West Cambridge a friend asked him to stop over. But Rugg cried out with a fearful oath, "Let the storm increase; I will see home tonight . . . or may I never see home!" For a while after this his wife on stormy nights thought she saw him doing everything in his power to stop his horse while racing past his own door. But soon her neighbors, who had been cooperative, refused to watch for him any more, and would say nothing about him. His friends, too, gave him up. One day they would hear of him in New Hampshire, the next in Connecticut, then in Rhode Island again. And there was what the toll-gatherer on the bridge between Charlestown and Boston had claimed. A horse and carriage had been rattling through the gate, in defiance of the charges, and once the man had tried to stop them, and had thrown his three-legged stool. But it was as if the missile had gone right through, he said, and he did not wish to discuss the matter any more either. This, concludes Dunwell, was all that he was able to learn.

The editor of the newspaper that published this communication knew no Jonathan Dunwell, and had no notion what the somewhat self-congratulatory name might be pseudonymous for. Swamped during four months with demands for information about him, he finally pleaded in his columns that it might be quite true that Peter Rugg could not get to Boston, but could his creator not get to the *Galaxy* office for the purpose of giving up his identity? The author never did. The story was reprinted in many books, often attributed to people who had not written it, and it was not for 17 years that an edition appeared under the name of the man who had.

That man was William Austin, a nearly forgotten citizen of Boston who deserves better of posterity. William would have represented the fifth generation of Austins born since 1638 in Charlestown, Massachusetts, except that the British intervened by burning that town, and his father's house, in connection with the event known (somewhat inaccurately, since the fight was on Breed's Hill, nearby) as the Battle of Bunker Hill. And so William was born, on March 2, 1778, in Lunenburg, Massachusetts. His father, Nathaniel, though a most prominent citizen, should perhaps be remembered for the fact that he once had the opportunity to say gallantly to a woman (as she fled in panic from the burning city of Charlestown with most of her possessions in her arms), "You've dropped your baby, ma'am!" whereupon he presented her with it. William's mother, Margaret, was of an old Tory family, and never failed to remind her son on Bunker Hill Day that they were commemorating a tragedy.

Austin went to school under the Reverend John Shaw (eventually the grandfather of Mrs. Herman Melville), and then went through Harvard College, where he had a good record and belonged to the best clubs—but not to Phi Beta Kappa, which he declined to join. He disapproved at the time of Harvard itself, and was distinguished there for an attack which he wrote on that institution in which he remarked, among many other things, that "should Homer himself revive and enter the university, he would turn in disgust from the Iliad, and Locke would detest his own essay." He intended to study law upon graduation, but needing money first he got a job with the U.S. Navy as a schoolmaster and soon became, in addition, the first man appointed by government commission as a Navy Chaplain. He served on the famous "Constitution," and in 1800 a case involving salvage arose and turned out fortunately for the temporary clergyman-schoolmaster.

Legal advice was needed, and Austin was sent to Alexander Hamilton to study the matter. Here he impressed Hamilton, got some money for his efforts, and Hamilton's commendation, and he went off to Lincoln's Inn to study law. In England he entertained himself with Washington Allston and wrote the *Letters from London*—on "men, morals, politics and literature"—which as a book were once widely read and (except by Federalists, who were already alarmed by his liberal views) enthusiastically praised. He attacked slavery, very early saw the dangers of large corporations, and soon got himself into real and highly illegal political trouble back in this country. A staunch Jeffersonian Republican, he attacked in a newspaper article the "pompous imbecility" of a prominent Federalist,

Major General Simon Elliot. The General's son, James, expressed the wish to Austin that "you will give me an opportunity to take your life." Austin told his second to get some pistols ("Mother—I suppose—has hidden mine"), and fought a duel in March of 1806—which was two years after the duel in which Hamilton had become involved. Austin fared better than his legal mentor, but unwell. Two shots were to be fired by each of the adversaries, at the murderous distance of ten yards, and feelings were so bitter that each fired an extra shot. Austin managed to miss with all three, and to get hit twice, but he recovered, and the event was kept very quiet. His own children learned of it for the first time after his death, when they found the record among his papers.

The rest of his career was less colorful. A highly successful lawyer, twice married and the father of 14 children, he also held various political offices as a Jacksonian Democrat. Despite his Tory background, his money and his relatives (he was related directly or by marriage to the most aristocratic families of New England's first 200 years—to Bradstreets, Dudleys, Cottons, Adamses, and Channing, Parkman, and Holmes) he remained until he died, in 1841, a progressive democrat.

As far as he was concerned, Austin's stories were a minor sideline. He wrote only five of them, apparently, and never took money for them or kept copies when they were published. But willy-nilly he was a pioneer in the development of American literature. He was, for one thing, a writer who "anticipates" Hawthorne in more ways than have been recognized. Like Hawthorne (and before Hawthorne, who read him, and like Henry James, later) he was able to give to events a quality whereby they seem neither real nor quite unreal. He gives in Peter Rugg a precedent for one kind of outcast that fascinated Hawthorne, as in "Wakefield," and his other first-rate story, "The Man with the Cloaks," is about a fellow who is a prototype for one of the principal figures in Hawthorne's work: the "unpardonable sinner," whose trouble is that his heart has "withered away."*

*It is worth noting that the "moral" to Hawthorne's story about the outcast "Wakefield" would serve as well for "Peter Rugg":

> Amid the seeming confusion of our mysterious world, individuals are so nicely adjusted to a system, and systems to one another and to a whole, that by stepping aside for a moment a man exposes himself to a fearful risk of losing his place forever. Like Wakefield, he may become, as it were, the outcast of the universe.

"The Man with the Cloaks," one of the very best early American short stories and almost completely forgotten, concerns a fellow who refused his extra cloak to a man who had none; in the chill of his guilt he has to put on another coat each day until before very long he is much too big

But Austin is of interest not simply as a precursor of Hawthorne or an estimable citizen but as a writer whose work deserves serious attention for its own sake, and he is the first American writer of short fiction but one, Irving, about whom this may confidently be said. In his own day his work was by no means unknown. "Peter Rugg" enjoyed a perfectly enormous popularity; the literary figures of the period—Longfellow, Higginson, Duyckinck and others—concurred in or promoted the general enthusiasm; E. C. Stedman, the poet, described himself as "daft" on the subject.

A few American writers have paid the story an even higher tribute by putting its "legendary quality" to their own use. And before they did, Austin himself, and a man who signed himself simply "Platt," attempted independently of each other to continue the tale of Peter's troubles. Published in three issues of the *Norfolk Republican* (of Roxbury, Massachusetts) in September 1827, Platt's efforts violate the spirit of the original and are of no interest. Austin's continuation is a good deal better, but it does not add much that is memorable either, except a final scene where Peter does get to Boston just as his estate is being auctioned. Here he is told by a voice from the crowd that "there is nothing strange here but yourself, Mr. Rugg. . . . Your home is gone, and you can never have another home in this world."

It is as a forlorn and hopeless man that Peter turns up next, as a part of Hawthorne's "Virtuoso's Collection" (1846). This story is about a fabulous museum which contains the manuscript of the Koran, Don Quixote's lance, the Flying Dutchman's autograph, and other treasures. It is presided over by the Wandering Jew himself, and when the narrator of the tale is asked the way to Boston by the establishment's doorkeeper he knows who asks the question. Much more recently, in *John Brown's Body* (1927), Stephen Vincent Benet also remembered the Jew and Peter together. When John Vilas and his daughter (and her child) wander in a horse and buggy in the backwash of the Civil War in search of the child's father,

> The story had gone on ahead of them . . .
> That made a fable of their journeying,
> Until you heard John Vilas was that same

for a room and must look out in misery at the world through the long tunnel of all his collars. Such a theme also suggests Hawthorne.

Lost Jew that wanders . . .
But cannot die . . . being cursed.

Vilas' own association, however, is more fitting:

. . . it almost seems to me
As if I were no longer what I am
But the deluded shade of Peter Rugg
Still looking for Boston through the storm. . . .

Two of America's better-known lady poets, both associated with Boston, both spinsters, and a generation apart, have given Austin's story their own full treatment. Louise Imogen Guiney's "Peter Rugg, the Bostonian" (1891) is a long ballad which adequately retells the tale. Caught in a storm, Peter's fiery horse gets off the route and he goes "forward and backward like a stone / The tides have in their hold." In the end he pleads to get home "GOD WILLING"—a chastened man upon whom a Catholic poet has bestowed repentance. Miss Guiney's ballad brought the wrath of those faithful to Peter down on her head, but the objections were not to her poetry, where they belong, or her piety, but to the fact that she had made a few apparently innocuous changes in the story—had given Rugg a son, for instance, instead of a daughter.

"A legend is something which . . . anybody is at liberty to rewrite," said Amy Lowell in the preface to her book *Legends* (1921). And in that book she printed "Before the Storm," her "polyphonic-prose" version of this particular "legend." She had been haunted by the tale, she says, from her childhood, when she had naturally thought of it as unauthored, and had had an "abiding fear" of the situation it describes. Her piece is better than Miss Guiney's, and preserves some of the force of the original. It also brings the story up to date; in the best scene, a pitifully comic one, Peter gets to Boston and is taken as a quaint advertisement, perhaps for some cereal product.*

More up to date still is the "Phantom Flivver" (*Saturday Evening Post,* January 28, 1950) of Frank Luther Mott, who as an authority on best sellers and magazine fiction could be expected to recognize a tale with

*Miss Guiney's and Miss Lowell's versions of "Peter Rugg," as well as the story itself, "The Man with the Cloaks," two other Austin stories, Platt's additions, and an account of Austin's life, are all conveniently to be found in Walter Austin's *William Austin, the Creator of Peter Rugg* (Boston: M. Jones, 1925).

popular appeal when he saw one. In his version the narrator, driving fast across Kansas a few years after World War II, passes and then a couple of hours later is startled to repass an old Model-T Ford. ("I feel queer," says his wife.) Later still, echoing Austin, the Ford goes right through the newer car. Piecemeal the man gets the story: the phantom driver is a "hant" named Peter Rugg who, accompanied by a small boy, has been driving nearly 40 years in search of a discontinued part for his beloved car, having vowed to drive all over America to find it, and not to come home till he does. Even an accident in which man, boy, and Ford are drowned in a river does not stay him; the part is finally located; Peter "sez thanks."

No other significant treatments of this story are known, and as happened in the case of Irving's "Rip Van Winkle" no one has come near equalling, let alone improving on, the virtues of the original telling. There have been, however, two successes with the same elements as make up Austin's tale, and they suggest how great an appeal these elements must inherently have. The first was Edward Everett Hale's famous *Man without a Country* (1863). Born on the site of the present Parker House in Boston in 1822, a bookish boy who grew up in the period of Peter's greatest fame, Hale could hardly have escaped knowing about him. In any event the theme of the best known of his many works is the same: defiance in an oath of the powers that be, and a condemnation to wander far from the place where the defier wishes to be. In Hale's story an officer named Nolan cries out in court, "D—n the United States! I wish I may never hear of the United States again!" and is sentenced accordingly. For 45 years he is transferred from ship to ship in the Navy, and never permitted to see in print even a reference to his homeland. So real did Hale make his account of Nolan's misfortune seem that a great many people took the thing as fact, and some claimed to have heard before of the man and his sad career. But the temptation to preach patriotism got not the feeblest resistance from the author, and for literate taste his didacticism overwhelms in the end the air of reality.

Peter's other popular reappearance, this time in deeper and probably unwitting disguise, came in a pleasing and widely publicized 1959 revival, by a group called the "Kingston Trio," of a politically inspired song opposing an increase in the Boston subway rates. The song, called "M. T. A." (Metropolitan Transit Authority), is about a man who got on the subway without the extra nickel and can't get off. Each day at one of the stops his wife hands in food from the platform.

Will he never return? No he never returned,
And his fate is still unlearned.
He will ride forever 'neath the streets of Boston,
He's the man who never returned.

This ballad owes a good deal to one of the nineteenth century called "The Ship that Never Returned," which was based on the unfortunate experience of an actual ship called the "Olive Branch," but Peter Rugg is at least a spiritual father of it.*

It is doubtful that patriotism and credibility will account for the great fame Hale's story once enjoyed, or that politics and three ingratiating singers with a good traditional tune will explain the presence of "M. T. A." on even a depraved Hit Parade. The missing part of the explanation for these successes lies somewhere in or near our response to such desperate and protracted wanderings as we also encounter, so much more forcefully, in "Peter Rugg."

People have of course responded to that state of affairs for a very long time, as to the myth of the Wandering Jew, which is alive and still being rewritten. This is, of course, the widespread story of a Jew, often a shoemaker, who has various names—Ahasuerus, Cartaphilus, Buttadaeus, Laquedem, and many others—who refused Jesus rest at his door when Jesus was carrying the cross to Calvary. As he pushed the Lord away he cried "go on!" And to this received the sad reply: "Truly I go, and that quickly, but tarry thou till I come," or: "It is thou who shalt go on, till the end of time." And so the Jew has done, a desperate, homeless man who can stop only to tell his story.† In some places his arrival is heralded by violent storms, and in several he has a specific inability in his wandering to get back to Jerusalem—but did once, and found everything so changed he couldn't recognize it.

Thus many of the elements that appeal to us in "Peter Rugg" have appealed to people for many hundreds of years. The story of the Wandering Jew had its first popular telling in 1602, in a widely printed and oft-reprinted four-page pamphlet which spread out from Germany to France,

*Peter might claim another offspring in Joe Btfsplk, "the world's worst jinx" in Al Capp's "L'il Abner." Joe travels under a black cloud, and gets to Boston, where he brings bad luck to the Red Sox.

†Most Teutonic versions of the Wandering Jew myth stress his inability to die—*der ewige Jude*—where the Romance emphasize his wandering—*le Juif errant*. Our versions apparently derive more from the latter.

England, Scandinavia and elsewhere; the tale was generally taken to be true, and many said that they had themselves talked to the poor man. But by 1602 the story was already old. In 1228 Roger of Wendover had written in his *Flores Historiarum* that an Armenian archbishop then in England was asked by some monks about Joseph of Arimathea, who had spoken to Jesus and was said to be living still. (The bishop replied that he himself had seen Joseph; his name before baptism was Cartaphilus; he confessed to having taunted the Lord.) And long before that a sixth-century monk named Moschos referred briefly but unmistakably to the same figure.

Nor does some sort of highly limited credence in the man appear to have entirely died out. Around 1800 a multilingual imposter in England was believed by many until he was exposed by learned men and disappeared; indeed the Wandering Jew is supposed to have reappeared as late as 1870 in Muddy Valley, Utah, to a Mormon named Michael O'Grady. Most recently George K. Anderson, author of the monumental *Legend of the Wandering Jew* (1965), remarks that he himself was introduced in 1948 to "a Wall Street broker [*caveat emptor*] who considered himself Ahasuerus." And he is still very much with us in literature; Par Lagerkvist devoted a whole tetralogy to him. In our own country he is Vachel Lindsay's "Scissors Grinder"; appears dimly in Hawthorne's "Ethan Brand," and prominently in O. Henry's "The Door of Unrest"; crops up in original versions by Ben Hecht, Maude Hutchins, Howard Nemerov, and so on.

Rugg was not Jewish, however, but of Dutch extraction, and the famous Flying Dutchman is perhaps his even more direct ancestor; most of the important elements of his story that are not in the religious myth are here. The Flying Dutchman of course concerns a ghost ship which is seen in stormy weather around the Cape of Good Hope, and is ominous of bad luck. In some versions this ship is doomed because of a foul murder committed on board. But in a commoner form, the one Wagner used in his opera, the trouble was that an old Dutch sea captain, Vanderdecken, in the middle of a storm had sworn an oath to round the Cape if it took him eternity. His curse can be lifted only if he finds a woman who will sacrifice everything for him. The helplessness of Peter to control his horse is anticipated by the fact that the ship of one Captain von Falkenburg, condemned to sail the North Sea forever, has neither steersman nor helm.*

*The myth of the Flying Dutchman seems also congenial to the American imagination. In *Life on the Mississippi* Mark Twain reports a tradition about a steamboat that couldn't round a bend that had been cut off when, as occasionally happened, the river suddenly shortened itself and took

The stories of the Wandering Jew and the Flying Dutchman, both very widely known, are both obvious sources for "Peter Rugg." But the figure of the condemned wanderer is of course far older than these. The antecedents for the Jew are where one would expect to find them—in the Bible and in Christian lore generally. There is first of all the notable example of Cain, with his sentence ("a fugitive and a vagabond shalt thou be in the earth") and his mark, which he bore lest any encountering him should mistakenly put him to death (the Jew has a cross on his forehead, or on the sole of his boot). And according to John (21:22), Christ did say to Peter of another disciple, "If I will that he tarry till I come, what is that to thee?" There are or have been other myths as well of the eternal wanderings of Biblical characters—Ishmael, Elijah, Judas Iscariot, St. Peter, and Jesus himself and Satan himself among them.

There is a Wandering Jewess as well—Herodias, who in one version of her tale was Miriamne before marrying Herod, and was punished because she showed contempt for the Magi when they passed Jerusalem on their way to the manger (in Sue's *Wandering Jew* she is Ahaseurus' half-sister, and suffers his fate); and there is Kundry of von Eschenbach's (and Wagner's) *Parzifal,* who is condemned to live forever because she laughed at Jesus. Closer to home there is Miriam, the temptress of Hawthorne's *Marble Faun,* who from one angle appears to be that Jewess herself in deep disguise.

In addition there are myths about dancers who were rude to the Saviour and are cursed to dance till Judgment Day, about the wanderings of the Gypsies as punishment for their refusal to shelter the Virgin and her child, about Samiri, the sculptor of the golden calf, and there are Odysseus, Coleridge's Ancient Mariner, and many others like them. Peter's relation to Christian tradition suggests also that his vaguely Satanic hue may have to do with a recurrent notion that the devil travels vigorously by horse and buggy. (Which association might help explain the somewhat mysterious fact that people weren't particularly sympathetic to Peter, and didn't want to have much to do with him after his fall.)

The chief prototype of the Flying Dutchman, in turn, is probably Woden in his role as leader of the Wild Huntsmen—those restless, wandering night-riders who arrive in or presage a storm, as do Peter and the Jew, and who probably trace back to ancient belief in the night-wandering dead. There is a mingling of Teutonic and Christian lore here, for in

---

a new, more direct course to the sea. The pilots tempted fate with their oaths, and Twain says that when he was an apprentice pilot watchmen told him that they had themselves seen the "phantom steamer," still trying to find her way out."

medieval superstition these spirits were often not men but Woden's avenging maidens, and therefore easily associated with witches, who ride in the night on brooms or goats. One of their leaders was Diana, goddess of the hunt in classical myth—which adds a Roman element to the Norse-Christian mix. The other witch queen was Herodias, the Wandering Jewess herself: she was sweeping, according to one story, when she showed contempt for the Magi, and she has travelled her broomstick ever since.

Stories of unending punishment and frustrated activity go back of course at least as far as Greek mythology, where their ancestors are to be found in the tales of such as Sisyphus, who was condemned to Hades eternally to roll a great stone over the top of a hill, its weight always driving him back just as he approaches the summit; and Ixion, who for aspiring to the love of Zeus's wife turns endlessly on a wheel in Tartarus, the depths of hell; and Callisto, who was placed by Zeus in the sky as a bear with her son Arcas, the little bear, and because of the jealousy of Hera, who persuaded the god of the sea to arrange it, is forbidden ever to descend into the ocean, and goes with her son, as Peter with his daughter, wheeling eternally about the sky, one of the few constellations that never set.

The last of these myths is a story that directly explains a natural phenomenon, and although the theory that it is proper so to interpret myths is distinctly out of fashion, it is impossible to get around the fact that whatever their origins some myths are very suggestive of great natural processes. Sisyphus's stone may once have been, á la Robert Graves, a sun disk with some very special meanings, but his endless, hopeless task naturally puts one in mind of the ocean tide anyway—or of the waves, inexorably ascending the naked shingles of the world toward an unattainable highest reach, and as inexorably withdrawing. Ixion on his eternal wheel, and placed next to Sisyphus in Tartarus, just as naturally suggests the sun as it appears to our eyes, revolving forever about the earth. In the same way, then, and related to his function as a breeder of storms, Peter Rugg—whirling about the countryside, approaching now from one direction and now another but endlessly headed somewhere—might be taken to represent the wind. Then, by extension, just as Sisyphus, especially, has become a ready and fairly eloquent symbol of the futility of human endeavor, or of life itself, so Peter can seem an expression of the aimless or rootless life—or American life, if we will—where things fall apart, the center cannot hold, and we are buffeted about by forces before which we are helpless.

Such notions may point to overtones to Austin's story that are in it, and ones which people have very faintly responded to in reading it. But they are much too simple, and will not adequately explain either its once-great appeal, which is not necessarily gone for good, or its function. Partly the matter of its appeal, first, is a matter of Austin's skill: very surprisingly the telling is fresh, and does not smell of the lamp at all. Apparently relaxed in style it is in fact spare, selective, and unembellished; its distinction lies in the way a desperate situation is related calmly, even somewhat whimsically, and altogether unsentimentally. Further, since Peter's punishment is highly disproportionate to his crime, our participation in his misfortune is perhaps enhanced: the void produced by an inexplicably excessive penalty may allow at least some to fill it with their own nameless anxiety. Indeed there are ways in which "Peter Rugg" is superior to the stories of both the Wandering Jew and the Flying Dutchman. It does not have their epic quality or sweep, but it conveys with more intensity and detail a sense of dreadful helplessness. It can almost stand comparison with Kafka, and especially calls to mind his "Country Doctor": "exposed to the frost of this most unhappy of ages, with an earthly vehicle, unearthly horses, old man that I am I wander astray."

The fact that inferior accounts of Peter Rugg have themselves been at least somewhat effective suggests, however, that the story's ability to attract cannot be explained in literary terms alone. Clearly the tale has the crude, obvious function of the sort that gives most very popular stories a part of their currency. The Flying Dutchman is a warning about the folly of pride and the needless tempting of fate; it reflects superstitions concerning the relation between naming a thing and, by sympathetic magic, bringing it about—an ancient superstition that is intact today in the notion of the "jinx." The Wandering Jew obviously functions as a fable of Christian instruction, and clearly implies a warning too: one should not in any way renounce Christ—look what can happen. And although propagators of this myth have remembered, for the most part, what Edward Everett Hale forgot—that insistence on a moral wrecks it, that on being pointed at certain messages vanish—in the Middle Ages the myth was used as sharply pointed propaganda, as testimony to the power and truth of Christianity as opposed to the error of Judaism. "Peter Rugg" clearly repeats the Flying Dutchman superstition and its orthodox lesson about pride—a New-English sin, as it were. But a good deal that is more subtle than this finds expression in Austin's story, and another reading of the myth of the Wandering Jew leads to some of it.

This figure has impressed many people as a strikingly apt, and by no means unsympathetic, personification of what long seemed the historical fate of the Jews, from the beginnings of the Diaspora, at the end of the Captivity, to the recent past. In the myth a symbolic account of their dispersion in the very early Christian era—first along the shores of the Mediterranean, then throughout the Greco-Roman world, and finally throughout Christendom and beyond it—is powerfully signified. The specific inability of Ahasuerus to return to Palestine, as Peter to Boston, is a sharp reminder of the time when the Jews themselves were expressly prohibited from entering that city, then in Roman hands, on pain of death.

In the same way Peter Rugg, galloping about the countryside north, south, and west of Boston, plausibly personifies what may (perhaps for the first time but legitimately) be called the "New England Diaspora." He is a symbol of the great waves of emigration that began just before Austin wrote the story—waves which broke first from Boston out across New England itself; then, after 1782 and the end of the Revolution, swept across New York and northern Pennsylvania; and then after 1812 and the next war rolled across Ohio, northern Indiana and Illinois, eventually to reach the Pacific. The tendency of the Jews after their scattering to hold fast to their own ways and their own culture helped to remind people that their true roots were elsewhere, and thus may have helped in turn to keep alive a myth which expressed that fact. In much the same way the tendency of New Englanders was to reproduce in their new locations a culture and a setting which were as much as possible like the ones they had known before. They often simply transplanted themselves, and built anew the towns (with Puritan traditions and tidy white homes and steepled meeting-houses around elm-shaded public squares) that are visible today hundreds and thousands of miles from their origins. In its own day the story of Peter Rugg must have been redolent of these tidal waves.

And so it would not seem exactly coincidental that the period of Peter's creation and greatest vogue was the very period, 1820–1840, of the most vigorous exodus from New England. The story was born of the complex of feelings this exodus aroused, and it gave voice to them. New Englanders were very touchy on the subject; they were intensely patriotic about their region, and greatly alarmed over its "depopulization." (Of course there are no exact figures on the emigration, but relative to the population levels of the times it is known to have been vast.) The people who didn't go disapproved, rather helplessly but deeply, of those who did; they felt a silent reproach to their own ways and allegiances, hence to themselves, in all this departure. This feeling emerges in the story rather forcefully in the fact that people were unsympathetic to Peter, and it explains what would otherwise be a mystery in the affair—especially in the harsh ending of Austin's continuation—that no fairly weak association of Peter with the devil or storms will entirely account for. The story indirectly but firmly disapproves of Peter Rugg. The modern reader's natural sympathy for him must oppose a forget-about-him feeling that is in the tale itself, for there Peter has become the black sheep who has deserted the fold, his name no longer spoken in family circles.

The passing of time, and the tremendous, homogenizing changes which have swept across the country in recent decades, have obscured what might be called the diasporac level in Austin's tale. But this loss has been erased by a promotion of its protagonist from regional to national stature, for there has been an enormous gain in the validity of a remark Count Alexis de Toqueville made about Americans, not just New Englanders, back in 1835. Peter Rugg, that is, personifies very well a quality to which de Toqueville, in his extraordinary *Democracy in America,* gave a whole chapter: "The Restless Spirit of the Americans." An American, observes de Toqueville,

> settles in a place, which he soon afterward leaves . . . and if at the end of a year of unremitting labor he finds he has a few days' vacation, his eager curiosity whirls him over the vast extent of the United States. . . . Death at length overtakes him, but it is before he is weary of his bootless chase of that complete felicity which is forever on the wing.

Death has not yet quite caught up with Peter, and he typifies even better than restlessness the "anxiety, fear, and regret" which, de Toqueville went on to say, keep the collective national mind "in ceaseless trepidation." No transplanted Dutchman or Jew, and no longer simply a New Englander, Peter is an American.

Such interpretations as these, however, cannot account entirely for the hold the story once had on people, or for the spell it still casts on readers who are exposed to it today. The impelling image that is at the heart of the tale is not reckoned with by them: the image of a powerful horse racing away with a desperate, helpless man and his little girl as a black cloud hovers over, signalling disaster. That is what distinguishes the story from its sources; it is that image that does most to arouse the story's emotional charge, the feelings on which rest its basic appeal. Clearly these feelings are primarily of anxiety—of fear combined (now that it's no longer possible to care about nineteenth-century emigration) with pity, and both unpurged. The problem is how the image goes about arousing these emotions.

As vivid, irrational narratives, myths often bear a close resemblance to dreams. Very closely allied in primitive cultures, the two are similar enough to suggest the possibility, however limited, of examining myths that people have responded to and remembered as though they were really dreams they had experienced and been able to reconstruct. If we are attracted to it, then, we could look at a myth as an expression—however dim and rendered always into symbols—of something that is going on in us. The events of the myth become external happenings with internal meanings, in somewhat the same way that our private desires and fears may be dramatized in our dreams.

Many myths, like the one of Pocahontas, are for the most part wish fulfillments, the kind of daydreams we have asleep. Some myths are nightmares, the moving pictures of our fears; and many, like the story of Rip Van Winkle, are complex mixtures of the two. In the bewildering and somewhat frightening way Boston seems to Peter to shift location, and in the way familiar scenes distort themselves, as well as in the central image, "Peter Rugg" is clearly a nightmare.

One modern theory of dreams posits a whole class of nightmares which come not from the fear of something external to us, but from a fear of our own impulses. In this type of nightmare a roaring lion, for instance, represents no retributive father or anything of that sort, but the feared outcropping of the anger that is normally buried in us. It is possible, then, to speak of the myth of Peter Rugg as though it were, for those who have responded to it, a nightmare which they themselves have had vicariously, and to think of it as a nightmare which produces an anxiety that comes to people as a fear of their own impulses.

Now the association of nightmares and sex is immemorial. The whole and specific aim of the *mara,** the incubus or succubus to which night-

*The "mare" in nightmare is etymologically distinct from our term for a horse of female gender. It originally meant "fiend" and is derived from the Anglo-Saxon *mara*—an incubus or succubus believed to be the source of bad dreams and derived in turn from the verb *merran,* to crush, cognate with Icelandic *mara,* Danish *mare,* Old High German *mara,* and so on (even into French, where the hag shows up in *cauchmar*?). Our mare is from Anglo-Saxon *mere,* the female of

mares were for so long attributed, was sexual abuse of the dreamer. If we turn for help to Freudian psychology, which has been no more reluctant in relating bad dreams to sexual problems than folk-belief, we are offered a choice of weapons, and a book *On the Nightmare* (1931) by Freud's biographer, Ernest Jones, comes readily to hand. Here Dr. Jones lays down a dogma (or, his term, a "formula"), to wit and flatly: *"an attack of the Nightmare is an expression of a mental conflict over an incestuous desire."* He claims further that the presence of an animal in a dream reinforces the theme of incest; further still that "dreams of *travelling* are almost constantly associated with sexual motives, such as . . . escaping with the loved parent away from the competing one. . . ." He submits both dreams and myths to exactly the same sort of analysis;* and thus it looks very much as if he would have to say here that "Peter Rugg" is, like other nightmares, an expression of the Oedipus Complex (or, despite the misnomer, the Electra Complex?), and presents us with a striking picture of a father and daughter in wish-fulfilling but *Angst*-ridden escape of the mother.

One of the most important consequences of the Oedipal situation is the sense of castration, remote from the ordinary consciousness of adults, but large in the unconscious mind. The notion of castration comes, of course, as a response, compounded of fear, guilt and the need for punishment, to the Oedipal wishes. Indeed Jones ingeniously connects a wealth of mythological beliefs about specifically—and of all things—horses with the whole problem of castration. Should we then take another tack and say that the essential anxiety in "Peter Rugg" is over castration? Should we gravely reconsider in this light Austin's request that his second get him a pistol: "Mother—I suppose—has hidden mine"? Is Peter's daughter now a substitute cast up by the machinery of censorship for his mother ("Some other Mrs. Rugg")?—or a curious symbol ("Peter") of the detached member?—or of both? And is her reproach now really the mother's reproach to Peter's infantile striving toward her? Or his wandering a search instead—for his mother, home, Middle Street, and the harbor of Boston?

As fast as that the amateur finds himself in murky water, over his head and unsnorkled. Fumbling around in the darkness, however, a few things

mearh, a horse. But by some obscure process mare and *mara,* horse and fiend, became associated in the imagination. Thus it is possible to say, remembering his horse, that "Peter Rugg" has doubly to do with nightmare. See Ernest Jones, *On the Nightmare,* new ed. (New York: Grove Press, 1959), especially Part III, "The Mare and the *Mara.*"

*Jones, *On the Nightmare,* 44, 70, 204, and 66.

may fuzzily emerge. For one thing, Jones's book, itself a bit of a nightmare, was written in those grand free-wheeling days before Freudian doctrine had undergone real testing, qualification and revision. It would not be unfair to say that his hypotheses are a bit unguarded. For another, we are searching for the story's appeal to the reader, not for what it might reveal about the writer; and in this context about all we could say is that the appeal is remotely to our own Oedipal guilt—which, if it exists at all, is buried so deep that most people, unable to detect even the existence of what's being appealed to, will hesitate to believe that any such communication is taking place.

Of course it may be that in the end we cannot really locate or explain the source of anxiety in "Peter Rugg." Indeed it may be that—as opposed to fear, where we know what we fear—anxiety is dread unable to identify its origins. It might even be that in pursuing Peter feverishly we have contracted his disease, and can't get home with the project. But in the ordinary rules of sport three strikes are allowed the batter: if incest and castration are a pair of misses then a third swing ought to be permissible. (If not, we can imitate Austin in his duel and shoot anyway.) Turning in but not from Freud, it might do to make use, finally, of his other trinity—somewhat more "available" than the Oedipus triangle: his three-part view of the human psyche. It's conceivable that this may seem, to return to a previous metaphor, a little like coming up for air.

For Freud the basic cause of anxiety is the fear of being overwhelmed by instinct, or appetite—the fear that the forces we normally subdue by repression will get out of hand and break through our defenses to destroy us. When for any reason the struggle between appetite and repression becomes intense, and pent-up drives threaten to break loose, people suffer from anxiety—especially because they fear not only disgrace or destruction in the eyes or at the hands of others; they fear as much the power of their own disapproval, of their "consciences." Anxiety, then, comes when we fear that the instincts, or the normally repressed unconscious forces in general (a crude description of the "id"), will overwhelm consciousness (the "ego"), and then our consciences (the "superego") will rise up and condemn us.

Subject to certain variations this theory is quite widely accepted, and it may throw light on the source of the anxiety that the central image of Peter Rugg occasions. This image presents an extraordinary vision of the destruction of control, of the usual self's precarious balance between appetite and conscience suddenly shattered. The looming and mythically powerful horse is passion, born of Peter's cosmic defiance, and broken out in spasms of vengeance for its normal suppression. Peter is the self, tied to the horse and hopelessly out of control. And the little girl increases his sense of guilt in sitting mutely by and providing a witness to the shameful display; her very presence is a grim reproach; she is, in short, conscience. The image presents a vivid and classic picture of the situation that produces anxiety. The horse, id, overwhelms Peter, ego, while the little girl, superego, sits in silent but terrible judgment. The horse and the girl are thus externalized aspects of Peter himself, and vicariously they are all symbolic aspects of ourselves. There, perhaps, is our nightmare.

Of course it is probable that for Freudians the horse in this nightmare would be a sexual symbol of appetite* whereas the passion that got out of Peter's control was rage or anger—his "terrible temper." But Freudian revisionists like Karen Horney have argued persuasively that the fear that rage or anger will break loose and destroy us can produce anxiety every bit as effectively as the fear of a loss of sexual control can do. Anxiety comes when *any* of our basic defenses against the onslaught of irrational impulse are seriously threatened. The anxiety that visits a man who, say, hates some superior and fears lest his anger burst out and cost him the position his false affability and compliance have built is extremely common. Peter's horse, then, is the symbol of Peter's rage, and this outbreak is no less awesome or terrible to behold than a loss of sexual control (to which our own dreams have accustomed us) would be. We see in Peter a man who, for the momentary breakdown of discipline and the defiance of superior power, has fallen clean out of comfort, home, place and time—and most of the other relationships which map our routes and define our roles. He has exploded right out of the grooves of his life. Anyone secretly knows how delicate is the balance whereby he maintains his security; anyone can participate through Austin's symbols in the anxi-

*Jung might well agree. In a chapter on "Dream Analysis" in his *Modern Man in Search of a Soul* he remarks that in myth and folklore generally the horse "carries one away like a surge of instinct"; it "represents the lower part of the body and the animal drives that take their rise from there." (Plato, in a startling section of the *Phaedrus,* said substantially the same thing.) For Freud all dreams of flight have sexual significance, and there are myths of flight comparable to "Peter Rugg" (Europa carried off by a bull, for instance) that seem transparently sexual. Some verse about another "Wild Ride" by the spinster Louise Imogen Guiney, written a few years before the poem about Peter's, has a refrain in which horses clearly suggest desire:

I hear in my heart, I hear in its ominous pulses,
All day, the commotion of sinewy, mane-tossing horses;
All night, from their cells, the importunate tramping and neighing.

ety of the man who was suddenly missing. Pity, we suspect, comes chiefly from the ability to see ourselves in the misfortunes of others, and when the horse and the little girl and Peter Rugg go riotously by in all the wrong directions we pity Peter because our own anxieties tell us that there, but for the precarious grace of control, go we.

1973

II.

Our Hemingway Man

4.

Hemingway and Me: A Rather Long Story

2 July 1961 it was, late of a hot bright Sunday morning, when dark amid a blaze of noon the phone rang with the news of Hemingway's sudden departure from the living. All the instruments agreed: the day of his death was a hot bright day, and the shock of it ran the whole world round. His scorn for the "cowardice" of self-destruction, especially as he had planted it in the thoughts of the protagonist of *For Whom the Bell Tolls,* seemed to rule it out for him—on the entirely foolish assumption that a man who had expressed his bitter distaste for suicide could not in another country, condition, and era commit it.

We were conditioned to expect that Hemingway's death would come with a bang when it came; following the airplane crashes in Uganda in 1954 there had already been obituaries. Most important, I had recently learned through an unusually direct and accurate operation of the literary grapevine that the author was a great deal sicker than the press, on his two hospitalizations, had announced or been in a position to know. But the news hurt anyway.

After great pain, claims the poet, a formal feeling comes. What came instead were more phone calls—later a couple of telegrams, later still letters—all excited and to the same effect: You called it, Young! These messages belong to a rare species of the genus Congratulation, but the recipient was not gratified. Nor was the remark particularly accurate, as anyone who reads my book will see, unless by extrapolation from it. But there is more to this than first appears, and it is fortunate that an objective statement of the problem already exists.

In a preface to the new edition of his *Art of Ernest Hemingway* the British critic John Atkins provides a sort of "Coming Attraction" for my tome:

> . . . shortly after my own book appeared there came an extremely interesting study by Philip Young. I understand that Hemingway tried to prevent the publication of this book. Its treatment was very intimate . . . and if its diagnosis was accurate it was a brilliant piece of work. If, on the other hand, the diagnosis was specious and only apparently consistent, it was a piece of impudence. According to Hemingway, it was a collection of mistaken conclusions based upon partial information. . . .

Fair enough, as a statement of a difference of opinion; and understandable enough the "irritation of Hemingway and his widow" toward Young that Atkins mentions later on. But then, with reference to Hemingway's first protagonist, Nick Adams, comes the trouble:

> Many of us had been puzzled by our own reaction to those early stories. . . . We felt they contained some deep significance. It is to Young's credit, I think, that he revealed this significance by showing the subject-matter to be the aftermath of fear. . . . All his life he had exposed himself (overexposed himself, claims Young) to things he feared. It may be a distasteful thing to discover, but I cannot help feeling that Young virtually foretold self-destruction.

"Distasteful" is not entirely adequate. But the question is, if the diagnosis were specious and mistaken, how could Young have "virtually foretold" suicide on the basis of it?

It is important first to get the picture hung straight. Move number one is to repeat that Young did not predict suicide. He described a situation, a pattern, a process in Hemingway's life and work in which the act of suicide would not be altogether inconsistent. Second move is to state that nobody I know of recognized such a prediction, nor was I ever aware of it, except by hindsight. But I think—I feel?—that there is a deeper problem only a very few have been tactless enough to raise.

Suppose, as is the case, the author had in advance warned his literary analyst of the enormous damage a psychological working over could do him. Suppose, further, he had mentioned a very long letter, almost certainly to the same effect, that he had composed but, since it could only, he said, give the critic worry, he was not going to mail. (To tell a writer he has neurosis, Hemingway did write me, is as bad as telling him he has cancer: you can put a writer permanently out of business this way.) Suppose, then, that critic, critic's critic, editor, and publisher all believed that Hemingway was needlessly and irrationally alarmed about the matter and so went ahead and produced a book which contains, among other things, a description of a syndrome the critic thought he had found in the author's work, which he believed the author's experience had caused him to delineate carefully there, and from which an after-the-fact prediction of death by his own hand could be, and was, imaginatively inferred. Could a head-on collision with such material conceivably have anything at all to do with the destructive way in which the syndrome worked itself out? If a diagnosis implies a prognosis can the diagnosis operate so as to induce the prognosis? Or help prevent it? Or have no effect at all?

Before questions of such complexity the critic is understandably mute. He does not know enough about the places and how the weather was to make even an impudent guess. Among the countless events that crowd a man's life, and this was a very crowded one, it is utterly beyond him to measure the effect of any single event. All he can know certainly is that for a year or two the "threat" of his book had an unmistakable effect on Hemingway and that in subsequent recorded interviews, right down to the last one, Hemingway was mindful of it.

But worry the critic has had—letter mailed or no. However his full discomfort, like his alleged prediction, came only after the fact. At the time of his struggle with the author, which developed into a struggle with himself as well, he simply could not get it into his head that a totally obscure $3,100-per-year instructor at the Washington Square College of New York University could actually hurt the most confident (apparently) American novelist of his age—and, next only to Faulkner, the best one. Neither could any of the others involved. Save only Hemingway.

In short, the critic is not as sure as he once was (once he felt quite sufficiently sure) that in his eventual "victory" a greater degree of right triumphed over a lesser degree. This is no matter of *mea culpa,* which would constitute an act of impudence to pass all men's believing. (Anyway, much of the tale is less morality play than farce.) And the critic will still defend the thinking according to which he and others, not knowing their own infernal strength, if Hemingway was right, built the case for publishing the book. Nor would he hesitate to make the case for bringing it out again. But it helps to admit at the start that like the ancient subterranean brook which is flowing still under Washington Square something is running under his reasoning, silently tugging at the foundations of it.

I had liked this writer for a long time, and had even ported a *Portable Hemingway,* along with a very few other books, halfway across Europe during World War II. But the story really starts later, with some well-remembered moments of a postwar afternoon in one of Iowa City's most wretched apartments for young marrieds when the pieces of my fragmentary reading of him began to fall into place—and, simultaneously, to align themselves with a recent and then-heterodox rereading of *Huckleberry Finn*. What I knew I had, if it would flesh out, was the argument for the subject of the doctoral dissertation I had to write. Flesh out it did, as things went along, in all kinds of ways.

The story consists more of endings than starts, however, and the first one came in 1948 when I finished the job—the first book-length study of Hemingway, I believe—and lurched off with the degree. There are two arguments among several to be found in that strenuous effort, as in this book, which are necessary to an understanding of subsequent events. First: the notion that the so-called "Hemingway hero" as I defined him was pretty close to being Hemingway himself. Second: the one fact about this recurrent protagonist, as about the man who created him, is necessary to any real understanding of either figure, and that is the fact of the "wound," a severe injury suffered in World War I which left permanent scars, visible and otherwise. I should also put it down for later relevance that in the beginning I answered a frequent question—What does *he* say about all this?—by explaining that since I knew roughly how he felt about critics and academics I was pretty certain he would not reply and hadn't asked him. When the question became oppressive I did write to ask if he wanted to comment and I was correct in the first place; he didn't answer. (At least I can take satisfaction in knowing that I did not start the procession of "these damn students" who "call me up in the middle of the night to get something to hang on me so they can get a Ph.D.") (Or, as he metaphorically looked at it, did I?)

The first of an impressive number of celebrations attended this ending; as for my work, it was supposed to pass and be forgotten with the rest. And, except for doing a nice little piece of business on the interlibrary loan circuit, it had begun that process even as my wife and I made our way to New York. But that first finish was undone when I was conned by some generous and well-intentioned people into a tedious interchange with a couple of university presses. And that misadventure ended when after eight months one unmentionable editor (he had once shot an antelope or something and was a great fan of *Green Hills of Africa*) returned the volume with the explanation that he was going to publish instead a work which would pretty much upset it. (Just how I was not to learn, since if that book appeared the secret never leaked.) Meanwhile, however, a good friend and colleague at N.Y.U., William M. Gibson, had read a copy and had sent it to a trade publisher with a college department, Rinehart and Company, where was employed a friend of his named Thomas A. Bledsoe.

Mr. Bledsoe was soon to figure largely in this story. He in turn became a friend and also established himself as the best all-around editor I ever encountered. He compounded at least one spectacular mistake of mine; he was forever on the road when we should have been in action back at 232 Madison Avenue; when he was there he was badly overburdened with all sorts of other books. But he worked with energy, intelligence, taste, and understanding from start of this to finish and I am still in his debt—especially for a couple of organizational and strategic ideas that worked.

The first smart thing Tom did was make a prompt offer, which was that if I would clean the thing up so as to get the Ph.D. out of it (largely because the subject resisted the same there was less of that than is normal), and if I would arrange things so that Hemingway shared less of the stage with Huck Finn, then Rinehart would publish it. Astonished and delighted with a new dimension to things, I attended my first of those let's-get-together-soon-I-mean-it New York luncheons, and became quite looped in a happy, expansive sort of way.

Thus for several months, exercising in the still night when only the moon raged, and the lovers lay abed, I remorselessly did the job over, chapter by chapter, adding one and junking another, until it was finally finished. But we only thought it was done, because right then, as if out of nowhere, came the announcement of Hemingway's first book in exactly a decade. This novel appeared initially in some improbable magazine; once each month I minutely observed the current idiosyncrasies of Col. Richard Cantwell, protagonist of *Across the River and Into the Trees*. Of all living readers only John O'Hara and Carlos Baker, I believe, have refused to call this near-parody of Hemingway a bad book. But I wonder when a critic-errant ever had a more astonishing adventure with a new work; it was precisely as if the author had got hold of my manuscript, incomprehensibly had determined to prove its notions to the hilt, and had brilliantly succeeded. For without pretending otherwise, the Colonel was about as close to his author as it is possible to get and still be called fictional, and now it was *Hemingway* who was demonstrating how his life had centered on that violent World War I misfortune. Here was staggering evidence for my argument, and nothing to do but put it in. Put it in I did. And finished again.

Even at this time I knew that when critic and editor have done all they can for a manuscript a common practice is to send it out to an Independent Expert. So I said if you're going to do this, how about Malcolm Cowley? He had been a friend of Hemingway's for many years, had himself written well and substantially on the subject, and was rumored to be available for such assignments. I had never met him at this point, but Tom knew him and thought he was a good if obvious choice. So the critic's critic was employed.

Cowley was to become the unintentional agent of a great deal of trouble, but at first he certainly earned his money. In April of 1951 he sent me directly a detailed interim report, which was a thoughtful thing to do, as I could begin considering changes at once. He related as well a good deal of factual information which I couldn't put in the book but which was reassuring anyway. In particular he brought up places where I had given impressions I hadn't intended and places where I had made bad guesses, and he objected to several things that I felt I wanted to leave the way they were. A month later he submitted his formal report, and I profited once more. He was gratifyingly enthusiastic about the first two and last two chapters, less so about the three in between, which I had already tediously reworked. But he had some solid objections, and I did a few things yet once more, finally in late May winding it up again.

The subsequent celebration took a nasty turn and became a wake. After reading the study Cowley had sent an informal account of it to Hemingway, commending much of it to him, and Hemingway had unaccountably got a very odd impression of what I had done. He proposed at once to stop it; and when Cowley had the letter to this effect, he reported it, with his hair on end, to Bledsoe, who had said nothing to me while I was still at work on this book of criticism. The letter was from Ernest to Malcolm and dated 22 May 1951.*

What Cowley reported in horror I read in shock. About this book of Young's, Hemingway wrote. He was absolutely determined that no biography of him was going to appear while he was alive to stop it. All he had to do was refuse to grant permission for quotation from his work, and then if the project went ahead all he had to do was turn it over to the lawyers. He was sorry, but every single time he had tried to be polite or helpful or frank to someone who was trying to make money out of his life it had gone badly. Thus if Mr. Young planned to publish his life while he was still in it, he would block him. He had no desire to be rude to Mr. Young or Mr. Bledsoe, but this was his considered stand and he did not intend to budge.

Perhaps this looks easy. I had most assuredly not written his biography—nor have ever wished to—and as for making money no one was more surprised than I, except the publisher, when the book did turn a profit. But to me it looked more than a little ominous. The book was criticism. But maybe you could call it "biographical criticism"; it did unfashionably contain enough biography to demonstrate that the experience of the hero was typically a refraction or projection of the author's. A sense of foreboding I couldn't account for distracted me even as words for a message of clarification began to form in my mind. But it was instantly decided that Rinehart would do the straightening out, and I acquiesced. Thus began what I still think of as The Year (it was really longer than that) of the Great Mess.

The struggle that followed was in large part real enough, but some of it was unreal and some of it was ridiculous. The real questions were, first: what are the rights of living authors, and what the rights of critics? Second: at what point can criticism become an invasion of an author's privacy? And how much privacy can a writer expect when he has allowed himself to become an internationally public figure, or even, according to

*Not even that date is a quotation (Hemingway didn't write dates in that fashion), and it may be necessary to make clear why it is not. In May of 1958 Hemingway wrote out an edict, with his wife as witness of it, to the effect that his letters, or even parts of them, were never to be published. One comes to understand his reasons. His letters are typically open and free-wheeling (and often very funny); he took few pains with the composition of them; he wanted to be remembered for his work, not his biography. But no one knows what "never" to be published, in this case, means. One thing it almost surely does not mean is "never." It certainly, however, does not mean "now." In savage retaliation to this policy I hereby refuse myself permission to quote from my own letters, or from Cowley's or Bledsoe's either.

some, had worked very hard at promoting the image? Lastly, and this was much the toughest of the lot: given a respect for the author, which grew as the struggle progressed, how far is the critic willing to venture, even in defense of the author against many other critics, in violation of the author's deepest wishes that certain theories about him not be published? (As I said, much of the debate was then as now as much with myself as with Hemingway.)

As for the false part: in addition to being no biography written to cash in on his life the book was in no way, as he warily seemed to feel, an attack on him. Quite the contrary. And as for invading privacy, I had from the start been careful to include absolutely nothing of a factual nature that I had not already seen in print, although I knew a great many other things. Only my organization of the facts, which was really a perception of how I thought and think *he* had, not far beneath the surface, organized them, was new. And as frustrating as anything was that the single impediment to publishing the book when it was ready was the preannounced refusal to grant permission to quote from his work and, if I quoted anyway, to take legal action. The joker in this pack was that nobody but Hemingway thought he would have a case. Despite his confident belief, which without any appreciable effect first Cowley, then Bledsoe, patiently explained to him to be almost certainly unsound, the considered opinion of the literary-legal experts like Morris Ernst was that if a case came to court in which a critic had without permission quoted for legitimate purposes and was not trying to sell the author's work as his own, the court would almost certainly find for the critic. (This was, however, a useless opinion in this instance, and Hemingway simply ignored it, probably figuring as I did that it didn't matter, since no reputable publisher at that time was likely to go to press without having satisfied the convention.)

In the light of the reality of central problems, however, it is remarkable how much of what happened was farcical. In the first place nobody, but nobody, except Hemingway answered his mail promptly. (When this eventually dawned on him he cut it out.) Indeed Bledsoe, who was in the naval reserve, went off at one critical point on an extended sea venture, having stowed away in his gear a letter that he thought he'd left behind for his immediate superior, Ranny Hobbs, to deal with. There was nothing to be done; I didn't even find out which ocean he was on.

Second is the fact that at this time Hemingway was living in San Francisco de Paula, which is a hamlet near Havana, Cuba. Now the mail clerk at Rinehart, whom I once or twice encountered on the elevator, appeared to be a nice enough girl. But I don't believe she ever did really master what I came to think of as the Cuba Concept. This had nothing whatever to do with politics, Castro not having yet been heard of. It was made up of the notion that Cuba lies outside the territorial limits of the United States. Thus mail journeying there by plane required three cents, I think it was, in extra postage to make the trip successfully, clear customs, and get unpacked. As a result of the clerk's failure to comprehend this, our letters, already long overdue, would typically wing south only to float back as it seemed on the trade winds, covered with blurred purple lettering which when deciphered and translated always turned out to signify Returned for Insufficient Postage, and had to wing it again. (The misconception must have been contagious; toward the end even Hemingway, in reverse, picked it up.) Then a fit of petty jealousy brought in the United States Post Office; two of our most winning bits of diplomacy touched base first at San Francisco, California, only later to take off, somewhat dispirited, in a proper direction.

And, Lord help us, there were the lawyers. Hypersensitive to Hemingway's pithy references to law and lawsuits, Official Rinehart (but never Bledsoe) ran scared all the way. I may not have all of it exactly straight, because much of this specialized activity, or inactivity, was not deemed suitable for my observation. But if the reports I got were accurate *three* firms had the manuscript to check out for libel—of which of course there wasn't any. One lawyer broke his hip, became intensely irritable, and refused to do any work during a lengthy stay at the hospital. After another long delay another lawyer announced, under some pressure, an Imminent Opinion ("by Monday"), whereupon he expired over the weekend. Then I heard that Stanley Rinehart and Charles Scribner appeared to have the thing about patched up on the front-office level when Mr. Scribner died. And all that time—it was nearly a year—until Hemingway wrote to ask why in hell he never heard from the *author* of the damned book, my hands were tied (and sweating).

Obviously things moved very slowly in this adventure-by-mail, which needs only a little cleaning up for family consumption and a little care in correcting the spelling (else one would be quoting).* We had not

*Hemingway had, to use his wife's phrase for it, "this crazy thing about spelling," which was chiefly that he usually inserted an "e" in words that do not conventionally retain it—e.g., liveing, writeing; the extra vowel in his *Moveable Feast* exists in honor of the practice. It is possible that he had some subtle purpose in mind here, but that would not account for the various ways in which

even got started with the correspondence when, six full months after Cowley's original shocker, he wrote Tom again. By this time the situation had become so miserable for him he wished he'd never heard of the wretched book. Word of it had apparently reached Hemingway from some additional source; anyway, we learned that by now the author was so disturbed that he had written his own publisher a whole *series* of letters on the subject. Since Cowley had commended the project to him in large part, he now seemed to Hemingway vaguely aligned with the enemy. Understandably, the critic's critic wanted to take his leave of the affair at this point—which only made Hemingway all the angrier at the man he referred to in one letter as an old, close friend (the same man who had done a good, honest job on the manuscript, and whose offer to return his check for it Bledsoe naturally refused). It is not pleasant to recall the time many years later when Cowley told me that following this mix-up he never once heard from Hemingway again. But I also know that Hemingway subsequently praised one of Cowley's books, and I remind myself that he has a compensatory privilege in being one of the very, very few who are going through all the manuscript Hemingway left behind.

Up to this point neither Tom nor I had written Hemingway, nor had we heard directly from him. On 3 December 1951, however, Tom did write, as Cowley had done and as we should have done six months before, in an attempt to bring the whole matter into focus. Some time later (due to insufficient postage our letter had only just arrived) the author replied at great length. And an open, rambling, and friendly letter it was. But it boiled down to his insistence that too much had already been written about his life. First there had recently been Cowley's own long biographical study in *Life* which, well-meaning as it was, had the effect of moving attention from his work to himself. Then there was the notorious *New Yorker* "profile" by Lillian Ross, another good friend. Despite her complacence, this had horrified him when he read it in proof, but he had done nothing to interfere with it. The result of all this (and much more), he felt, was that his writing was being judged from the standpoint of these widely read biographical impressions and not on its own merits. He had not discouraged any of these people (they had all needed the money) but

---

the word "psychoanalytic" was later to appear; nor does it make his position impregnable when in the *Feast* he kids Fitzgerald for having known him "two years before he could spell my name" (which usually came out "Hemmingway"). (But truth to tell it is doubtful that Fitzgerald could have survived the first cut in a fourth-grade spelling bee, while Hemingway, if he put his mind to it, could.)

by now he had had bloody well enough. Although he had been a very long time hearing from us and wondered why and intended to be firm, he did not wish to seem rude or intractable, he said. He predicted that pretty soon there would be no writers, only critics, who would go off to Hollywood and be wrecked by the movies. What did we want to bet that Arthur Mizener wouldn't soon be on TV? All we had to do was get him another Scott Fitzgerald. I have nothing against Professor Mizener, but it was a most ingratiating letter, which ended wishing us a good holiday.

The holiday was Christmas, and better than a month was to elapse before Hemingway was to get a response to his most friendly overture. But it should not be assumed that Bledsoe and I were idle all that time. Indeed not; we were busy making things infinitely more difficult. Christmas time, for all healthy-minded college and university English teachers, is also Modern Language Association time, when we stage our own peculiar version of a convention. The proceedings that winter were in Detroit and I had been invited to read a short paper on Hemingway. I did, it was a mistake, and when Bledsoe finally answered Hemingway's letter (he'd been extensively on the road again), he reinforced the error, proudly describing the reception of the talk, which he had attended.

Tom's letter, again returned for more stamping, arrived on the evening of 16 January. The next morning Hemingway replied to it and by now his patience was tiring. He pointed out that in a frank and friendly way he had spelled out his position, only to wait a month for a response to it. If Mr. Bledsoe was too busy, why didn't he hear from Mr. Young? Was it true that Mr. Young was corresponding with a critic in the Sudan?* He couldn't understand why, if Mr. Young had time to be traveling about giving papers on his work, he couldn't find time to write the author about it. *And* send along a copy of the talk. He closed, but on 31 January added a postscript explaining that he had put the letter aside for two weeks so that he would not be the only person involved who answered his mail. He also stressed his eagerness to read my paper: he felt it might help him in his present efforts.

The trouble was that, as assigned, my effort (restricted to something like twelve minutes) was a critique of three Hemingway papers that preceded it. Two of those papers were by chance psychoanalytic in approach—John Aldridge's "Jungian," and Frederick Hoffman's "Freudian." To establish the widest possible area of agreement among us I

*Probably a reference to Atkins, who was, I believe, in the Foreign Service.

followed the lead, voted for Freud, and, carrying the tendency of Hoffman's remarks to what seemed a logical conclusion, ended with what I still take to be the appropriate psychoanalytic terminology. Hemingway's sense of indignation at this vocabulary did not surprise anyone. My position is what needs explaining.

There were two lines of defense at this dreadful juncture. One is that I stumbled on the psychoanalytic theory and its terminology *after* I had completed my own analysis of the wounding process and its results, which I felt Hemingway had delineated carefully only to have the whole matter ignored by his swarming critics. I remember this clearly. As part of my General Education, back in Iowa, I was reading *Beyond the Pleasure Principle* when it suddenly broke over me that Freud was writing about precisely the kind of thing I had constructed out of Hemingway's scattered descriptions of it. Told that Freud had undergone a lot of modification, I got hold of Fenichel, recommended to me as the most authoritative of the post-Freudian Freudians, and there I found a more detailed account of the same business. What I had called, in a very special sense, "primitivism," Fenichel called "primitivation"; I had written "shell shock," he called it "traumatic neurosis." All I had done in the paper was to supply these and other terms, and to remark how skillfully Hemingway had illustrated them in fiction.

The second point is that for the MLA there was no need to waste even thirty seconds acknowledging the obvious fact that the critic was no trained analyst. I have a recent anthology called *Psychoanalysis and American Fiction,* which has fifteen contributors; all of them, including myself (but not on Hemingway), are English professors or literary critics or both, and not one of them felt the need to point out that he has no medical license to practice. It might have been unreasonable to have expected Hemingway to know this, but in our branch of service, as the saying goes, it goes without saying.

Rinehart clearly was betting no money at all on my diplomatic talents; before my first letter to Hemingway had passed a board of review Bledsoe had written again, and on 12 February received an eloquent reply. First noting that for once sufficient postage had been supplied, only to have the letter go to California (he enclosed the envelope), Hemingway gritted his teeth and remarked once more how much he looked forward to hearing from me in person and reading my paper. But he said he had a real objection to people who won't leave writers alone to do their work (precisely why, except for my reluctant, unanswered letter of years before, he had not been aware of my existence until hearing from Cowley). And people don't wish writers luck. They annoy them and worry them instead of simply hoping they will be healthy, live a long time, escape financial and female difficulties, and most of all go on writing. Writing is very tough work, he said, yet it requires mechanisms as delicate as the most delicate mechanisms imaginable. If someone comes along, not himself an expert, and takes the machine apart for his own benefit, it's all very well to say that he has a right to take any old machine apart, but Hemingway did not feel the right existed while the mechanisms were still in good running order. And that was what he meant when he said some criticism constitutes an invasion of privacy.

A man who cannot, first shot, put down two English sentences in a row that are nowhere barbarous did not need telling that writing is an extremely difficult way to pass the time. But the important fact to me was that on 6 February I had the first chance to present the case myself—which, despite the cogency of Bledsoe's and Cowley's letters, I probably should not have relinquished in the first place. I explained my previous silence, pointed out that the connection between himself and his recurrent protagonist was not in my mind the central idea of the study, and tried to salvage what I could from the Detroit debacle. I expressed my admiration for his work, noted that my own book had come to mean quite a bit to me, too, and closed.

At this point Hemingway went on a fishing trip, and it was one month to the day of my first effort when he sent the most memorable reply I ever got from anyone. It began with a simple offer: if I would give him my word that my book was not a biography disguised as criticism, further that I was not psychoanalyzing him alive, then he had no objection to my publishing it. He was not going to go over the whole business again, he said. But then he wondered if I really understood how damaging it could be to a practicing writer to tell him he has a neurosis. It damages him with all his readers and could so injure the writer himself that he could no longer write. He said he had found my Detroit paper, which I had so kindly sent him, very interesting; but he was shocked by my use of serious medical language. He repeated it: the paper he thought interesting, and likewise the conclusions of it, but he was shocked by the terminology when there were no medical qualifications for employing it.

What followed, as he tried to explain the amount of trouble I had caused him over the past ten months, shocked me. It surely seemed to him, he said, that there were enough dead writers to work on to allow the living to work in peace. So far I had caused him serious worry, hence a serious interruption in his work. First there was Cowley, who had disturbed him with that first report, and next, leaving a mystery, had washed his hands of the thing. Then there was all the rest. The disturbance caused by me, he said, had been very bad for a man who was trying to keep his mind peaceful during a year which had already seen the death of his first grandson, the serious illness (cancer) of his father-in-law, the death of his mother, the death of a former wife (mother of two of his three children), the suicide of the maidservant of his house on the heels of a previous attempt, the death of his last old friend in Africa, and then the death of his very dear friend and publisher, Charles Scribner. On top of everything were piled the menace of my book and then the neurosis or neuroses charges made in Detroit. Out of all this he said he sincerely hoped my luck had been good; his assuredly had not. (Many of his letters had been composed on an obviously decrepit typewriter but this one was handwritten, three pages of it, and he explained that the lines were askew because of the hot day, which made his forearm sweat on the paper.)

The effect of seeing myself in the company of such events was nearly catatonic, so that, although I thought of little else, two weeks elapsed before I was able to respond and to clear the response again with the board. I had begun to think my initial sense of doom was profoundly justified. There did not seem much point in explaining that I had studied a good many writers, most of them dead, without coming up with a set of ideas that would support the like of my doctor's thesis and the consequent book. What I said instead was that the easy way would be to give the word he asked for. I could satisfy the letter of his conditions. But I was less sure about the spirit of them. He had been so decent throughout this business that I couldn't tell him less than the truth. The biography part was simple, but not the psychoanalytic; perhaps I should have offered simply to remove what little I had got from the analysts. I was glad to read, eventually, Mark Schorer's judgment that this material was handled with "great sensitivity," but a couple of other reviewers were to remark that my case would stand without it, and as already noted there had been a time when it had not been around to cut. But the shoe I handed readers to put on if they wished seemed to fit so well I could not resist offering it, and I tried instead to explain. There were only a few hundred words of offensive matter; it dealt with *nothing* but the wound; *I* had not done the psychoanalyzing—had, rather, quoted from two analysts and called their theories plausible and incomplete. One thing I was trying to show,

I wrote him, was the remarkable resemblance between a psychiatrist's description of how a man acts who has been badly hit and his own account of, say, Nick Adams fishing the Big Two-Hearted River (which he had complained no one had ever understood). I also told him that however much things had gone astray I had surely never intended to injure him in any fashion. If a critic could hurt a writer with his readers, then it must follow that he could help; I hadn't wasted the better part of the last few years trying to knock anybody down. I said I felt badly about having caused him so much trouble, and that I did, very much, wish him well.

It was not surprising when at this point Hemingway lapsed into a complete silence. As the weeks went by, it became clear that we were on dead center. Ranny Hobbs sent a cable asking for a favorable decision on my letter; a few days passed; then he received a cable from Hemingway saying that he was thinking my letter over as I had done his. He would write soon. But he did not, for a long time. The situation had ceased to be bad and had become desperate; conceivably the whole project should have been dumped at this point. But that did not really seem an option to me, because of a scarcely less serious situation that had developed simultaneously with these events.

Following the postwar G.I. bulge of students, enrollments at N.Y.U. dropped precipitously, and as an untenured instructor in 1951 who had not published anything breathtaking, I was perishing fast. Although no one had told Hemingway this, I was, by the time now reached in the story, unemployed for a whole year. Except for the mercies of the American Council of Learned Societies, which paid a small wage to keep me from leaving the profession (as I had come near doing in Detroit), and for the fact that Carolyn, my wife, had a part-time job as hostess in a tearoomy sort of restaurant, I don't know what we would have been eating. Further, I had no job for the next year, and when I eventually landed one it was strictly a temporary appointment, so that I faced unemployment again for the following year. Lastly, since the book had long ago been announced all over the place I was receiving a certain amount of static from the wrong quarters about not being able to deliver.

Thus I felt that if I was unable to get Hemingway's go-ahead for what I thought the right reasons I had very little choice but to try to get it for the wrong, and so on 23 May 1952 I wrote again, explaining very briefly my predicament. I also said that, although it was none of my business, it was hard for me to understand why, because she needed the money, he had assented to Miss Ross's "murderous" *New Yorker* profile but would not permit a book which made the strongest case it could for his importance. Anyway, I felt now there was only one thing I could do. If he would not grant the conventional permission then I was quite prepared to rewrite the book paraphrasing all the quotations. I was positive he would prefer his own language to mine, but it was up to him how it went. Bledsoe wrote to confirm it: Rinehart would publish the book that way. Five days later I had a cable from Hemingway telling me to inform his editor that permission to quote was granted. He said he hoped I was happy.

Over the years I had accumulated a good deal of circumstantial evidence of Hemingway's generosity. He liked very much to be generous; perhaps for some reason he needed to be. I thought then that however much he deplored what he thought I was doing to him, he seemed now to want to be generous with me, and I wrote to thank him. I remarked that I could scarcely be happy when it was so clear he was not, but that I was grateful and accepted his kindness not only because I needed it but because I thought—as Cowley thought—that he would be pleased with much, not all, of the book.

The insufficient postage problem originated with Hemingway this time, so that two weeks later I got a letter that had been written before the cable was sent. It was a warm letter. He said that as a matter of principle he would maintain his stand with Mr. Bledsoe forever, but that however mistaken he thought my book, he felt badly at its being held up and my chances for making a living impaired. Since he was granting the permission, it would only worry me to have a very long letter he had written me, so he was not mailing it. Then it was as if all his skies cleared and the sun poured down. He would tell Scribner's, he said, to pay to me instead of him his share of my permission costs (this was done), and if I had practiced economy in quotation to hold down expenses, he would be pleased if I would quote more extensively. (I hadn't realized the quotes were to be paid for, so there was no need of this.) Lastly he wrote that he was real sorry, buddy, if I was in crummy shape financially. He could let me have a couple of hundred and I could still feel free to call him a bastard if I wanted. If I was broke I couldn't be sued.

I did call on the Scribner editor, Wallace Meyer, who gave every appearance of having expected a man with at least two heads. Settling down, we went over the principal quotations I was going to make; I seemed again to have passed some sort of examination; then I wrote Hemingway at once (no board of review any more) accepting his generosity with the permissions fees and declining with thanks the two hundred dollars. I listed each and every quotation, including bits from things not published by Scribner's, and assured him that there had never been a moment when I felt like calling him a bastard.

There followed a rapid exchange of entirely cooperative and cheerful letters. After discovering precisely and down to the tiniest detail what words of his I was using, and commenting on several passages of them, he approved them without protest, exception, or change. Habitually he would extend the friendliest of best wishes, remark the heat, and include some little diversion such as an anecdote. I did what I could to reply in kind.

Negotiations had been going on for over a year now but the end was once more in sight; the manuscript, all tattered and torn, was once again at Rinehart ready to go. And then publication of *The Old Man and the Sea* was announced. I had known "a new book" was in the works. Hemingway had written that he hoped I would like it—that although he had gone through it over two hundred times it still did something to him. Mr. Meyer had predicted I would like it: there was not, he said, a single four-letter word anywhere in it. (Not even, I thought, "this" or "that" or "fish"?) But I had not known publication was imminent. So back from the printer came all my pages. I read an advance copy on its arrival, and did at that time like it, and wrote a new rousing climax to the chapter on the novels which (hopefully) had already climaxed twice. Then a few months later my book, officially dated 1952, unbelievably did appear—on the twenty-sixth day of February in the year of our Lord nineteen hundred and fifty-three.

I remember little of that celebration except driving back late from Tom's house on Long Island, with a knowing but now silent and vicariously exhausted Carolyn beside me, and finding myself irrevocably committed to the George Washington Bridge, hence to New Jersey—which would not have been absolutely unacceptable but for the fact that we were then living in the Bronx. I remember, too, the morning after, when of all books published that day the *Times* reviewed mine, and Charles Poore offered me a medal for composing the atrocity of the year. (February was pretty early in the year for that, but then it turned out he was editing a Hemingway omnibus for Scribner's.) I stifled an immediate response to the gist of his attack: he must be crazy to say that I had said Hemingway was crazy, thereby proving that I was crazy. And that was the last bad review I saw.

* * *

Partly because I had not realized in how many out-of-the-way places book reviews are made, I was astonished by the number that appeared. (For instance, there was the *Public Spirit* of Hatboro, Pennsylvania—"highly recommended"—which metropolis I had never heard of.) The book came out shortly afterward in England, where reviews were equally generous, and then, translated, in Germany, where sales were excellent. It was published as well in Spanish, and has long been postponed to appear with Hemingway's *Collected Works* in Italian. A substantial piece of it was in a French journal, and bits of it came out in such unlikely tongues as Telugu, Bengali, and Marathi. Best of all, it was pirated in the Argentine, and when Rinehart went to collect it was discovered that the publisher, a Peronista, was both bankrupt and in jail, which is the start of a saga the reader is to be spared.

From feature stories in the papers to solemn academic exercises, several writers paid the honor of plagiarism. (If imitation is the sincerest flattery, then what's plagiarism?) (Almost as good as piracy.) There were television plays, at least two movies, and one live play (which happily closed before it ever got to Broadway) that revealed a bungling study of the book. So much of this went on that I finally decided to crib myself, and by invitation wrote another *Ernest Hemingway,* the first pamphlet in the flourishing Minnesota series on American writers. This has now appeared in three English versions, three Japanese, two Spanish, and one each in Italian, Portuguese, Arabic, Korean, and Pushtu (which, according to my *Britannica,* is the language of the Afghans, 90% of whom are, it says, illiterate). The book itself, reverting to type, went out of print the very week it was voted into the new White House Library, and it took nearly three months of real effort to locate a fresh copy for Washington.

Mindful of this run, the original question left unanswered becomes central: what did Hemingway say? Several reviewers had wondered about this; the *Times Literary Supplement* had asked it, and more, with a vengeance: "Though simple and at first sight devastating, the argument is solidly based on a thorough analysis. . . . What will happen to Hemingway when he has read this book?" Curious to find out about this myself, I mailed him the first advance copy I got hands on, and in view of his great alarm, followed by the enthusiasm, I was surprised at the speed with which he returned it—the wrapping reversed, my name and address carefully lettered in. Very well, I thought, it can't hurt him a whole lot if he doesn't read it. That returned parcel was the last contact.

Before long, however, I began hearing from people who knew him, and it became clear he had read the book all right. Then, when he took the Nobel Prize, *Time* ran a cover story on him, and the anonymous interviewer who went to Cuba asked him what he thought of it. "How would you like it," he asked, "if someone said that everything you've done in your life was because of some trauma?" Also, with reference to the amazing list of his physical injuries I had compiled, he objected that he didn't "want to go down as the Legs Diamond of Letters."

Many years later, in August of 1965, *Atlantic Monthly* ran some free verse of doubtful quality by the author and along with it an interview by Robert Manning, which seemed to have been conducted in the same period as *Time*'s and remarkably resembled it. On this occasion Hemingway is reported as saying of the book: "If you haven't read it, don't bother. How would you like it if someone said that everything you've done in your life was done because of some trauma? Young had a theory that was like—you know—the Procrustean bed, and he had to cut me to fit into it." (The mystery of the similarities is cleared up by our man in Havana, who submits intelligence to the effect that there was only one interview—and some correspondence: the *Time* reporter was Robert Manning, too.)*

An indecisive but somewhat different exchange took place later in *Paris Review*. Editor Plimpton:

> Philip Young in his book on you suggests that the traumatic shock of your severe 1918 mortar wound had a great influence on you as a writer. I remember in Madrid you talked briefly about his thesis, finding little in it, and going on to say that you thought the artist's equipment was not an acquired characteristic, but inherited, in the Mendelian sense.

Ernest Hemingway:

> Evidently in Madrid that year my mind could not be called very sound. The only thing to recommend it would be that I spoke only

*Mr. Manning had added a little to the record by noting in a letter the great care with which Hemingway had obviously read the book and the good-humored way in which he rejected it, so that his remarks, Manning says, look more hostile in print than they sounded in conversation. In a subsequent and only mildly obscene letter to his interviewer Hemingway rewrote my list of his wounds so as to make it hilarious. He also added to the reference to Legs Diamond his disinclination to enter literary history as a clay pigeon.

> briefly about Mr. Young's book and his trauma theory of literature. Perhaps the two concussions and a skull fracture of that year made me irresponsible. . . . I do remember telling you that I believed imagination could be the result of inherited racial experience. It sounds all right in good jolly postconcussion talk, but I think that is more or less where it belongs. . . . On the question you raised, the effects of wounds vary greatly. . . . Wounds that do extensive bone and nerve damage are not good for writers, nor anybody else.

To which one can only say that the gulf between these remarks and Mr. Young's trauma theory (which is of course by no means original with him) could not be bridged in a sentence—and wouldn't require a chapter either.

The only other reports received on the subject of the author's reaction to the critic's book have come from old acquaintances unforgot, and the last one reliably described came not long before Hemingway's death. Professors Leslie Fiedler and Seymour Betsky, both then of Montana, had called on the author in his Sun Valley home. A short time later Fiedler was in my house, where he briefed me on the shocking, unpublicized condition of the writer's physical and mental health—which is why I was not as startled as many by the news of his explosive end, while at the same time being perhaps more moved by it. Fiedler was unable to recall what had been said about the book, but Betsky did remember and wrote me that to the best of his recollection Hemingway's exact words were: "Mr. Young is a good man and he is certainly entitled to his opinion of my work. But I think in his book he was riding a thesis and I think the thesis distorts the work somewhat."

I wish I had expressed that last myself. All theses distort the work in some degree. In trying to get at the figure in the carpet (to give a tired metaphor just a little more exercise) the man who thinks he has found the essential pattern ignores, at least for the time it takes him to demonstrate it, the whole of the rug for the figure in it. But when he is done, he hopes that the pattern will sink back into the carpet, and the carpet none the worse for wear. Even, maybe, if the revelation was truly new and sufficiently convincing, all the more to be valued.

1966

5.

To Have Not: Tough Luck

KENT. *Vex not his ghost; O, let him pass! He hates him*
That would upon the rack of this tough world
Stretch him out longer.
—King Lear, v, 3

It is somewhere recorded that long ago a broker named Chapman approached a man sitting peacefully in a club and said "So you're Hemingway . . . tough guy, huh?" and pushed him in the face. The assailant lived to regret having been right on both counts. A foolish one, Mr. Chapman, or at any rate a drinking man. But he was only one among many who did not believe Hemingway was as tough as he sounded. The doubt was, ironically, a simple-minded perception of a basic truth. The writer was quite tough enough to take care of belligerent drunks and all threats that a man exposed to lions, bulls, and bombs may encounter. And yet as a very young man, he had managed, through his prose, to suggest to a few readers at least that his "primitivism" was actually the product of a sophistication and delicacy that called the masculinity of his fiction and his press into question. The masculinity was no pose, however, nor the artistry a delusion. An old *New Yorker* cartoon of the hairy-chested writer clutching a single rose in a big fist expressed the incongruous truth. Fist and rose, both were real.

But it will still come as a surprise to many that *To Have and Have Not* is the only hard-boiled book Hemingway ever wrote; further, that there are almost no tough guys among the leading characters in his fiction, and only a few in minor roles. The most important single fact about his central, recurrent and loosely autobiographical protagonist—Nick Adams, Jake Barnes, Frederic Henry, Robert Jordan, Richard Cantwell—is that he is *not* tough. The front looks solid enough, at least from a distance, but it was built by will and courage to protect what is damaged inside. "No," said Nick, rejecting a reference to his bravery under fire. "I know how I am and I prefer to get stinking."

Hemingway does stand, however, in some sort of relation to the Hard-Boiled School of fiction—more of an influence on it than anything else. If the genre really got started in the magazine called the *Black Mask,* which was founded in 1919, then Hemingway could have learned something from it. But if, as alleged, "the first full-fledged example of the hard-boiled method was Dashiell Hammett's story 'Fly Paper,' " then the method got started too late to have much influence on him, since that story did not appear in the magazine until 1929, by which time Hemingway was almost completely established in manner and method both. Two parts of *To Have and Have Not* (1937)—the fight in the bar and Marie Morgan's final soliloquy—are obviously indebted to Joyce's *Ulysses*. But the hunch is that Hemingway's "tough" owes a lot less to his contemporaries than to a few forebears, and his own imagination. The similarity of some of his work to the Tough Detective School (particularly to the novels of Raymond Chandler, the only member of it Hemingway once said he could read) is the result of his effect on them. "The Killers," surely one source for the American gangster movie, was published in 1927, and so was "Fifty Grand," which features his first real tough guy, a prizefighter named Jack, who is a clear forecast of Harry Morgan, protagonist of *To Have and Have Not*. Like Jack, Harry has no sons, only daughters;* like Jack he can think very fast in a pinch. If not entirely amoral, both men are highly illegal; both are pitiless and both *very* tough.

A remoter precedent for Harry is more obvious: his namesake, Henry Morgan the pirate, who once ravaged the coasts off which Harry works, who like Harry was really hard, but brave and resourceful too. Where the

*"Funny we didn't get no boys," Harry says. His wife replies, "That's because you're such a man. That way it always comes out girls." Oddly enough, the author got only boys.

parallel breaks down, we get what may be the main point of it: following his capture by the law Henry was knighted; Harry was killed. A closer precedent is more obscure: a minor Hemingway story called "After the Storm" (1932), which also features a fight in a Key West bar, and also deals with a self-reliant, tough, modern pirate (an exact working-sketch for Harry), who takes off in his boat and discovers a sunken ocean liner he is unable to loot.

A real curiosity, however, lies in the fact that if Hemingway's book does not have origins in the nearly-forgotten, turn-of-the-century, primitive branch of American naturalism, then the coincidences are astonishing. Frank Norris's *Moran of the Lady Letty* (1898)—a rather ridiculous novel—is built around a Have and Have Not Contrast (again the rich are effete, the poor robust); there is brutality, as in Hemingway, for the Chinese, and a lot of deep-sea fishing. Further, the Moran of the title is the image of one Morgan, Harry's wife Marie: a great blond woman, too big and strong to be pretty but a wonderful mate. And as if that were not enough there is Jack London's *The Sea Wolf* (1904), which comes directly out of *Moran,* and presents another original for Harry himself in the person of Wolf Larsen, a virile, hard, amoral loner whose survival-of-the-fittest ethic seems, like Harry's, the central concern of the plot. The novel is again a sea story, full of violence and cruelty, and even the apparent "message" is the same: no matter how potent and pitiless, a man has no chance alone.

That is the instruction that Harry Morgan provides, and it is always taken to be the message of *To Have and Have Not.* Also taken to be the book's climax, when Henry speaks his last words, "No man alone now . . . No matter how a man alone ain't got no bloody f——ing chance." But the trouble is that these words do not seem as they should to put a finishing touch on the novel's structure. Indeed, it is hard to see how any lesson could, so faulty is the book's architecture. The story of how it got built and then knocked apart is the story of how Hemingway's tough novel became Hemingway's tough luck.

Kidding around one day some years after publication of the book, Hemingway described it as a "frail volume . . . devoted to adultery, sodomy, masturbation, rape, mayhem, mass murder, frigidity, alcoholism, prostitution, impotency, anarchy, rum-running, chink-smuggling, nymphomania and abortion." That may be too many things for a relatively short volume to devote itself to. But when the author agreed with those of his critics (not this one) who regarded the novel as his weakest effort, he gave a different reason: "The thing wrong . . . is that it is made up of short stories. I wrote one, then another when I was in Spain, then I came back and saw Harry Morgan again and that gave me the idea for a third. It came out as a new novel, but it was short stories, and there is a hell of a lot of difference."*

That was an explanation which the "publishing history" of the book more or less bears out, and not an excuse. Hemingway didn't make excuses, but if he had wanted to, he had a good one: his deep involvement in the Spanish Civil War. He didn't make speeches, either; even his own Nobel Prize address was delivered by someone else. And he didn't believe that writers should have political affiliations. But so committed was he to the Republic that he did make one speech, his only one and a good one, to the Second American Writer's Conference in Carnegie Hall in June of 1937. And so it was that *To Have and Have Not* became the only book he ever published that he did not care much about at the time.

It was after publishing the second of the three stories that he made the unlucky decision to build a novel, and arrived at the equally unfortunate decision to put a theme to it. The theme, he wrote his friend and editor Max Perkins, was to be "the decline of the individual" (which hasn't come through to many readers as what the book is about). The first idea, of writing a full-scale novel, was an unhappy one because if he had kept within the good old Unities, and restricted himself to the three Morgan stories, he might have had a successful "novelette." Instead, however, he tried to flesh out the stories with the portraits of some contrasting Haves—particularly with the story of a well-to-do pseudo-proletarian novelist, Richard Gordon. Presumably to point up Morgan's masculinity, he also provided him with a wife. But neither the emptiness of Morgan's pocket nor his curious virility needed emphasis, and anyway Gordon is treated so sketchily that he cannot possibly stand up to a contrast. The brevity of his role is one result of yet another mistake.

Until quite recently, readers had no way of knowing why it is that there is such an imbalance between the considerable space devoted to the Have Nots in this book and the small room given the Haves (which is

*Apparently, Hemingway refers here to yet another source of his overdetermined protagonist: Joe Russell, owner of a charter-boat out of Key West from which Hemingway often fished in the days before he had his own boat built, and before Russell settled into the operation of his Key West bar. It was here that many war veterans, temporarily employed by FERA depression projects, came on pay days to get drunk and fight.

one reason for its failure—if it can truly be said to fail). But now we know that the disproportion springs from a very bad guess on Hemingway's part as to just how much he could print about certain living Haves and get away with it. In the end he had to dump a good deal of material, and didn't bother to put anything in its place.

We have this information from Arnold Gingrich, publisher of *Esquire.* He reports that when the book was done he was flown to Key West and handed the "finished script." He read it, and out of his own experience of such matters came up with the opinion that three people in it were "libelled right up to the eyeballs. They were Dos Passos, and Janie,* and her then husband, Grant Mason." Hemingway protested a good deal, particularly that Dos Passos would sign a "release," but in the end, Gingrich says, he "mutilated . . . large portions of the *Have* sections . . . without any sort of replacement of the deleted elements. I thought the least he might have done would have been to change the title, because, as the book appeared, the title applied about like the "fifty-fifty" recipe for hamburger: one horse, one rabbit. It was a little disillusioning."

It was worse than that. Beyond inequity, here was a perfect case where the whole amounts to less than the sum of its parts—for the simple reason that the parts don't appear to "add up." Though not vintage Hemingway, many of the fragments are good. The Morgan stories are vivid, mostly convincing, and occasionally exciting. If Hemingway had struck objectively to Harry, they could have had power. There are good things, furthermore, beyond Morgan. Gordon breaking up with his wife is one; the portrait of Professor MacWalsey (a little reminiscent of "Owl Eyes" in *The Great Gatsby*) is another; the vets' fight in the bar (toughness become positively sickening, as the author intended it should) is a third. But the ex-soldiers are made to contrast with some corrupt yacht owners, and the relationship is too obvious. So is the contrast between the real Marie and Gordon's fatuously ignorant thoughts about her; so, later, her equally unknowing glimpse of him. So too the dragged-in comparison between a rich bachelor's depleted income (still plenty) with that of a fisherman and his family (insufficient). Hemingway was underlining with a crayon what at his best he would have felt no need to remark at all. An elaborate

*Hemingway pointed out to *his* then wife, Pauline, that "Jane was flattered when people took her for Mrs. Macomber in that story" ("The Short Happy Life of Francis Macomber"). "Well," Mrs. Hemingway replied, "I can't imagine that her husband would exactly feel set up about that." Mr. Gingrich told the story in the December, 1966, issue of his magazine. As he himself points out, Jane Mason became Mrs. Gingrich.

rationale for all the switches in point of view the novel undergoes does exist, and it may reveal Hemingway's intentions quite accurately. But the changes actually accomplish very little beyond momentary confusion, and they increase the sense of fragmentation.

These are minor difficulties. A major one is that the book's ostensible message, a man alone has no chance anymore, seems inserted by Hemingway rather than extracted from Harry—perhaps to fit that "decline of the individual" business. Now this is one place where the tough guy fiction of the Thirties more or less crosses with the depression novel. As Carlos Baker has pointed out, Hemingway clearly intended us to see his Key West as America in small—or at its worst—in that grim decade; and meant us to see that Morgan, in the foreground, showed that the age of the gutty, self-reliant American pioneer was over and done. Minor figures representing capitalism, communism, and fascism meet with Harry's bitter disapproval and the reader's. All right, a plague on all your houses. But what's wrong is that the social cooperation implied by the "no man alone now" message has nowhere to go and just stalls.

Another impediment to implementing this "moral" is that a sensitive reading of the book will show some of the Haves, whom we expect to despise as the villains, to have been drawn with considerable sympathy. The result is a temporary emotional confusion, which is not straightened out by the perception that in practically everything but money, sex for instance, it is Hemingway's Haves who have not and his Have Nots who have. On first meeting Richard Gordon, for example, it is easy to dislike him, as expected. He is clearly an ass. "A writer," he says, "has got to know about everything. He can't restrict his experience to conform to Bourgeois standards." But after his wife decides to leave him, and has denounced him in the most spectacularly abusive speech in American literature, it is hard not to feel sorry for the man, particularly as we learn how much he loves her, and as the delusion that he had been good to her in bed crashes about him. Similarly, it first appears that we are supposed to deplore Professor MacWalsey as a professor, a useless drunk, and—far worse in Hemingway's scheme of things—a tourist to boot. But this man is really a very good person, and the author quickly brings us to like him a lot. In the same way, the evocation of the recent Haves who lost their money, particularly the capitalist "who shot himself early one morning before breakfast," brings little but sympathy. Conversely, Hemingway does not permit us to like some of his Have Nots.

In the end many of the things that once seemed clear about this novel have blurred extraordinarily. Harry Morgan, for instance. He is usually thought of as one of Hemingway's "code heroes" (and never more confidently than by the present writer). As defined, however, this figure in Hemingway is a man who makes a basic moral compromise and then sticks to his bargain come what can. He may throw a fight, play crooked cards, guide the unlikable rich on safari and service their women. But after the first compromise there is no other. Morgan, on the other hand, makes his bargain ("chink-smuggling" instead of rum-running) and then betrays it quickly as he is able, having intended to all along. As a matter of fact it is not even certain that he may legitimately be called "tough," though he can surely take it, as we say, and dish it out. But following his planned, cold-blooded, bare-handed murder of the Chinese Mr. Sing rather early in the book, the question is whether he is tough or simply brutal, which is not at all the same thing. Even Eddy, Harry's rummy companion (whom he was going to kill too until chance made it unnecessary), is shaken by that one, and asks the reader's question for him, "What did you kill him for?" Harry's answer, "To keep from killing twelve other chinks," is not completely convincing.

If then we have misgivings about Morgan as a tough hero, if his dying words do not function well as a "moral," if the announced theme is seldom felt to be one, and if our sympathies extend to several of the Haves but are withheld from a few Have Nots, then we are caught up in some sort of maze. But there is a way out. And, good news: it leads to the discovery that this just might be a better novel—more meaningful, more nearly unified—than Hemingway or his readers have believed. Despite the title, here is surely not another of those books about the well against the badly off, where allegiance is easy to pledge and the point easily got. What the novel really says, most steadily and conclusively, is what Hemingway had been expressing all through the Thirties, and it didn't have anything much to do with depressions or tough guys. It was simpler: a profound loss of hope for the lot of man. A savage civil war was going to bring him back, but that was later. *To Have and Have Not* comes in the darkest night of the soul, not the dubious dawn of social pronouncement. Its real message is not cooperation, it's desperation. It is not expressed by Harry but by Marie. It is not forced, but grows naturally out of all that's happened, and arrives with an air of finality at the finish of the novel in the last sentence of the following passage. Harry is dead, his wife widowed, and she is wondering what it's going to be like for her now: "How do you get through nights if you can't sleep? I guess you find out like you find out how it feels to lose your husband. I guess you find out all right. I guess you find out everything in this goddamned life."

Though not at its very best, *that* is the authentic voice of Hemingway, speaking through one who has survived to learn the lesson. It hasn't a lot to do with having or not having things—nor primarily with losing things you had, though that is much of it. What Marie has epitomized is the anguish that pervades the book. Rich or poor makes no difference in the very end; disparate elements are gathered into a unity brought about by nothing but Hemingway's unflagging awareness of mental and physical pain, his memorable sense of what a beating people take from life. The world he saw this time is a very rough place indeed, and the feeling that stays with you is of pity for anyone who is stretched out and racked up on it.

1968

6.

"Big World Out There": The Nick Adams Stories

I proposed publishing this book almost 25 years ago; maybe I should be excused for taking a special interest in it. Bring out all of Hemingway's Nick Adams stories in one volume, I presumptuously suggested in a 1948 letter to Charles Scribner, and print them in the chronological order of Nick's advancing age. There were 15 of these stories then, several of them pretty well known, like "The Killers" and "In Another Country," and all of them in print for 15 years or many more. But Nick himself was scarcely known at all; people had practically no idea who he was or what he was like, the main reason being the jumbled ages at which one met up with him in the various collections of Hemingway's short fiction. He would surface as a soldier, say, then as a boy, then a child, a married man, and a soldier again. The coherence of his adventures was obscured, you might say, and their overall significance was just about invisible.

Mr. Scribner replied that since he did not think Mr. Hemingway would approve of the idea there was no point in pursuing it, and the matter was dropped as far as I was concerned. There it lay, as in a corner, twitching once in a while, until the fall of 1967, when I began going through the Hemingway manuscripts in an attempt to identify things. It

This essay was originally conceived as an introduction to the chronological collection, *The Nick Adams Stories* (1972), which included eight previously unpublished tales and fragments. A brief preface by Philip Young now introduces that book.

was rather early in the game that I happened on something called "Summer People," 40 sparsely-covered sheets of pen and ink—a Nick story, and very likely the first one. Mary Hemingway had already given me a typescript of a much later and longer, though unfinished, piece of Nick fiction—the last one—which she called "The Last Good Country." And it was at just this time that Scribner's asked me to "have an idea" for a book. I don't quit easy, and soon found myself proposing to Charles Scribner, Jr., what I had prematurely recommended to his father—*The Nick Adams Stories,* with two new entries.

I didn't have that title in mind, and it was certainly not my idea that the rest of the new material that was uncovered (much of it by Carlos Baker, at Princeton) be printed here. The notion that We Must Have It All—every scrap that turned up and had Nick in it—has prevailed, which is to say that the trade publisher has out-pedanticked the academy. (The fact that Hemingway never destroyed these bits and pieces means little; he didn't throw out grocery lists, and didn't plan to print them someday either.) A lot of people are wondering how the author would have felt to know that such trivial fragments as "Crossing the Mississippi" and "Wedding Day" have been presented to the public as "stories," and that his new book opens with something called "Three Shots," which he discarded as a completely false start before beginning again from scratch to write "Indian Camp." It's a pretty safe bet that he wouldn't be happy about it.

One last disclaimer for the record: I didn't edit anything, either. Indeed there has not been much editing, except in the case of "The Last Good Country," where a good deal has been cut from what Hemingway wrote. But here the judgment is favorable: the cuts were either necessary, to piece together two long and different openings present in the manuscript, or desirable, where the text was wordy, or the pace slow, or the taste dubious. The job has been done skillfully by Scribner's.

Beyond the trivial Preface, the only other things I am indeed responsible for in this book are the selection and ordering of the "real stories"—matters that are not as simple as may first appear. Actually there isn't any completely satisfactory way to arrange them all, as readers are going to discover when they confront Nick as an adolescent veteran of the great war; and on that puzzle, one of those debates that delight some of us, and enliven (a little) the lesser critical journals, is already getting under way. But enough of the record; if we back away from it to take the large view of this book it is clear, whatever else may be said, that as we follow Nick across the span of a generation in time we have got a story worth following. As it turns out, Hemingway arranged it (consciously or otherwise) in five distinct stages—that is, the original fifteen stories occur in five segments of Nick's life, three stories to each part. "The Northern Woods," as the first section is called, deals with heredity and environment, parents and Michigan Indians. "On His Own" is all away from home, or on the road, and instead of Indians, prizefighters. "War" is exactly that, or as the author put it later on, "hit properly and for good." Then "A Soldier Home": Michigan revisited, hail and farewell. And fifth, "Company of Two": marriage, Europe revisited, and finally looking backward, a sort of coda.

Maybe it will also appear now and at long last that in Nick Hemingway gave us the most important single character in all his work—the first in a long line of fictional self-projections, the start of everything. Later protagonists from Jake Barnes and Frederic Henry to Richard Cantwell and Thomas Hudson were shaped by Nick, were all to have (if only tacitly) his history behind them. So had Hemingway. Not that everything that happens to Nick had happened to him. Indeed the author remarks right here, in the fragment called "On Writing," that "Nick in the stories was never himself. He made them up." To an extent that is of course true; the autobiography is transmuted. But it is bemusing that at the very moment when the writer is categorically disassociating himself from his persona he makes him interchangeable with himself, as the "he," the consciousness of the piece, shifts from Nick to Hemingway back to Nick again. But the real point is that this extended and disciplined self-portrait became a significant story in its own right: the story of an American born with the century, complicated in boyhood and badly hurt in a war, who came to terms with what happened and turned it to lasting fiction. And now, after all these years, it's time to have at this episodic narrative for the last time—to uncover, with the help of the biographers, its roots in the author's experience, assess the new material, remark what has not already been remarked to death about the old, and attempt a new judgment of what it all adds up to.

I

The earliest scent of Nick's trail can probably be picked up in a little story called "Sepi Gingan" which the author published when he was still at

Oak Park High. A juvenile but already violent tale, apparently set in Hortons Bay, Michigan, the heart of Adams country, it is told by an Indian (who will appear in a mature Nick story) to a nameless boy who is Nick in all *but* name, about another Indian who was killed by a dog and left on the Pere Marquette railroad tracks, where a train "removed all the traces." Another Indian, drunk, who had "laid down to sleep on the Pere Marquette railway tracks and had been run over by the midnight train," figures in a new Nick "story" (it has no plot) that is here called "The Indians Moved Away," and relates how that happened. (An early piece, it was found in the manuscripts without a title; also found was an early title, "They Never Came Back," without a story; they probably should have gone together.)

Indians figure as well in all the stories Hemingway published alive about Nick as a young boy, of which "Indian Camp" is first in several ways. It was the first Nick story to see print; it is the earliest according to his apparent age; it is the opening story of *In Our Time,* the first real book of stories. It is also perhaps the most violent, and unintentionally portentous, of all Hemingway stories, and it lays down what was to become the basic pattern of all his fiction, which is to expose a character to violence, to physical or psychological shock, or severe trial, and then to focus on the consequences. The consequence of violent birth and death in "Indian Camp" is muted—a calm discussion of suicide between Dr. Adams and his small son, the portent being that the originals for both of them were destined eventually to commit it. The story itself, with its jack-knife Caesarian, is invented. "Of course," Hemingway once remarked (again in the piece called "On Writing") "he'd never seen an Indian woman having a baby. . . . He'd seen a woman have a baby on the road to Karagatch and tried to help her. That was the way it was."

The way it started, however, in the eight longhand pages that Hemingway discarded but Scribner's prints as "Three Shots," was on a fishing trip. Uncle George (Ernest's uncle) and his brother, Dr. Henry Adams, were out fishing at night. Nick was back at their tent and frightened. But he was not so much afraid of the dark as "of dying. . . . It was the first time he had ever realized that he himself would have to die sometime." In throwing out this section of the story Hemingway was struggling, successfully, with what he once called the most difficult problem for writers: "knowing what you really felt, rather than what you were supposed to feel. . . ." Thus at the end of "Indian Camp" as we have it, Nick "felt quite sure that he would never die." What you were supposed to feel has given over to something subtler and deeper. Children don't really believe in their own demise. Death is obviously something that happens to other people.

Perhaps it was because he had been camping that Dr. Adams set off to deliver a baby with no better equipment than a knife and some gut leaders. He is an ambiguous figure generally, who does not unwrap his medical journals; and on his next appearance, in "The Doctor and the Doctor's Wife," it's his courage that's in question. Two Indians, Dick Boulton and Billy Tabeshaw (of "Sepi Gingan"), come to cut wood for him. When Boulton tries to pick a fight, only to have the doctor walk off, the problem of whether his exit was sensible or unmanly can be left to the reader. The author probably did not intend a choice; he said that the story, based on an actual incident, is about the time he discovered that his father was a coward. On the other hand Dr. Hemingway said he liked the piece, and at the end when Nick has to choose in a small way between the doctor and his wife (who is a Christian Scientist) he immediately chooses his father.

"Ten Indians" appeared two years after the story of the doctor's dilemmas and in a different book. But a little something was lost before the two stories were brought together, and tensions in the Adams family are seen against the cheerful ease with which the neighboring Garners get along. This pair of tales must also have been linked in the author's mind in another way. As the Garners return in a wagon from Petoskey with Nick aboard they pass the slumbering bodies of nine Indians, who have excessively—and inappropriately—celebrated the Fourth of July. ("Them Indians," says Mrs. Garner.) The tenth Indian is Prudence Mitchell. And now there are none: Prudie does not appear in the story, but she was Nick's girl, and when he gets home the doctor tells him he has seen her "having quite a time" in the woods with another boy. What we are not told is that in life this Indian girl, who sometimes worked for Mrs. Hemingway, was Prudence Boulton, daughter of the man who perhaps humiliated the doctor—who in turn may take satisfaction in telling Nick what he saw.

As for Nick, he is about to learn again what he really feels. "A Broken Heart" was the original title of "Ten Indians"—an ironic one, since Nick is about to learn that his own heart is quite intact. But we are not done with Prudie, later Trudy. She figures in three episodes of Nick's life, and the author often spoke of her, especially in connection with the loss of his virginity. His authorized biographer, Carlos Baker, put this down as "wishful thinking," which is probably right. But another biographer, Constance Montgomery, reports having been told that Prudence Boulton died young, perhaps in childbirth, and she passes along a rumor that the child was Ernest's. There are *no* grounds for believing this, and it would not bear repeating but for the fact that, before it was cut from "The Last Good Country," it came out that Nick indeed had got Trudy pregnant. And in his last appearance he will think back on this girl who "did first what no one has ever done better."

II

Hemingway left home in October of 1917, heading for Kansas City by train, and some years later he remembered in a very brief sketch how as Nick he first saw the Mississippi from a coach. It had been away from home, or on the road, that Nick's adolescence was spent—but on freights or on foot, not in coaches. And one would be "ill advised," as Hemingway once remarked, to think of the first of these stories, called "The Light of the World," as a "simple tale." He tried once to explain it by saying that although it is "about many things," it is really

> a love letter to a whore named Alice. . . . And the point of it is that nobody . . . knows how we were then from how we are now. This is worse on women than on us . . . and that is what I was trying for in the story.

This helps in reading the piece, but leaves out *too* many things, one of which is the religious note sounded by the title. The reference to Jesus is crucial ("I am the light of the world. . . ."), for it is what points to the fact that the champion prizefighter named Ketchel has become, in the minds of the two mammoth prostitutes, a sort of fire sale Christ crucified: "I loved him like you love God," "His own father shot and killed him. Yes, by Christ, his own father," and so forth. At the end Nick (clearly, though he is not named) and Tom (in life an Indian boy named Mitchell) seem to have nowhere much to go. It is getting dark, and as they leave the railway station where they listened to the whores arguing over which of them had been loved by Ketchel it looks as if the point of the story is really that the light of the world has gone out. In *Winner Take Nothing,* moreover, Hemingway put this story right after "A Clean, Well-Lighted Place," the most pessimistic of all his stories ("Our nada who art in nada. . . ." and so on). With the breakdown of faith and "light" in both stories, it is a good bet that he thought of these as another pair, thematically related. He coupled them again when he said of "A Clean, Well-Lighted Place," "May be my best story. That and 'The Light of the World,' which no one but me ever seemed to like."

Perhaps no one but he ever seemed to understand all of it. For that we need an answer to the unresolved question of Ketchel's first name. Alice and Peroxide agree that it was Steve; a homosexual cook asks if it wasn't Stanley. It is usually assumed that there was only one Ketchel, that everyone has in mind the same fighter, and that in the argument over which woman had actually loved him it is Alice who is telling the truth. But the point this time is that both women are lying (it's worse on them than on us): neither one of them has got her lover's first name right. The facts are that the boxer who "knocked Jack Johnson down" was Stanley Ketchel, as the cook thought. He was murdered in 1910, but not by his father. In 1915 Steve Ketchel fought Ad Wolgast to a draw.

The facts are further that Ad Wolgast had won the lightweight championship of the world from Battling Nelson in the year of Stanley Ketchel's death. It was one of the bloodiest brawls of the era, and Wolgast eventually became punch-drunk. In 1917 he was declared legally incompetent; ten years later he was committed to an asylum in California where he died in 1955. From small-town Cadillac, he was known as the Michigan Wildcat, and when Nick encounters him in "The Battler" Hemingway calls him Ad Francis.

Nick is traveling alone in "The Battler," but along the same railroad (The Grand Rapids and Indiana) as before. Hiking along the rails after having been knocked off a freight, he encounters Ad and a companion in a sort of two-man hobo jungle. It turns out to be a tough experience, and for the first time—but as a striking forecast of things-to-come—we see Nick definitely shaken at the end. When in "The Killers" he meets up with some gangsters and Ole Andreson, the fighter who will no longer resist being killed, he is shaken a bit more.

Hemingway once said that Gene Tunney had asked him, "Ernest wasn't that Andre Andreson in 'The Killers'? I told him it was. . . ." (This was astute of Tunney; Andreson was so obscure that, next to this story, his best chance of being remembered was for falling clean out of the ring and knocking himself out—or so he claimed—when boxing a much smaller man in 1915.* Hemingway also once explained what his story does not—"why the boys were sent to kill" him:

*Oddly there was also a fighter named *Ole* Anderson whom Tunney knew, since in the third round of a bout held in Jersey City in June of 1920 he knocked him out.

> the Swede was supposed to throw the fight but didn't. . . . All afternoon he had rehearsed taking a dive, but during the fight he had instinctively thrown a punch he didn't mean to.

He is also said to have told Tunney that "the town wasn't Summit, New Jersey, but Summit, Illinois. But that's all I told him because the Chicago mob that sent the killers was and, as far as I know, is still [1955] very much in business."

Exactly what at that late date he might have said that would have meant a thing to any gangster if Tunney had passed it along is very far from clear. The point seems to be that Hemingway continued to spin fictions about his fiction even after the fiction was in print. On many occasions he presented actual events as tales, and sometimes he told tales as fact. "The Last Good Country" is a good example of the latter practice. The final story of Nick on the road, and hitherto unpublished, Hemingway used to tell it (invent it, actually) about himself—about how *he* as a boy had escaped the game-wardens by taking off into the Michigan forest. It was good practice, and in 1952 he began inventing the tale for Nick.

The way it all got started is that about a week after his sixteenth birthday Ernest was working at Longfield, the family farm across the lake from Windemere, when two "beastly, insinuating, sneering" wardens came to the house "on business": "How about that young man about eighteen . . . ?" (Mrs. Hemingway is writing this to her husband, back in Chicago practicing medicine; the letter is mentioned in the story.) "They had two witnesses that he had shot a big game bird—had it in his boat, and they were after him." As soon as they went, she sent his year-older sister Marcelline "to row at top speed to the farm and warn Ernest to go to Dilworth's and stay until further notice."

> Now here's what happened. He shot a crane. . . . He wrapped it up and left it in the launch. . . . When he returned . . . he found it gone and a young boy who said he was the game warden's son came up to him and asked about the bird . . . "just drumming up business for my father. . . ." I don't know whether he had best risk it to come back to Windemere or not.

At this point there is a disagreement on details, but the result was that Ernest paid a fine and the incident was ended. He identified the bird as a great blue heron, biggest he had ever seen, and explained that he had taken an impossible shot at it only to drill it right behind the eye. (Why in writing the story he changed it to a deer is hard to understand.) But the older he got the more he embroidered things, until he had the narrative of a runaway boy and his sister Littless—probably based on both Ursula Hemingway, who used to run away and "meet Ernie in Petoskey," and Madelaine (or Sunny) Hemingway, who was the family tomboy.

Familiar voices, familiar rooms. Prominent in the story, Packard's general store and post office at Hortons Bay on Lake Charlevoix appeared in "Up in Michigan" and in "Sepi Gingan." The Dilworths, to whom his mother sent Ernest, lived there, and there like Mrs. Packard in the story Mrs. Dilworth served the public fried trout or chicken dinners. Like Nick, Ernest brought her rainbows (illegal if he sold them) and split wood. The girl of "Up in Michigan" was a waitress there; so was Marjorie, with whom Nick was to have an affair later on. The hotel the Packards also run in the story must be the Echo Beach Hotel on nearby Walloon Lake, where the Hemingways used to stay before it burned down and they bought Windemere. Trudy we have met before. Mrs. Tabeshaw is probably Billy's wife. Michigan was a small world.

Although we may read "The Last Good Country" as a short story it is obviously not one. Rather long already, it is nowhere near finished when it simply stops. If the plot at its original pace were to be resolved, Hemingway was clearly headed for a full-length novel. For once, however, there is a "plot plant," so that one can guess, at least, how Nick is going to get out of the jam he is in: a warden with curious feet is going to have to call off the hunt—*and* his son, if the boy is on the trail—in exchange for continued silence on Packard's part regarding a far more serious and unpunished offense than Nick's. And though we leave off in mid-air, Hemingway has already accomplished a great deal. We get to know Nick better here than we have ever done before. And the "Hemingway heroine" is never more real than in her youngest appearance as his kid sister. Right down to the short hair, Littless is the wonderful if slightly unreal child that grew up to be a Catherine Barkley and all the others. Indeed the piece immediately attracted, on publication, such damaging epithets as "mawkish" and "puerile." And it is true that here, for the only time with Nick, Hemingway treads the boundaries of sentimentality (his characteristic brinkmanship), occasionally trampling them.

But this does not automatically disqualify or cancel out the story; its real distinction lies in the fact of its genre, which is related to sentiment and unprecedented for Hemingway: sky-blue pastoral, with but one cloud in sight to keep things real and moving. Up to now, "idyllic Michigan" has been mainly an exaggeration on the part of his critics. But we leave these children on a level of peace and contentment he never occupied before—in mid-air suspended. And in this sense if in no other the story does "end." There is nowhere to go from a dream. Or from a myth: the familiar American story, most notably Huck Finn's, of a magical journey from the irritants of civilization to an unspoiled state of nature, an odyssey of a loving couple in escape of society—and of its epitome, the law. A Michigan forest was prefigured by the Mississippi River, and the kids' camp in it by a raft.

In this passage one is never alone. Van Winkle in the Catskills, Thoreau at Walden, are incomplete. To make it work there must be love. But the love must be forbidden: two males, Huck and Jim, Ishmael and Queequeg, Deerslayer and Chingachgook—or siblings, Nick and Littless. Only in Hemingway's version are sexual overtones explicit (some were cut), and only here is the partner of another sex rather than race. But as she says, Littless is not *really* a girl yet. Indeed she is something of a boy. For just as Huck dressed as a girl, in calico gown and sunbonnet, and "practiced around all day to get the hang of things," so Littless wears overalls and a boy's shirt, cuts her hair short, and moves around "practicing being a boy." But in all these stories, hints of physical love serve always to highlight the innocence of actual relationships. Without the overtones, we would never think to realize how immaculate is the conception. "The Last Good Country" is at one with its precedents in expressing a yearning for escape from ordinary life into a charmed kinship under the ennobling conditions of earth or water in the new security of a new home: raft, ship, or campfire.

And if it seems a stubborn truth that these are after all a boy and his sister in the forest, different overtones are also audible. Hansel and Gretel were not entirely happy with their mother either. They lived by a great forest, where they too picked berries and bedded down in a sort of "cathedral," as the Adams children call it, where an evil witch (or warden's son) may find them. Hemingway gets by natural means the magic that the fairy tale achieves with fourteen white-winged angels and the sound of heavenly music.

III

There is a time limit on adolescence and enchanted forests. And the title of an unpublished poem, "Killed. Piave—July 8, 1918," indirectly conveys the reversal in Nick's fortunes whereby after leaving him at Camp Number One, as happy as he will ever get, we pick him up again as a soldier, miserable and badly wounded, in Italy. The date commemorates the night on which the author was hit "for good" ("killed" is what almost, or metaphorically, happened; Piave is the river where it happened) at Fossalta, which is north of Venice. Hemingway did record the fact of Nick's wounding directly, but he slighted the event by entering it in an untitled, one-paragraph sketch (here reprinted from an inferior early text), placed between two actual stories of *In Our Time,* where readers scarcely noticed it. A more effective transition between Michigan and Italy was severed when in 1925 he abandoned at page 26 a novel called *Along with Youth,* that appears in this book as "Night Before Landing," in which Nick was crossing to France in May of 1918 on the liner *Chicago.* Hemingway had, of course, been in Italy as an ambulance driver for the Red Cross, and a week after his wounding he was shipped to a Red Cross hospital in Milan. The most badly damaged part of him was a knee; after two months he could walk to the Ospedale Maggiore for physiotherapy. Returned to the front to see his friends, he came down with jaundice and was sent back to Milan, where he had fallen in love with an American nurse he hoped to marry. Out of these events and their effects he wrote, in addition to *A Farewell to Arms,* three stories of Nick Adams.

In "Now I Lay Me" Nick is suffering from insomnia, one result of his wounds. As befits the title he thinks back to his childhood and says his prayers "over and over." The reader is meant to recall a later line of "Now I Lay Me"—"If I die before I wake"—as Nick remarks that he

> had been living for a long time with the knowledge that if I ever shut my eyes in the dark and let myself go, my soul would go out of my body. I had been that way . . . ever since I had been blown up at night and felt it go out of me and then come back.

This story, set near the front, is closely linked to "In Another Country," which is set in Milan. Both stories—which were originally two parts of a single one, as the manuscript shows—deal with the effects of Nick's wounds, psychological and physical. In the first of them his Italian orderly tells him he'd be all right if he'd only get married; in the second a bereaved Italian major tells him he must *not* marry, must find things he cannot lose.

In "A Way You'll Never Be," which falls chronologically between these two, it is clear that the psychological damage is more severe than the physical. Hemingway once explained his title saying he wanted to show a girl who was going crazy that Nick had been "much nuttier" than she was going to get. The story deals, he also said, with "things that happened to me in a trench outside Fornaci," which is near Fossalta. If so, things were really grim; Nick's mind goes utterly. And it may be that what particularly "frightened him so that he could not get rid of it . . . that long yellow house and the different width of the river," is the scene of his wounding—and Hemingway's, Lt. Henry's, and Col. Cantwell's, who also "had been hit, out on the river bank."

But the best of these, and one of the best of all Hemingway stories, is "In Another Country." "It opens," Scott Fitzgerald wrote long ago, with "one of the most beautiful prose sentences I have ever read": "In the fall the war was always there, but we did not go to it any more." It was like a sport one has lost interest in. The visiting team was the Austrians, meeting the Italians, at home; Nick, a ringer, is benched as befits his incapacity. He takes his therapy in Milan, but the focus is on that major—"in another country," as Marlowe's famous lines go—whose "wench is dead." Hemingway himself was not to make out much better with his girl, Agnes von Kurowsky, the Red Cross nurse who became Catherine Barkley. She did not follow him home to the States as he expected, and he turned his bitterness into a "sketch" which he later named "A Very Short Story." He did not call the jilted soldier Nick, however, and the piece remains more sketch than story. Thus Hemingway returned to Michigan from the war, "blown to pieces," according to a Petoskey doctor, and still alone.

IV

"It's the account of a boy on a fishing trip," to call again on Scott Fitzgerald, writing this time about "Big Two-Hearted River." "Nothing more—but I read it with the most breathless unwilling interest I have experienced since Conrad first bent my reluctant eyes upon the sea." In 1926 Hemingway was happy to settle for such published praise. But Fitzgerald might have asked himself why nothing more than a fishing trip should have galvanized his attention. If he had done so he might have discovered that he was responding perfectly to what Hemingway called in those days "my new theory that you could omit anything if you knew that you omitted . . . and make people feel something more than they understood." The things he had left out before were never really crucial, but this time an omission made all the difference. As he pointed out years later, "The story was about coming back from the war but there was no mention of the war in it."

There is no doubt, however, that the perilous state of Nick's nervous system, unmentioned in the story, accounts for the intensity of the writing, which is what arrested Fitzgerald. Here is the quintessential Hemingway style: simplicity, forged under great pressure, out of complexity. The trout, "keeping themselves steady in the current with wavering fins," reflect as in a mirror. He decides not to fish "the swamp," which would be to complicate things; besides, that's where "the river narrowed," which may remind him of the "different width" of the river at Fossalta. Acting, and not thinking, his trip proves a remarkable success. He will carry his scars, but will never be badly shaken again. Fishing is better therapy than Milan's; for Nick the war in Italy ended in Michigan.

"If he wrote it he could get rid of it," Nick will think later on. "He had gotten rid of many things by writing them." And in his next appearance so much has been purged that he seems—most disconcertingly—less the struck-down veteran of a war than a prewar adolescent. But Hemingway was still writing out of his own experience—seeing himself, at each stage of the narrative, as Nick—and the events that gave rise to the next three stories took place in the postwar summer of 1919, through half of which he was in fact still the teen-ager that Nick seems. Indeed a year later, Marcelline observed, her brother was "more like a boy of sixteen than a man approaching his twenty-first birthday." Nick at this age will bear her out, and several details in the stories date them as postwar—rum-runners, for instance, and the business about "not thinking."

"The End of Something" and "The Three-Day Blow" are as closely related as chapters in a novel. In the former Nick breaks off his affair with a girl named Marjorie. Just as Hortons Bay has run out of the logs that made it a lumbering town, leaving nothing but the foundations of the mill, which she calls "our old ruin," so their relationship has run its course and is left in ruin by Nick—one of the things, perhaps, that he got rid of by writing it. But the break-up, it turns out, was a plot in which a friend named Bill conspired, and in "The Three-Day Blow" they discuss the matter, along with the joys of bachelorhood and literature—especially Maurice Hewlett's *Forest Lovers,* which at points strikingly resembles "The Last Good Country"—as they get happily drunk on Bill's father's whiskey. "Now she can marry someone of her own sort," Bill tells him, which suggests that what Hemingway omitted this time is that in life, as already mentioned, Marjorie (Bump), though a respectable high-school girl, was a summer waitress at Mrs. Dilworth's Pinehurst Cottage. Nick is uncomfortable about the whole business, but then he realizes that just as love can run out so estrangement is not necessarily permanent, and he feels better.

"You are constantly aware of the continual snapping of ties that is going on around Nick," Fitzgerald wrote of this pair of stories—an observation so acute that it reads more like a prediction, since it is in "Summer People" that Nick really begins snapping his ties to Michigan, and there is no evidence that Fitzgerald ever saw the story. At any rate it has never been published before, or even typed.

Ernest went into a church on September 30, 1920, one of his biographers tells us, with a girl named Kate. He burned a candle, prayed for everything he wanted and was rewarded, he wrote in a letter, with a small "Adventure with a touch of Romance." If the Kate of "Summer People" was the Kate of actuality perhaps she was the reward, which is sexual. In any event, Nick has one last adventure up in Michigan, and it tells us as much about him and his maker as might a chapter of factual biography. Imperfectly paced, and itself rather boyish, it is not the best Nick story we have. Nor is it the least of them, but it is almost certainly the first: the manuscript shows repeated vacillation on the protagonist's name. Nick, Hemingway writes, and crosses it out; Allan the same; Wemedge, which becomes here as before Nick's nickname, the same; again and finally Nick, all the way through.

As an apparent first-try at a very early story, "Summer People" is remarkable for the deftness with which seemingly unlike things are brought together. Nick plunging his arm into a cold spring on a hot night at the start sharply prefigures his small adventure with Kate at the end. Along the way, the swimming, diving, conversations, thoughts, ambitions—as well as the interlude with the girl, and a prayer—are gathered in the boy's realization that he is "different," which is presumably the point. Different in all the ways of the story. Even if he does not entirely act on it, his knowledge of girls is "beyond his years"; the manner of his diving is unusual, and another prefiguration of the intercourse later on; he swims underwater, not on top of it, and so forth. All differences culminate in the crucial one, the hope and belief that he will be a great writer.

Evidence in the manuscripts shows clearly that Hemingway intended to revise and publish this story, which raises the question of why he never did. Perhaps he thought it was unprintable at the time, at least in this country. (Gertrude Stein told him that "Up in Michigan" was *inaccroacha-*

ble, and at the time she was right.) More likely, though, he "didn't want to hurt living people," the reason he once gave for why he didn't write a "wonderful novel" about Oak Park. His summer people were not just living; they had been his very closest friends. Most of all, "Summer People" would have hurt Hadley Richardson, his first wife by the time he wrote the story. It was Kate, Hadley's close friend, who had introduced her to Ernest. (He was in turn to introduce Kate to a close friend of his, the late John Dos Passos, whom she married.) Indeed in September of 1921 when Ernest married Hadley at Hortons Bay, the town of the story, near Windemere, where they spent their honeymoon, the original for every single character in "Summer People"—Nick, Kate, Bill, Odgar, and the Ghee—was in the wedding party. Kate (sometimes Butstein or Stut, just as in the story) was Katharine Smith, a bridesmaid. Bill, the same Bill as in the two previous stories, was her brother, William B. Smith, Ernest's best friend and an usher (who eventually became a speechwriter for Harry Truman). Odgar, or Carl, also an usher, was J. Charles Edgar, an older man but long-time friend who had housed Ernest when he worked in Kansas City for the *Star.* The only person involved who would not be hurt was another usher, the Ghee (significance unknown)—Jack Pentecost, who was along on the trip to the Fox River that became "Big Two-Hearted River."

Kate Smith was eight years older than Ernest, and her brother states categorically that "Ernesto did not have an affair with my sister." But Hadley was just as old. Anyway it didn't matter, Hemingway thinks for Nick later on, that the best of his writing was "made up." "None of it had ever happened. . . . That was what the family couldn't understand." (Perhaps because a lot of it had happened.) But "Summer People" was far too close to home. And by the time the family was mostly gone, and Kate decapitated in an automobile accident, her husband and brother and Hadley still lived, and Hemingway was in far other country. He published no Nick Adams fiction after 1933; by the time Kate died his manuscripts were widely dispersed; he may even have forgotten the story. But it is a significant one—of Nick's graduation into a bigger world. Summer people are insulated; they matter but for a season, don't really belong. Nick is at the center of this transient population, but he has a secret that neither summer nor year-round people are in on: because he is different he can have what he wants, as he thinks. And that entitles him to belong elsewhere. If his final prayer comes true he is not temporary at all, but the man for all seasons he became.

At this point, however, Nick can only aspire to be a writer. He's not old enough yet, and, as he remarks, doesn't know enough. ("Wait.") As with Hemingway, the wait proved short, and it's a reasonable guess that the end of "On Writing" records the very moment when the mature career began. Irrelevant anachronisms concerning bullfighters and so forth set aside, the piece emerges as Hemingway's Farewell to Michigan. Nick is Letting Go: relinquishing the past, the Northern Woods, summers, friends, and even fishing. At the end the piece moves into action. Nick releases the trout he has caught and kept alive, simply cuts the line he had been fishing with that snagged, then relieves the rabbit of two ticks on its head that were killing it. He is freeing everything for one thing, "work." This because he has a sort of tick in his own head—very different from the one that agitated "Big Two-Hearted River," to which this material was once illogically appended. It has dawned on him that he has learned (from Cezanne, as explained) how to build in prose the land and landscape that contain "Big Two-Hearted River." Nick, in other words, is off to start the story that Hemingway had just finished. It won't be long now.

V

Meanwhile Nick has married Helen (Hadley in the manuscript of "Wedding Day"), and once again the scene shifts abruptly to Europe, where things turn out to be relatively uneventful—two episodes only, loosely connected in that both involve skiing and touch on marriage. "An Alpine Idyll," about the peasant who used to hang a lantern from the mouth of the frozen corpse of his wife, is said to be a tall tale told tourists by natives in Austria. (Nick asks his friend, "Do you think it's true?") In "Cross Country Snow" it is again the stubborn reality of a woman's body that impinges on the skiing; Helen is pregnant and Nick is taking her back to the States to have the child. (If he remembers what Bill told him, "Once a man's married, he's absolutely bitched," we do not hear about it.) And on this dying fall, taking "the run home," Nick's adventures—but for a reprise—are abruptly ended.

They needn't have been, had Hemingway chosen to pursue that marriage to Helen, for he wrote several stories in which Nick could have easily been the husband, and Helen the wife. But he tended to smuggle certain things away in his fiction; if they were compromising or shameful and he wanted to get rid of them he chose masks less transparent than Nick's. In "Soldier's Home" he had disguised his misery on returning to

Oak Park from the war by giving Harold Krebs an experience of battle different from his own or Nick's, and by moving both his mother and Oak Park to Oklahoma. "Up in Michigan" was based on personal experience at Hortons Bay, and he set it there, but cast himself as Jim Gilmore, a short blacksmith with big mustaches. Similarly he skirted the breakdown of his marriage to Hadley, but did write a group of stories which are set abroad and show a marriage very like his own in a state of progressive disarray. He once called "Out of Season," where there is only a hint that things may go bad, a "literal transcript" of himself and Hadley. And although he said that the man and wife of "Cat in the Rain" were a "Harvard Couple," they sound like much the same people. In "A Canary for One," "I and my wife" are separating, and in "Homage to Switzerland" Mr. Johnson is being divorced.

That child, however, was born—a son called Schatz in "A Day's Wait," a story which could have been included in this book, except that it is really about the boy. In life John, or Jack, or Bumby Hemingway, he figures prominently in the Bimini section of *Islands in the Stream* as Schatz again, or Thomas Hudson, Jr., oldest son of the last major protagonist. He is also the son in "Fathers and Sons," in which Nick looks backward to his boyhood and rounds it off. Nick is now thirty-eight and a writer; the son is about the age of Nick when he first appeared in "Indian Camp." The action has covered a generation. The doctor who discussed suicide with his boy in the first story has now committed it, though we are told only that he is dead—another important omission. And as Nick remembers how useless his father was on the subject of sex, which he learned about from Trudy instead, so now he cannot talk to his boy about the doctor's death, though he knows that sooner or later they will have to visit "the tomb of my grandfather" (the boy has been raised abroad). A son is now father to the son, things have come full circle, and in his collected *First Forty-Nine Stories* Hemingway put this one forty-ninth.

The tale is told, but if Nick's history seems in retrospect to amount to slightly more than the sum of its chapters it may be because his progress through the first third of our century is at once representative, distinctive, and personal. Representative as a national passage from the innocence of a shaky prewar security through the disillusionment of a European ordeal-by-fire, and the rejection of much that a previous age had stood for, to "normalcy." Distinctive for memories of specific experiences the exact like of which we never had. And personal as the recreated autobiography of a culture hero of his time. But if anyone still feels more than he can account for in remembering Nick, he might ask what if anything Hemingway omitted from the story as a whole. The answer is so obvious that it might never dawn on us. The Nick Adams fiction is about leaving Oak Park, but there is no mention of Oak Park in it.

The text may be taken from Marcelline. When Ernest was flopping loose in their suburban house on his return from the war he spoke to her one day about "all the other things in life that aren't here. . . . There's a whole big world out there. . . ." What he omitted is what he escaped from. What he escaped to, for the rest of his life and all of his career, moves against a background he expunged. Oak Park was rejected for Michigan, and when that became a small world it was in turn put behind for a greater one. All that is simple to understand. But it is hard to realize today how great was the *need* for rebellion—how preposterous were things *At the Hemingways,* the name of Marcelline's affectionate book. Home was a Victorian matriarchy, and it has been said more than once that Hemingway was the only man in the world who really hated his mother. She had considerable pretentions to the arts; she sang, composed, and later painted. Her response to *The Sun Also Rises* was "I can't stand filth!" Her husband, though a busy doctor, kept house far more than she did. ("Dr. Hemingway did most of the cooking. He'd fix the kids' breakfast and then take the Mrs. her breakfast in bed.") She raised Ernest as closely as possible as a twin, a twin girl, to Marcelline. They looked alike, and were "dressed alike," his sister writes, in "gingham dresses and in little fluffy lace-tucked dresses. . . . We wore our hair exactly alike in bangs." (Harold Loeb, Robert Cohn in *The Sun Also Rises,* traces the source of Hemingway's insistence on his masculinity to this. It was as if he were forever saying "Damn it, I'm *male.*")

Few could have outdone Grace Hemingway in the intensity of her middle-class respectability, but for all his profession, and love of the outdoors, Clarence Hemingway was one who did. A lifelong teetotaller, he "abhorred" the playing of cards in any form, and would not permit anyone in his presence to say darn or gosh. Dancing school was morally repulsive—" 'leads to hell and damnation,' he kept muttering." When *in our time* was published he sent back six copies, returning even the single one his wife wanted to keep. "He would not tolerate such filth in his home, Dad declared." Later on when his son was becoming famous he is known to have answered sadly the question of how the boy was making out: "Ernest's written another dirty book."

What Hemingway called "Mr. Young's trauma theory of literature" is not retracted: the wounds in Italy are still climactic and central in the lives of Hemingway and all his personal protagonists. Nor is there any reason to withdraw the notion, which the author also objected to, that he wrote chiefly about himself; he was not lacking in imagination, but to live his life as he wished, then to write about it, was the way he basically operated. Neither is there any reason to abandon the idea that the adventures of Nick Adams were foreshadowed by *The Adventures of Huckleberry Finn.*

But a different emphasis can be put on this combination. Huck's rebellion was of course from Aunt Sally—and St. Petersburg, which Twain did not omit. Nick's rebellion is a given—omitted but as basic as the wound, and prior to it. Almost nothing Hemingway ever wrote could be set in Oak Park; it is extremely doubtful that he could have written a "wonderful novel" about the place. What he could write about happens "out there"—an exact equivalent for what, departing "sivilization" for the last time, Huck called "the territory." In the overall adventure, life becomes an escape to reality. No reward whatever is promised, and the cost in comfort and security is high. Out there can kill you, and nearly did. But it beats "home," which is a meaner death, as Ernest tried to tell Marcelline.

1972

Hemingway's Manuscripts: The Vault Reconsidered

As learned scholars and masters of our trade, you will all remember how Whitman once paraphrased Emerson:

> Do I contradict myself?
> Very well then I contradict myself
> (I am large, I contain multitudes).

So permit me a little paraphrase of Whitman:

> Do I repeat myself?
> Very well then I repeat myself
> (I am small, I contain platitudes).

For no one is more keenly aware than the present speaker that he is already in print—three times!—on the topic before us, which was assigned. This is a story that I wrote up once for the *New York Times Book Review,* revised and updated for a journal, and reprinted in my last book (which is called *Three Bags Full: Essays in American Fiction,* Harcourt Brace

This paper was read at The Pennsylvania State University Conference on Bibliography, held at University Park, November 29–December 1, 1973.

Jovanovich, newly out in paperback and attractively priced). Not to mention the fact the principal result of all this effort—everything that was presented to Mary Hemingway as a book, called *The Hemingway Manuscripts: An Inventory*—is, though never exactly a best-seller, still in print too (Pennsylvania State University Press).

Nor did I realize until I read our program that this was supposed to be some kind of "keynote," which I see defined as "a policy line to be followed, set forth authoritatively in advance by formal announcement." If I should here inadvertently establish any key, major or minor, or accidentally sound any note, tonic or dominant, then this Conference is cursed, damned, and doomed before it ever saw light of day. (Faulkner.) But as some of you know, the impresario of this get-together is a very hard man to say no to. So here we are, back at the old stand.

In 1950 Hemingway wrote someone or other a letter that I have seen in which he says he figures to have all his papers and uncompleted manuscripts burned when he is buried; he doesn't want that sort of crap to go on. Well, as some of you also know, quite a bit of stuff escaped the flames (which will ignite later), and so it goes on all right—precisely as here and now. But I do not really wish to seem cynical or sarcastic about this. Going through all of Hemingway's manuscript (I doubt that a single sheet of *it* was destroyed) was a profoundly rewarding experience that I never for a moment even dreamed of having, but definitely had. It was the high point of my vicissitudinous "career," and, as I have said before, I could never be happier working than I was in that vault if I lived to be a hundred.

I suppose that for present purposes the place to start is at the point when, following her husband's death in July of 1961, Mary Hemingway realized that she had the responsibility of gathering up all the manuscript of a man who moved about a great deal, kept practically every piece of paper he ever wrote a word on, and left it behind, without regard for hardly any of it. Chiefly this meant going to Key West, where large boxes of stuff were stored away in a back room (no longer there) of Sloppy Joe's, and to Cuba—then as now completely out of bounds. She hasn't told that story yet, since she is saving it (I think) for her autobiography. But it would appear that there was some sort of deal with Castro here, whereby in exchange for the Finca, their house in the country outside Havana, and the Pilar, their boat, she was allowed to retrieve such manuscript as was down there, as well as an extremely valuable collection of paintings. Then, via an empty shrimp boat, I've heard, she got the cargo to this country—first to Ketchum and the house where he died, which she still summers in, then to New York, to her penthouse and the vaults of a nearby bank, where the papers rested for several years before being shipped to Brookline, Massachusetts, where they await the building of the Kennedy Library, if that ever happens, in which they will be magnificently housed and displayed in a special room, which Charley Mann will apparently have a hand in designing.*

Some of you already knew a lot of that, and this, too: the story of how Charley, and before that I—the most unlikely choice conceivable, given all the nasty things Hemingway said or wrote about me (these letters keep turning up)—got the opportunity to be first to go through all that paper. It actually starts in a barbershop in downtown, or metropolitan, State College, Pa., where I was reading in a magazine a prepublication excerpt from Hotchner's *Papa Hemingway* with what you might call considerable interest. I had already read in the *Times* that Mary was trying to stop publication of the book, and what I quickly realized was that there was more wrong with it than she could possibly know—for instance that one sentence, there put in the mouth of Frank Capa, was taken verbatim from a book I wrote. I had read someplace that Mrs. Hemingway shared her husband's lack of affection for me and my work. But I was going to New York in a few days anyway, and so, after surmounting the difficulty of getting an unlisted phone number, I called her up and asked her if she'd like some more ammunition. She gave me a rather wary Yes, and I paid her a visit. She was very wary indeed. I underwent the first elaborate security check of my civilian life, prior to entering her lair, and things got off to a fairly stiff start. But she made me the biggest bourbon on the rocks I have ever downed, also a smaller drink for herself, and after a little conversation things got more comfortable; we exchanged damaging information for a couple of hours. We were both kind of exhilarated when I left and I couldn't resist it: I gave her a big hug and a little kiss, and was rewarded with a short sentence that sticks yet in my ear: "Carlos," she said, "would never do that." One up.

What we got out of this was a split. She eventually lost her suit, but my attempt to discredit the book was (by all fair-minded people) thought successful.† I will skip the rest of that (including some funny business

*Until his death in 1998, Charles W. Mann Jr. was Chief of Special Collections at Penn State's Pattee Library. With Philip Young, he was co-editor of *The Hemingway Manuscripts: An Inventory* (1969).

†"I Dismember Papa," originally published in *Atlantic Monthly* (August 1966) and included in *Three Bags Full*.

where Hotchner refused to face me on "Mike Wallace at Large"—we appeared separately). The only point is that in the face of a common enemy Mary and I had become friendly. And that is how she happened to take me to look in the bank vault one day, which is where it dawned on me that here was buried treasure, rich enough to rival any legendary pirate's, and never dug. Except for a few prominent items—such as the manuscript of what became *Islands in the Stream*—absolutely no one knew what-all was in those enormous safe-deposit boxes (I had no idea they come so big). I offered my services, and was accepted; Charley Mann was signed aboard to "help" me, whereupon he became a Hemingway expert so fast you wouldn't believe it unless you've worked with him. We started out in a state of excitement that must have been truly marvelous to observe, and though that wore off it was quite a while before we really touched earth. I was gratified, later, to learn rather dramatically that the excitement was not peculiar to us. I knew there was interest in what was in those boxes, but underestimated it; on the day that our list of their contents was published the story was on the front page of the *N.Y. Times*; and as if one weren't enough I did two interviews with Hugh Downs on the "Today" show.

It was first and foremost—at the time and in retrospect—an experience, roughly comparable, for literary persons, I should think, to being suddenly called to Washington to listen privately to the Nixon tapes. The sensation of being grabbed almost bodily into literary history was overpowering: the cheap, crumbling paper of Chicago and Paris days when he felt, as he wrote later, "like I was making the whole world"; the heavily rusted paperclips that had to be removed but could not be replaced without gratuitous damage to the pages (before I gave some of them away I was the world's foremost holder of used Hemingway paperclips), the worm holes (we had a favorite, a heroic fellow who made his grand way through a good three inches of heavy paper), the teeth marks where mice had made off with the corners of many pages (probably in Sloppy Joe's)—there was an awful lot of what I think is called "color." Hemingway had long ago accused me of invading his privacy, which I really did not feel I had done, but I was acutely aware that I was now invading it massively: examining faulty early drafts of things now famous, of things discarded or unfinished, seeing the names of real people before he invented new ones for print—hardly an hour ever went by that we did not discover something previously unknown, and to us, anyway, worth knowing. Eventually we identified almost every sheet of paper that was there—over 19,000 of them—even down to one that had but a fragment of a sentence on it (which was, first guess proved correct, for "Fathers and Sons").

I will never forget finding, very early in the game, what is clearly the first Nick Adams story Hemingway wrote, "Summer People," which was not known to exist and had conceivably not been read by anyone before me—anyway I'm pretty sure he didn't show it to Hadley his wife. Or my first sight of those seven French schoolboy notebooks labelled *Fiesta,* in which he wrote the first draft of what, completely rewritten, became *The Sun Also Rises.* Even stronger were my sensations at finding, carefully folded and tucked away in notebook three, a scrawled ten-page, unsigned letter by Scott Fitzgerald, written after he had read the final typescript of the novel, giving Ernest the very devil for certain things—as the result of which Hemingway junked the first chapter and a half of his book, though it had already been set in galleys (which I found in a cabinet in Mary's study).* And so many other things. The first draft, called "The Matadors," of "The Killers"; a draft of something called "The Happy Ending," which turned out to be "The Snows of Kilimanjaro"; "The Great Man," which became "The Battler." And so on—at some length. Little never-published things, too, like "The Autobiography of Alice B. Hemingway." And a substantial unpublished essay on "The Art of the Short Story," self-conscious and really quite bad, but containing some interesting comments on his own stories. (Some of Hotchner's better "Ernest said to me's" came from this manuscript.)

Indeed I don't see why I shouldn't mention a couple of these comments here, specifically two which deal with two of his most famous stories, "The Snows" and "Francis Macomber." On the subject of the mysterious leopard in the epigraph to "Kilimanjaro" Hemingway says he is *omerta.* There is a note in the margin there in Mary's hand where she says she can't find that in any dictionary, but it is of course Mafia for "Silent," or better "a conspiracy of silence." This leads me to suggest, anyway, that the leopard in that epigraph is an enigmatic or untranslatable symbol (hence not in the ordinary sense a symbol) precisely because the author had no definable secondary meaning in mind; what cannot be explained has got to baffle—and reverberate—as this leopard has done. The other remark has to do with the famous problem of whether Margot Macomber shot her husband intentionally or by accident, and resolves it

*The letter is printed and annotated in "Fitzgerald's *Sun Also Rises*: Notes and Comment" by Philip Young and Charles W. Mann in *Fitzgerald/Hemingway Annual* (1970), 1–13.

to my satisfaction (here I commit the International Fallacy) since it confirms what I have always said, and have got a certain amount of hell for saying. Hemingway's words are, "No, I don't know whether she shot him on purpose any more than you do. . . . The only hint I can give you is that it is my belief that the incidence of husbands shot accidentally by wives who are bitches and really work at it is very low." Well, this was fun. From dog house to penthouse it was great to be back in New York—employed.

There were trivial discoveries as well. The one I remember best was in a file of letters beside some big-game rifles in the closet of that same study: a letter which the author had written me back in 1952—half almost hysterically abusive, half funny—and never mailed. Indeed I was to learn that on May 26 and 27 of that year he wrote me four long letters in which he told me (although he had not yet seen a line of my book, which had not yet been published) how I had damaged him in the eyes of his wife and children, completely stopped him from writing for several months, and so on. A man doesn't know what to say to that kind of thing, so I won't try. But some of it is funny. He wrote, for instance, a series of letters to Charles Poore, which have been (however illegally) published, and so according to current practice I can quote from them. In one he says that Young "must be a strange character. If you shot him he'd probably bleed footnotes." (He had a lot of ideas that were worse than shooting me.) But after seeing my picture on the back of the book he decides "I'm just going to let him hang and rattle." In another he says "I think we ought to get him to his analyst. . . . I'd say he was pretty well around the bend already. . . ." The last one I'll mention may be a little less trivial, for I think it really gives insight into the special kind of person Hemingway was. One day in that file of letters I came across maybe the fourth reference to something or other that "non-combat characters" like me can *never* understand, and I went into the living room where Mary was and I said, "for crying out loud where did he get this non-combat stuff? I've got three battle stars and a medal." Mary hesitated no more than a second, then looked at me straight and said "Philip, if Ernest had known that there would *never* have been any trouble." (I don't know what to say to that, either.)

The reason I am taking so long in getting to an actual "Reconsideration" of what I learned in going through all the pages we examined is that Reconsidering has not got me much of anywhere. There are, however, two or three things I had not thought to say before that I can mention now. One is that I learned in the bank something that Hemingway himself may never have learned, unless in his deepest depression, which is only a form of knowing: that he was not a particularly good judge of how well or badly he was writing, from day to day, over some *very* extended periods of time. If this were not so it is hard to see how he could have persisted month after month and into years in the composition of things that just weren't working out. There are three very large manuscripts that did not: *The Dangerous Summer,* his return to bullfighting in Spain, an "African Book,"* which is another return, and a very long and tedious novel called *Garden of Eden*. Hemingway seems to have had whatever it takes to convince oneself that one is writing well when he really isn't—which is why, I suppose, for so many years he could go on composing poems that would have convinced most of us—though some of them are amusing—that we were something less than cut out for the genre.

A possibly related thought is that Hemingway never really had either an agent or an editor. Of course he did have a lawyer who did many of the things an agent is paid to do, and technically he had as editor the one and only Maxwell Perkins. But Alfred Rice, the lawyer, never gave him any literary advice so far as I know—nothing like the shrewd criticism I get from my agent, for instance. And I find no evidence that, as Hemingway's editor, Perkins ever did any editing. I am not an expert in this matter, and haven't committed any homework, but all Perkins seems to have done was tell Hemingway he was great, which he probably thought was all Hemingway ever wanted to hear. Emerson says somewhere—and I doubtless misquote, because I can't find it—that dear to us are those who love us, but dearer by far those who find us wanting. Perkins should have thought of something like that. How would you like it if your copy of *The Sun Also Rises* began with the statement that "This is a novel about a lady," which is something less than the truth, and that Robert Cohn is the "hero" of it, which is the reverse of the truth? Well, that's the way it would read if it hadn't been for Scott Fitzgerald, my point being where was Maxwell Perkins?

A third reconsidered thought is that, as he himself once or twice said, Hemingway did not revise very much. I had always thought of him as a writer who must have polished and polished endlessly, but the evidence

***True at First Light* (Scribners, 1999). This was the last manuscript remaining in the vault to be published.

is that, another personal for instance, he often did about one-tenth as much revising as I do. He would make large cuts, often, but not always, judicious; he would discard and start over, and also, of course, abandon; but although he occasionally revised heavily, the practice was more occasional than habitual. As we all know, he wrote very slowly—slow enough, that is, to get it pretty close to right first shot. (I'm reminded here of John O'Hara, who wrote very fast and got it right first shot—but only as right as he could.) So much for startling revelations. I trip south, where my experience with the manuscripts has a little postlude.

Shortly after Charley and I had finished with the bank, Mrs. Young and I were in Key West, one of her favorite places, which I had never visited, for a few days. Hemingway of course had lived and worked here for many years before he moved to Cuba, and of course we went to the touristy shrines: the House on Whitehead Street, Sloppy Joe's, etc. But people seemed to sense that we were not exactly tourists; we detected a sort of guarded curiosity in a few of them, and soon I was getting highly veiled questions about how much old Hemingway "papers" might be worth. What kind of papers? Well, papers. Manuscript? No, just old papers. It had only begun to become a story of mystery when we met up with the Bruces, who still live in Key West. Toby Bruce was Ernest's long-time friend, handyman, chauffeur, and jack of many trades—a genuine character and marvellous raconteur. Betty, his wife, was the person who had helped Mary dig the manuscripts out from the great piles of junk Hemingway had left behind him when he took off for Cuba long ago. He never seems to have tossed out anything: cancelled checks, old grocery lists, lists of fish boated, expenditures for liquor, old newspapers, ticket stubs, programs, what-all. Mary wanted all that destroyed, so that *it* would not "go on," and the plan was that Toby's truckdriver (Toby was in the appliance business) was to take them to the city dump where they were to be burned. Then of course it dawned on us what must have happened. Some of the stuff actually got to the dump (hence the false rumors that had reached me that Mary was down there burning up manuscript), but some of it didn't, and the people who had or have it wanted to know how much they could get for it. (An apparent example is the owner, at that time, of Sloppy Joe's, who was said to wish to see me, but twice failed to show up at his saloon at an appointed hour in order to do so.) This was five years ago, and I don't know what has happened since, but there could be a small fortune in Key West. For instance, Betty Bruce had a whole stack of cancelled checks—there may be hundreds more—

and handed me one which I kept, dated March 4, 1932—$20.85 payable to the Key West Colonial Hotel and signed Ernest M. Hemingway. Just the other day in *Hemingway at Auction* I saw such a check (from 1959, payable to a tax collector) advertised in 1970 for $75. You may be sure it sold.

The point of all this is that the weather cleared, my wife, way out in the Gulf Stream caught a fine kingfish (I caught nothing), the Bruces had a cocktail party, and Bernie Dickson, the owner of the house on Whitehead Street, took everyone to dinner. And it was right along in there that Betty began, shyly and piecemeal, to trot out for us manuscript of legitimate literary interest. These were things that Mary had given to the Key West Public Library, which Betty was custodian of—plus a couple of things she had simply given Betty. And so we had excuse for staying on an extra day, at the Bruce's Tennessee Williams sort of house, going over things and making notes after the manner in which Charley had instructed me. I remember especially the galleys for *Winner Take Nothing,* where Hemingway had substantially revised the text of a few stories, and where he himself (this was news) had censored all the four-letter words he had written and the printer had set. And the galleys for *Death in the Afternoon,* where there is a rather good ending to the book that was set in type but never published. Also a big chunk of corrugated cardboard which he had covered with practice titles—e.g., "The Manner of the Accident," for "The Short Happy Life of Francis Macomber." And a list of topics for stories to write. But most of all a nearly blank notebook, dating from the very start of his career, where he had listed the various ways he liked to think of dying—mostly suicidal, contradicting everything else he wrote about that—and not including by shotgun.

And so, as I said, this business of the manuscripts was in retrospect an experience, or rather a series of them. Exciting, memorable, sometimes fascinating. Most especially in the bank, in the midst of early drafts of now-famous things, and in the best of the unpublished things, some of which no one knew existed and even the author had probably long ago forgot. We were deep in what I have called the mess and mystery of the creative process—one that has become a part of history—and it would have set an iceberg tingling.

1974

8.

Hemingway Papers, Occasional Thoughts

"Few Americans had a greater impact on the emotions and attitudes of the American people than Ernest Hemingway. From his first emergence as one of the bright literary stars in Paris during the 20s—as a chronicler of the 'lost generation,' which he was to immortalize—he almost single-handedly transformed the literature and the way of thought of men and women in every country in the world."

Those sentences make up the opening paragraph of a four-paragraph tribute to Hemingway which appeared in a special issue of the *Mark Twain Journal* for Summer, 1962. They were signed by John F. Kennedy, and though a rigorous textual analysis would probably not support me, I would like to think he wrote them. I do not think he wrote the other paragraphs, which read like the work of a subordinate (very) who had located the subject in a reference book. The President of course knew quite enough about the writer to make a statement. As we all know, seven years earlier in his *Profiles In Courage* he had thought of him at the first mention of the word "courage. 'Grace under pressure,' Ernest Hemingway defined it." As not everyone knows, though Theodore Sorensen passed it along, Kennedy once added that "grace under pressure . . . also described a girl he knew by that name."

This essay was presented on July 18, 1980, at the dedication of the Hemingway Collection at the John F. Kennedy Library.

Kennedy and Hemingway. Back when I was getting ready to bring out a *Reconsideration* of the writer, I was struck with similarities between two of my favorite people, both so suddenly and violently gone. Both were serious, realistic, witty men, who aimed for the top and made it. Both were great readers, both men of style, both students of courage who drew portraits of it. Curiously parallel were their grievous injuries, illnesses, and brushes with death. Knowing a little of the author's admiration for the President, I wrote Arthur Schlesinger, Jr., to ask if Kennedy had perhaps not felt some kind of affinity with Hemingway. Yes indeed, was the friendly response. Schlesinger, who was just finishing his book on Kennedy, said that he "obviously felt an affinity of some sort" with the author. Although when "I got to know him well," he added, the President had pretty much quit reading fiction, "he appeared to have read most of Hemingway at one time or another," and was a "great admirer." He recalled how distressed Kennedy was by the writer's death, and how touched he had been by the message received from the Mayo Clinic at the time of the inauguration. *A Thousand Days* says the same things, and its single epigraph is a passage we know that begins "The world breaks everyone. . . ." Kennedy believed that the health of society related to the health of the arts, which is chiefly why so many artists, including Hemingway, were invited to his inaugural. I don't remember that any professors were asked. But for the present occasion it might be noted that when the White House library was, in Sorensen's words, "restocked and restored with the best in American literature," two critical studies of Hemingway showed up in the acquisitions.

It would be unwise to attempt an extended account of my own relationship with John F. Kennedy. (My mother used to push me in a baby carriage to the neighborhood grocer's in Brookline, and only long afterward realized that the infant perambulated there by Rose Kennedy—recognized by all as Honey Fitz's daughter—had become our senator, then our chief executive. Though the Youngs lived adjacent to the Kennedys—they at 83 Beals Street—we did not know them; like so many in that town, they were Democrats.) But a different sort of connection might be briefly invoked. On or about February 3, 1968, Charley Mann received a note from Mary Hemingway which read:

> By chance I spoke a moment tonight with Robert Kennedy, told him what you and Philip Y. are doing. He appeared very

> pleased, and said whenever the inventory was ready, he would like very much to have a copy of it.
>
> This is not to harrass or hurry you; only to suggest that the original catalog—or listing or whatever you prefer to call it—have another copy made, not waiting for Philip's printed thing for libraries. . . .

On the back of the envelope she wrote "P. S. We should make one for Mrs. Kennedy too."

February 3, 1968, was the day Senator Kennedy opened his presidential campaign in Concord, N. H. Charley and I were at that point far from ready, but thought it might become us anyway to hurry, and before long we sent Mary copies of a substantial listing. Neither of us recalls what happened next, but by then R. F. K. was well along the trail on which he died in June. In the aftermath of yet another catastrophe we asked nothing, and suppose he never saw what we put together for him. (Asked about this in the Hemingway Room at the time of the dedication, Mrs. Onassis said she does not think she ever saw it either.)

It is hard to think of a time when a rapprochement between the arts and the White House seemed more real than during the Kennedy administration—a sense of rapport, of which the present ceremony is a pointed reminder. It is precisely the ceremonial aspect of all this that attracts me. Similarly it is the remarkable existence and bringing-together of the Papers, more than the use to which they can be put, which I find exciting. But I think we should be mindful, in the presence of such treasure, that if the author had had his way—at least as he once expressed it thirty years ago—we would all be somewhere else today and the Papers would be nowhere. Posterity, Hemingway wrote Arthur Mizener in 1950, can take care of herself. What he figured was "to have all my papers and uncompleted Mss. burned when I am buried. I don't want that sort of shit to go on. . . ." It is not specified in the letter what sort that might be, yet I do suspect that the activities we are engaged in would qualify. Nor do I believe that this sentiment of the author's was aberrant or fleeting. It fit his wish—as he expressed it, anyway—that attention would focus exclusively on his published work, not its creator. Also the belief that by issuing a sort of edict he could forever prohibit publication of his letters.

But surely it had been an awful loss if all this paper had gone up in smoke. When I consider the scope and profundity of the universal debt owed the author's widow, I am most impressed by the number of situations in which she must have had to weigh her sense of the writer's wishes against other interests, such as the public. It is not just the enormous energy and effort she has expended, or the skill and judgment with which she has managed things, but the moral quandries she must have endured (so I imagine it) and have had to resolve. We have long honored Max Brod for violating the wishes of his friend Kafka, and issuing posthumously the uncompleted work on which much of a great reputation rests. But Mary H. was not just a friend.

The thought that led to the permanent repository of so much cherished wealth, furthermore, was inspired. What is awkward is the matter of one's own contribution to the program. I first thought it was to be occasional and the truth is that I have not, as advertised, "utilized the Papers in recent years." (It's been over a decade since I glimpsed them, and I never so much "used" as identified, listed and simply read.) Moreover, as some of you know, I have subsequently passed along such thoughts as I could summon up at meetings of this sort in Texas, Oregon, Idaho, Pennsylvania, Alabama, and Florida. The cupboard is very close to bare, and only after some poking around have I managed to locate in its recesses three bits of business commenced yet unfinished. These are, first, an updated report to stockholders in the Hemingway Industry, and, second, a bulletin on the recent fortunes and misfortunes of a book called *The Nick Adams Stories,* which grew out of the Papers. Last there is what may be a final thought on the situation which once nearly stopped the speaker before he ever got started in these affairs.

That story, with which I begin, has been a long time ending—particularly as new insights have appeared. I told it many years ago: the epistolary argument between author and critic, his strong objection to publishing his biography, which critic did not propose to write, and to a psychological analysis of his work—hence him, which I would attempt. To that narrative I brought all the understanding that I possessed. But I never did truly comprehend Hemingway's fear of what I was doing: most especially his warning (which to be honest I did not believe) that I could put him absolutely out of commission as a writer. All this had come to a head in late May of 1952. But one day long after, while looking for manuscript in a closet at Mary's, I came across several letters he'd written me back then and hadn't mailed. One of them, dated the 27th, is unfinished but representative. In it the author warns that by publishing my book I was about to "damage him, his wife and his children . . . gratuitously and without necessity." I was, he wrote, "at temporary liberty to attempt to destroy me as a writer. . . ."

I wished no such freedom, but since I had written about nothing Hemingway had not himself written about, whence such terrible power? In the context of the letter, it clearly related to the importance I placed on his wounding in Italy in the first World War. He said that in view of all the other wounds he had suffered, many of which he recapitulated, it seemed "silly" that his writing "should have been the result of a wound which was not my first. It was the worst. . . ."

It was also the only meaningful one, as far as his fiction went, and all I was doing was underlining and elucidating the significance he ascribed to it. A piece of a puzzle was missing, and in 1977—a full quarter century later—it turned up. Actually it had been resting in a letter I read that year, which Hemingway had written to Malcolm Cowley back in 1948, in connection with the latter's biographical piece on the former, forthcoming in *Life*. Published in an auction catalog, it is dated October 25th, and reads in part

> . . . look, Malcolm, if you want to do me a favour only put in about Italy . . . that I was wounded on such and such a day . . . had such and such decorations . . . and leave out everything else . . . As you must know from A Farewell to Arms and from In Another Country and A Way You'll Never Be (two uninvented stories) Italy and that part means more to me than I can ever write. I was in very bad trouble there and if you write anything about it *somebody will start digging around and I will,* eventually, *be in bad trouble again.* . . . I was hurt very badly; in the body, mind and spirit and also morally . . . hurt bad all the way through and I was *really spooked* at the end. (Emphasis added.)

As it happens, I had just that summer (in a doctoral dissertation) finished digging around in exactly that area of the writer's *fiction,* pointing out how much "Italy and that part" meant to him and his work. But beyond the well known fact that he like his protagonists had himself been wounded there, all I had to go on was what he had chosen to publish. As I now understand it, what he feared, when I came to his attention three years after he wrote Cowley about this, was that I was digging around in that area of the writer's *life,* and gone into his bad trouble during that period instead of the protagonist's. Then, I imagine, he was afraid that reading all about how it had been, and knowing others were doing the same, would resurrect the demons to spook and incapacitate once more. This was an investigation I never even thought of making, would not have known how to undertake, and would have found distasteful anyway. Biographical details would have been, as he said, gratuitous and unnecessary. Whether they could or would have done the damage he worried about, no one can say. We can only respect his apprehensions, and turn to less painful matters.

I have in mind what are now called "Hemingway Studies"—to me a self-conscious, heavy-handed, and complacent term, which effectively connotes the academic institutionalization of a literary subject. Some time ago, I reported on the considerable growth in this "field." Bemused by it, I thought now to review its history quickly, to extend the survey of productivity into the 70s, and to inquire into its meaning.

We begin by observing that in Lewis Leary's *Articles in American Literature, 1900–1950,* Hemingway titles take up 2¼ pages. (For purposes of comparison, Faulkner fills 3⅓, and to broaden it: Hawthorne and Melville get 7 each, Emerson and James 9, Mark Twain 12, Whitman 12½, and Poe 13½.) One notes that the first Hemingway item appears in 1923: "Hemingway: a Portrait," by Gertrude Stein. (The second, 1925, was Burton Rascoe's and the third, 1926, Scott Fitzgerald's.) By 1950, 91 articles had appeared, for an average of 3 + per annum since the start. It might also be remarked that "serious" Hemingway criticism appears to have begun in the Thirties with J. Kashkeen, John Peale Bishop, and Edmund Wilson, and continued in the Forties with Malcolm Cowley, Robert Penn Warren, and Alfred Kazin out front. Mass production did not get under way until the Fifties, when (working now from the annual *MLA International Bibliography*) the average number of publications per year jumps to 16+. (In erratic fashion, from a yearly low of 8 to a high of 31; Faulkner's average was 38.) Book-length studies began to appear in 1952, and if anyone was watching it must have looked as though by the end of the decade, at the latest, the important things had been said, and Hemingway Studies must decline before they had achieved that title.

What of course happened instead is that the rate of production in the Sixties better than doubled to an annual average of 42+ entries. (Again spasmodically distributed, from a low of 18 in 1960 to 53 the next year and higher in '69.) And then in the Seventies, with the last year not yet reported, the rate nearly doubled once more to an average of almost 81 items. (Output was also steadier; the championship season was 1974 with a score of 98. And if some of these things are but notes, others are books: "It all evens up"—as, after a few drinks, Nick Adams once remarked.)

The question, I take it, is obvious: whence this snowballing activity? And so, I suppose, is part of the answer: it is a product of the academic situation. Currently, not always. Hemingway criticism used to issue from as far outside collegial walls as it does now from within. (Not one of the pre-1950 names I mentioned strikes us as essentially professorial, though I could have added Oscar Cargill's.) But in three decades things have reversed, as the cloistered pressure to "publish" steeply mounted. Add to this the sharp increase in the number of individuals suddenly belonging to the trade and newly subject to its demands. Hemingway Studies are one result.

Add to this in turn what happens when the study of a literary figure becomes what we now call an Industry. Such a business operates by its own laws. Production, for example, stimulates production. One piece on the now-famous dialogue in "A Clean, Well-Lighted Place"—did the writer get the waiters mixed up?—has spawned twenty others. (With more on the way, though I do believe that David Kerner very recently demonstrated that it was not Hemingway who was confused: Scribner's ought to put the text back the way they had it, and not worry about the cost.) Production creates new opportunities. To choose an obscure one, there is now a little literature on baseball in *The Old Man and The Sea*: what's to be said about that? Another industrial law, as I observed it some time ago, is that the more that's written on a subject the more significant the subject seems, and the more significant it seems the more secondary (tertiary) will be the matters that seem worth going into. For a sobering experience, skim the bibliographies and see how much more important and comprehensive the Hemingway titles become as you move backward in time. Things badly needed a boost when the Papers began to become available for research. Someone with a better prognosticatory record might estimate how long this will keep the ship afloat.

None of this, however, really accounts for the fact that the boom in Hemingway production—like that in Faulkner Studies—has exceeded the general increase in productivity. It was a decade ago that William White announced that the five American writers who had attracted most attention in print were Hawthorne, Melville, James, Faulkner, and Hemingway. The question becomes: Why Hemingway? Why should he have overtaken Whitman, Twain, Emerson, and Poe? Faulkner does not surprise me. For one thing, I remember Hemingway's telling Cowley that if he had Faulkner's talent "I would outwrite him 50 to 1." For another, Faulkner presents—like Melville and James—problems and complexities (and, like Hawthorne, ambiguities) that Hemingway by and large does not. One might think that our man offered less to write about. And what, exactly, does all this attention mean? That he is a more important writer than Whitman or Emerson? (And if so, why?)

I do not personally think we have that in mind. In considering alternative explanations, one thing that occurs is that if challenges offered by "difficult" writers invite some they put off others. Access to Hemingway is relatively easy. He has never given middlebrow readers any great trouble, has never appealed to highbrows alone if at all, was never cultish or modish or avant-garde in a bewildering way or a secret prized by an intelligentsia. For over a half-century, people who read fiction have enjoyed reading him. A few go on to study, and a few of these stay to write. His academic popularity, in other words, may not differ in kind from his general popularity. Though they may be detained by deeper and subtler qualities, who is to say that his scholars are not initially drawn by the same ones that attract the reading public? If you are going to work on something, who says you can't like it?

Lots of people—or so, once upon a time, it seemed. You couldn't, for example, get credit for reading anything like *A Farewell To Arms* when I was an undergraduate. The idea was that you read it on your own. Advanced academic work, for the most part, was (is?) precisely what you would not do on your own: the dissertation on Lanier's prosody, Thoreau's reputation in Italy. Past that, it looks as if the profession, having insisted on publication, was forced to admit subjects that may be undertaken with pleasure.

Practically anyone can speculate on the causes of a long bull market. It is more likely that I can contribute something by turning finally to an announcement of second thoughts on a matter where I have been taken severely to task. This reference is to a volume called *The Nick Adams Stories,* 1972, which I gather is widely read. I accept certain responsibilities for it. The original idea of the book was mine, the ordering of the stories is essentially mine, and so, aside from some of the fragments, is the selection of the stories. Likewise a trivial Preface, which replaces a more substantial introduction to the book that, as it turned out, Scribner's did not want. Thus in the book there is no mention of a problem I had wrestled for a long time: where in Nick's chronology to put two tales, "The End of Something" and the related "Three-Day Blow." It was to these stories that the banished introduction referred when it admitted that "there isn't any completely satisfactory way to arrange them all, as readers are going to discover when they confront Nick as an adolescent veteran of the great war." The problem has not gone away.

For a long time it had not seemed to exist. I had thought of Nick in these narratives as an adolescent only; clearly they came before the war. Then in 1966 I learned from Constance Montgomery's *Hemingway In Michigan* that they had grown directly out of events in the author's life that occurred during the summer following his return from Italy. I already knew from *At The Hemingways,* his sister Marcelline's book, that a full year later, when he was almost 21, Ernest seemed to her about sixteen. In writing the stories, was he seeing himself as Nick at the time of the events, boyish as he seems, and thus—"most disconcertingly," as I put it—thinking of him as a veteran? When I came to put together the book, I explained the problem in a letter to Charlie Scribner. The circumstances of the stories—as well as of the newly found "Summer People"—belonged to the author's first postwar summer; his persona seemed distinctly prewar. By this time, Carlos Baker's biography had verified and expanded on Montgomery; Charles Scribner consulted his copy, confirmed the biographical data, and that apparently decided the matter. In the book, the stories come after the war—which is where I had with misgivings placed them. I say "apparently": it was about this time that I was dismissed from the project along with my introduction. With this, much of my interest in it dissipated, but I did observe and report on its initial reception, which was mixed. I also remarked that later and more considered responses in the journals would outweigh the first ones, and for the present occasion I examined four "essay-reviews" of the book, which are unfavorable.

Essentially it is the ordering of the stories which is causing trouble for the book's critics. Douglas Wilson (*Western Humanities Review,* Fall, 1973) objects first that the volume contains no statement of what constitutes a Nick Adams story; thus tales are included in which he is not named, and others excluded where he may *be* the "nameless hero." Wilson wants to make Harold Krebs of Oklahoma (which he has Kansas) Nick Adams of Michigan, and he calls another item "in the truest sense, a Nick Adams story" because of a character in it named Horace. (Actually Hemingway used names like Harold and Horace to disqualify them.) But Wilson objects even more to the chronological placement of the stories, and concludes that "nothing . . . is really gained by rearranging" them. He does not explain what the previous arrangement was, or where the new materials go. Robert M. Davis (*Southern Humanities Review,* Spring, 1973) wants them rearranged in the order of composition. (He also wants "Cross-Country Snow" to appear before "Big Two-Hearted River," which would make Nick a married man and presumably a father on that fishing trip.) More emphatically he wants "The Three-Day Blow" put before the war—chiefly because of some conversation in it about the trade of a ballplayer named Heinie Zimmerman to the New York Giants, which occurred in 1916. Most of all he would like to bench the present writer: father of "errors likely to plague a whole generation of students."

So would Bernard F. Rodgers, Jr. (*Fitzgerald/Hemingway Annual, 1974*), who deplores my having "dominated," so he alleges, and "distorted Hemingway scholarship" with a biographical emphasis. One was right in 1952, he says, in putting "Three-Day Blow" and its companion piece before the war: look at Heinie Zimmerman. Look at him a third time, says Stuart L. Burns (*Arizona Quarterly,* Spring, 1977) without mentioning previous observers. But it turns out it's Burns who must be watched. First he thinks the book is a good idea—for quite mistaken reasons and even though a "logical chronology" for the stories is in his view "impossible." Then, having got the year of the author's birth wrong, he appears to attempt what can't be done by figuring Nick's age along the way on the assumption it is the same as Hemingway's (in which case forget Heinie Zimmerman). Finally, as if a chronological ordering did not turn out to be profoundly thematic, he concludes that a thematic arrangement would be best. He is full of questions which a quick reading of the book's deflected introduction (by this time long in print and reprinted) would have answered. Not one of these people profitted from it.

Perhaps this one may benefit from them—if only to concede that the decision on where to put "The End of Something," "The Three-Day Blow," and very likely "Summer People" probably went the wrong way. I would now call these stories dysynchronous, in that Hemingway did not adjust the time of his own fictionalized experience to that of the world's. (The history of the N. Y. Giants, for instance.) Put before the war, I still think the stories anachronous as well: as yet unknown were the rum-runners mentioned in "Summer People"; unless Nick had been in Italy I don't believe he would have planned, as he had, on taking Marge there. As I said before, there is no completely satisfactory place for these stories. But presenting them before the war would have caused less trouble. It would also have fit the fact that the writer was probably seeing himself in them as a prewar protagonist exposed to postwar events—which would indeed have better suited the younger character.

But if I am to end with second thoughts, better they should deal with that remark of Hemingway's about the destruction of his papers at his death. I do imagine that it satisfied him to think that all this material would go to eternity in silence. I suppose the idea of strangers or even friends poring over it would have been displeasing. On the other hand I have a hunch that if he had known about, and had a chance to think about, the honor his widow and the Kennedys have paid him, he would have come privately to rejoice in it. It is evident that the personal attention he tried to avoid in life he also sought. In middle age, anyway, he not only welcomed praise and reassurance but had continual need of them. In his last recorded literary conversation, what struck Leslie Fiedler was "his fear that he had done nothing of lasting worth. . . ." Praise and reassurance on that occasion would have been useless. But it would be hard to dismiss the tribute of the clean, well-lighted place that has been permanently established for him. Or to wish it away.

1980

Hemingway: The Writer in Decline

As experts all in the study of American letters you will remember how Walt Whitman once paraphrased Emerson:

> Do I contradict myself?
> Very well then I contradict myself
> (I am large, I contain multitudes).

Permit me then a little paraphrase of Whitman:

> Do I repeat myself?
> Very well then I repeat myself
> (I am small, I contain platitudes).

Things are worse than most of you think. I have, for example, had to use even this opening business before. (That was when I was outrageously conned, if anyone cares but me, into writing not for the second but the third time the story of going through Hemingway's manuscripts in the bank vault.) It ought to be easy to dodge this sort of thing, but some-

This paper was delivered at the Alabama Symposium on English and American Literature, "Hemingway: A Revaluation," held in Tuscaloosa in 1976.

times—as on the conned occasion and now on this one—it is not. One does, however, come to wonder what in the world people expect. After writing off and on for over 25 years on the subject of a single author, what can you possibly have to say that will be neither stale nor wholly trivial? I don't know, and it won't happen again. It's been five years since I last even attempted to accomplish anything fresh with Hemingway; in the mean time I've done a book which is as far as I can get from my familiar topic (it isn't even "about literature"), and I'm well into another that's a sort of sequel to it.* But even as I hear me saying "Never Again" it pops into my mind that I have been described, in print, as "the Sarah Bernhardt of Hemingway criticism." (I took that for some kind of dirty crack, but was calmed by the explanation that the reference was to this thing she and I appear to have shared about giving Farewell Appearances.)

Well, in thinking how I could conceivably contribute to the present coming-together it occurred to me first that I have never expressed myself publicly on the subject of what I take to be a special reason for Hemingway's general descent as a writer of fiction over his last decade or so. And second that this partial explanation of that falling off has a great deal to do with the next-to-biggest objection he had to my understanding of his work. Further, that although I have told the story of his biggest objection—the complaint that I was psychoanalyzing him alive—I have never said much about his other chief grievances. The concern here is of course not the critic's notions, which some of you know anyway, but how in responding to them the author reveals something of what he thought about his own fiction. My hope is that this will serve.

Arnold Toynbee observed that history shows how the same traits that made nations great eventually led to their downfall. Precisely, it seems to me, the case with Hemingway in my present view of him. What made him great were of course things like extraordinary talent—"gifts"—originality, courage, absolute dedication, and so on, but I am taking these things as givens, common in varying degrees to most important writers. My notion of the special quality, marked in Hemingway from the start, that promoted his early success as a writer of fiction was what I will call "confident self-absorption"; in his decline it became an insecure obsession with self. The very early ability to look objectively to himself for a protagonist, and to write realistically and impersonally of his own experi-

**Revolutionary Ladies* (New York: Alfred A. Knopf, 1977) and the uncompleted *Dark Lady of the Republic.*

ence, while transmuting it to fiction, was an act of daring. To believe that one is significant enough, and what happens to one, too, and to start a career on that basis took guts. I have specifically in mind "Summer People"—almost certainly the first story Hemingway ever wrote about Nick Adams, his first protagonist. The confidence here was that the reader could be interested, as he generally is, in Nick's youthful thoughts, ambition, conversation—even in the way he swims and dives!—and most of all in his assurance that he is "different": that because of "something in him" he could "have what he wanted"—which is not, chiefly, the girl of the tale, whom he does have, but to be "a great writer."

I would hope to do justice to the early fiction that emerged from such confidence. It took repeated acts of moral courage to break through, in those first stories, so many conventions that people were unwilling even to call them "stories" (they were *contes,* etc.). Here was a new kind of prose, a new objectivity, a brilliant economy, a startling freshness of view—even a willingness to put up with complaints about some of the tales that "nothing happens." It took fantastic discipline, still at the start of a career, to write a long story (I'm thinking of "Big Two-Hearted River") while intentionally omitting the one crucial fact that would explain it. (It's equally astonishing that he got away with it, by which I mean that the story was widely admired long before it was completely understood—if it is yet: I'm thinking about that "tragic" swamp.)

Obviously I am assuming that in both the fishing story and in "Summer People" the author was seeing himself as Nick, in the summer after his return from the war. Thus I am still registering the identification that Hemingway first objected to in me long before my book on him was published.

The identification did not, of course, begin with me. Rather, though I didn't know it then, with his parents and siblings. When most of the Nick Adams fiction remained to be written, Hemingway had Nick thinking (in an abortive ending to "Big Two-Hearted River," later published separately) that "Everything good he'd ever written he'd made up. None of it had ever happened. . . . That was what the family couldn't understand." Possibly because, like the fishing trip to that River, some of it had happened. In any event it was immediately after thinking this that the passage goes on to say "Nick in the stories was never himself. He made him up." But in context it is clear that it is "he, Nick," who thinks or says that—which amounts to saying—it does indeed say—that Nick was never Nick: it is precisely at the moment when the author attempts to distinguish writer from character that he confuses them absolutely, which is to say identifies them.

Hemingway must have sensed that I would relate him as well to Jake Barnes, as I did and do. Not literally, of course; everybody knows how in those Paris days Ernest was married to Hadley and the father of Bumby. But I did believe that in many real ways—in his attitudes, interests, thoughts and general character—Jake would be hard to tell from the author, who wrote to inform me that he was specifically *not* Jake. This figure came, he explained, out of his own wounding when some pieces of cloth were driven into his scrotum so that he got to know soldiers with other genito-urinary wounds, in particular a boy who had suffered Jake's special disaster. He had got to wondering what a man's life would be like in this condition and so took *him* and made him a foreign correspondent in Paris, which is of course what Hemingway had been. It was at the time as far from his mind as from mine that I would one day be leafing through the start of the first draft of what he was calling *Fiesta* without encountering the name Jake Barnes: there *was* a young man known as "Ernie" or "Hem." (The author also thought to mention Francis Macomber in this connection. Was that him? He knew very well it was not, and I agree.)

It's my belief that it was when Hemingway put on a mask that depersonalized himself—as Nick, Jake, or Frederic Henry—that the autobiographical method worked, and awfully well. Nick, indeed, is almost im-personalized, or played down as a person, at least until he appears in the late-written and posthumously published "Last Good Country." With these three protagonists, further, it seems pretty much the same mask.* No matter. Hemingway deeply resented my thought (which was scarcely peculiar to me, though I went farthest with it) that these protagonists were based loosely on himself and his experiences. To take the case of Nick alone for a moment, it is easy to see his position. "Indian Camp," for instance, does not describe an ordeal that Ernest went through any more than he'd had the adventure related in "The Battler," or run off

*A very small thing, but has it been noticed that the same three—Henry, Barnes, Adams (as in "In Another Country")—and Hemingway all recuperated in Milan and at the Ospedale Maggiore (the last two going there for physiotherapy)? Several years ago I gave a talk to the faculty and students in American literature at the University of Milan, fatuously remarking for their satisfaction that Hemingway had recovered in that city. After the lecture a professor came up and said, "In this city? In this Building." As Nick remarks, the "hospital was very old and very beautiful. . . ." It was explained to me that when the bombers completely gutted the structure in World War II, leaving the ancient walls more or less intact, the hospital was rebuilt elsewhere and a modern interior constructed inside the shell, which now houses Milan's university.

with his sister following his shooting of a great blue heron as in "The Last Good Country." But many of the stories involving Nick do reflect or build on things that had happened to the author. It was he, not I, who said that the little Nick tale called "The Doctor and the Doctor's Wife" is "about the time I discovered that my father was a coward." (I do not believe that is what the story is "about," and the identification of himself with Nick here is more absolute than I ever made it.)

The idea that Hemingway wrote often of himself, in whatever disguise, and out of his own experience needs of course to be qualified. An important qualification is that he often romanticized things—or even more simply "wish-fulfilled" them. This was especially true of his female characters in their relationships with the hero—and right from the start. In "Summer People," for example, Kate gives herself most willingly to Nick. She was in life named Kate, and I once heard from her brother Bill (Smith), who appears in the same story as he did in "The Three Day Blow." The original Kate was much older than Ernest, and seems to have thought of him as a likeable kid; Mr. Smith was absolutely positive that Ernest had never slept with his sister (who became, incidentally, Mrs. John Dos Passos). Likewise, as you will remember, Nick had a colorful introduction to sexual fulfillment in "Fathers and Sons"—in the woods with the Indian girl Trudy; in a brief passage that was removed in editing from "The Last Good Country" it is revealed that Nick indeed had got her pregnant. Carlos Baker reports that in letters Ernest occasionally boasted that Trudy provided his own initiation; it is Baker's conclusion that the whole affair was something the author wished had happened. In *A Farewell to Arms* the same process is at work: Lt. Henry's love affair with Catherine Barkley is what Hemingway in writing dreamed of; what actually and very differently happened in his relationship with Agnes von Kurowsky the author presented in a little piece called "A Very Short Story." Similarly Hemingway does not appear to have more than fantasized the affair with the youthful Italian Adriana Ivancich, who became Renata in *Across the River and into the Trees*. And no ex-wife (whom I take to be modeled on Marlene Dietrich) turned up in Havana for the sexual interlude described in the "Cuba" section of *Islands in the Stream*. Which leads me to the third and last thing about my book that got under Hemingway's skin, as again I did not know until I saw the letters he didn't mail.

The sore point here was that I thought the "Hemingway heroine"—meaning Catherine, Renata, and Maria in *For Whom the Bell Tolls*, to which list now might be added Hadley in *A Moveable Feast* and Littless in "The Last Good Country"—seemed day dreams of the author's: as females, too good to be true, submissive and devoted to the hero beyond credibility and to the near-extinction of their own personalities. This, Hemingway explained to me, was because I knew so pitifully little about women. If he wrote of his lovely wife Mary, or of his late wife Pauline, or of Ingrid Bergman or Marlene Dietrich I would call them fantasies. (I note that he did, according to him elsewhere, write of Ms. Bergman: he inscribed her copy of *For Whom the Bell Tolls* "To Ingrid Bergman who is the Maria of this book"; she played Maria in the movie; I did say she was a fantasy.) In another unsent letter he wrote at considerable length about my knowledge and experience of women, remarking that we had moved in different circles. (I had, one night, sat right behind Ms. Dietrich at the movies, but I expect that doesn't count.) According to Professors, Hemingway said (how rapid my promotion from Instructor!), women are like professors' wives. Some of them look like Mrs. Whitaker Chambers, others like Priscilla Hiss. Or better, the women I knew were like the Catholic Communist he once met on a ship: instead of a mons veneris she had a mountain of dialectics; one breast was for Marx and the other Engels; the only open orifice was for fouling Trotsky. Professor, he wrote, she would have been your dream girl. (He cut that off remarking that he shouldn't joke with anyone as mentally understaffed as me; especially, I thought, unless he could be funnier.)

He had already made the point that his heroines were "invented from life"; as little as he wanted to hear it, so too were his proper heroes invented out of his own life, in an act of imaginative self-dramatization. As long as the raw material—Hemingway—was strictly under control, disciplined and objective, the method worked. It worked for that matter in *For Whom the Bell Tolls* too, and in the non-fictions called *Green Hills of Africa* and *Death in the Afternoon*. It was in *Across the River and into the Trees* that things got all out of control: it is my argument that this was largely for the reason that as his career moved toward its close, the author was less and less willing or able to turn himself into a protagonist who is anything different from or more than himself. In this novel Richard Cantwell is an almost exact and utterly indulgent self-portrait, and it was out of the assumption that he could be made fascinating—and moving—for those reading about him that disaster struck. There are very fine passages in this book not open to this objection; for the rest we get the Colonel's banal and downright embarrassing conversations with the girl, and worse ones with her portrait. (In her book, Mrs. Hemingway remarks that at the time of writing it was her hope that these parts would be "improved" at Scribner's, but I at any rate am unaware that her husband ever did, alive, get any editing there, though like the rest of us he could sometimes have used it.) In other places, Cantwell appears to be under the curious delusion that he is being interviewed; people hand him implausible questions so that he can pontificate. This book is a parody of the grace of execution which once made its author distinctive. No one has made fun of him as effectively as he does himself; once exposed to it it is hard to forget the moment when Cantwell is having a little wine, and reaches for the champagne bucket "accurately and well."

The Old Man and the Sea seemed at first a happy turn away from the self-absorption that deluded Hemingway into believing that his readers could subsist on portraits of the artist as a middle-aged man. But even here it is my ungenerous reaction that the old Cuban fisherman is distractingly impinged on by the author, who gives him thoughts and phrases characteristic not of such a figure but of the writer. "I am a strange old man," Santiago thinks twice—as Hemingway was much given to saying of himself (to Lillian Ross, among others) in that period of his life. (As *I* read it, this was a way of saying how mysterious, ineffable, are the gifts of the great artists!) At a couple of points, Hemingway intrudes on Santiago to the extent that he seems more a writer (or *the* writer) than a fisherman. His lines are "as thick around as a big pencil," and "He kept them straighter than anyone did." The boy, who stands in for the Hemingway heroine, tells him "There are many good fishermen, and some great ones. But there is only you." He is soon doing "that which I was born for"; he had proved it many times and "now he was proving it again"—which is to say he was writing a book. We recall being told that Santiago lost his prize because he "went out too far," though he did, after all, catch his fish, and the sharks who took it from him are also present much nearer shore. It seems to me that Hemingway is saying that it was he, in his recent *Across the River and into the Trees,* who had gone out too far—farther than the critics could go (so he remarked of their failure with his experiment "in calculus"). *They* were the sharks who had devoured his enormous trophy.

Thus *The Old Man and the Sea* does not, for me, contradict my argument: *A Moveable Feast* does. The author is almost wholly preoccupied with himself in it, and he wrought a minor masterpiece. What was always needed between himself and his protagonist was distance. If the triumph of this book is as I feel it to be enchantment, it is distance that lends it—a distance of nearly forty years. I was once very mistaken in my understanding of the writing of this memoir. Having read Mary's story about finding some old notebooks which had reposed in the Paris Ritz for some thirty years, and believing that the prose of *A Moveable Feast* was comparable to the prose which distinguished the artist at the peak of his Paris power, my hunch was that those notebooks contained at least sketches for what would become these chapters, and a big leg up on them. The facts appear to betray me. The only manuscript I found in the bank that clearly derived from the Paris days and made its way into the posthumous volume was a single sheet of paper containing what was published as a headnote to the Fitzgerald chapter. ("His talent was as natural as the pattern that was made by the dust on a butterfly's wing. . . .") Carlos Baker found a few sentences in a blue notebook labeled "Paris 1922" that did not become any part of the *Feast*; they are printed in his biography. The only notebooks *I* found were marked "Fiesta a Novel"—the first draft, of course, of *The Sun Also Rises*. Thus it appears that Hemingway wrote his Paris book from scratch, as the manuscript also indicates. (The only exception to this I know of is that until the author in galleys struck the first chapter and a half of *The Sun Also Rises* the Ford Madox Ford episode of *A Moveable Feast* was presented, in embryo, in the novel.) *How* Hemingway managed to write the memoir when he was, so much of the time, unwell—and was also occasionally working on a long bullfighting piece that I would one day be unable to get through—I have no idea in the world.

The process whereby the author became increasingly his own, undisguised subject is writ plain in *By-Line Ernest Hemingway,* the 1967 collection of his journalism.* At the start a youthful reporter is filing stories on Mussolini, a Genoa conference, Swiss hotels, and a lovely one on Christmas in Paris. By part II he is a famous man writing letters to *Esquire*; by part IV he is himself being interviewed, and part V is entirely about him, his wife, and places where they lived or adventured. The reporter had hit again on his natural topic—sometimes managing very well with it, too. His *Four Stories of the Spanish Civil War,* published in book form in 1969 but written at the time of that struggle, show the same tendency far earlier. They are autobiographical fictions so dominated by the presence of

*See Young's introduction to the British edition of this collection (London: William Collins Sons, 1968).

the author that they scarcely seem fictional: personalized feature stories, rather, much like the wire-service dispatches reprinted in *By-Line.*

If *A Moveable Feast* came to me, anyway, as a superb surprise, I have to confess that *Islands in the Stream* brought disappointment. (Not at all in the editing, by the way; from such looks as I had at the manuscript I would say that the very best that could be got from it was gotten.) But the problem of self-absorption and -dramatization was never (unless in *Garden of Eden*) more painful than here. Indeed in the "Bimini" section, which I like much the best of the three, it seems possible to say that for the first and only time the authorial ego grew so big it took two characters to contain it. By that I mean that Thomas Hudson is transparently autobiographically drawn, and his friend Roger Davis is whatever of himself the author thought was left over once Hudson was established. (When I first saw the start of the manuscript—which appeared much the least finished part of it—I wondered if perhaps these two men were really a single persona, Hemingway not having yet decided—such was occasionally his practice—which name to use.)

For me the chief weakness of the book is what I have in general been talking about: the lack of distance between writer and hero, the apparent conviction as well that readers could be caught up in this character as the author was. But it is impossible so to be caught. The peerless Hudson assumes the posture of the tragic hero for no assignable reason. He is, further, a suffering stoic who—save for two failed marriages—has nothing in his past but success to explain the stoicism; behind the pervasive despair lies a great void. I reread the novel for the present occasion, but am still at a loss to know what is the "point" of "Bimini." The "Cuba" section, made up of unfunny high-jinks in and around Havana, with episodes involving cats, a bar, and an ex-wife, seem not only pointless for all I can perceive but also ill-related. "At Sea" strikes me as simply that—"neither here nor there," as we say—a straight adventure story lacking in excitement, which I thought the purpose of adventure stories.

Worst of all, to my taste, is the unaccountable adulation of Hudson in the book—by his sons, women, servants, friends, *and* cats. When it dawns on one, as it does very quickly, that the object of the adulation is the author himself, the response can be excruciating. Then self-admiration turns to self-pity, the unloveliest form of charity. As Hudson finally drives himself half to death in a mission of undemonstrated importance, one of his men (speaking for their leader) says "the poor son of a bitch . . . and covered him carefully" in his slumbers. I can find no meaning in the book beyond this one. The central fact about Hudson is his despair. One can search the pages forever without finding the cause of it—not, that is, beyond the desperation shot at one which misfires, the deaths of the man's three sons, which seem utterly fabricated on two separate occasions to substitute for what is not understood. One way of putting this point would be to say that Hudson's despair was Hemingway's, but John, Patrick, and Gregory Hemingway are alive and well and living all over the place.

Carlos Baker and now Mary Hemingway both make it clear that among the author's troubles in his last years was the loss of the very thing I say helped to make him as a writer—confidence—along with a growth in preoccupation with self that I believe helped undo him. What I am not clear about, however, is how the author had still, in his last decade, confidence enough in what he was doing to keep on doing it. The manuscript of *The Dangerous Summer,* written in the late 1950s, runs over 900 pages; the "African Book" [*True at First Light*], a little earlier, is nearly as long; *Garden of Eden* runs to 28 chapters. They did not appear to be going anywhere, and it seems to me that a man who has begun to lack faith in what he is doing should not have been able to do so *much* of it. I'm missing something here.*

What does strike me over and over in reading Mary's book is how the literary problem I've been talking about was so clearly a personal problem—which, when the author is his own topic, is not very surprising. As she and Carlos both show, the ego in life was gigantic. It is Mary who tells how—like Col. Cantwell—Ernest was given to acting as though he were being interviewed, a situation in which he rejoiced. (When he was *actually* being interviewed, I note, he usually complained about it.) There was an obsession with self; the need for flattery at times nearly determined his life—as when in Cuba, expecting the visit of a young lady, "He could barely stand," Mary writes, "the waiting for Adriana's bright, admiring glances." (Which suggests that it was mostly her admiration of him as Col. Cantwell that had the old soldier so gone on her as Renata in *Across the River and Into the Trees*) Leicester Hemingway made much the same point long ago. Hemingway needed the conviction, which was hard to come by, that he was still, like Santiago down on his luck, the Champion. No one will gloat over such a picture, as all these biographers

*In response to this point at the Alabama conference, Mrs. Hemingway suggested that her husband, sensing the decline in quality, may have driven himself to increase the quantity. I believe that this is at least part of the answer.

know. One hurts for the man as he gets personally into the trouble his books reflect. Never more than in the unexplained despair of *Islands in the Stream* that I was just speaking about. When Hemingway told his wife "I'm just a desperate old man" I cannot help remarking that he was seven years younger than I am. "You're not old," she told him, wishing she could help with the rest of it.

At one time "the world," as Gregory Hemingway writes and no one has said much better, "had flowed through" his father "as though through a purifying filter, with the distillate seeming more true and beautiful than the world itself." The son thought that his father drank to cover up the loss of talent; a psychiatrist I once talked to, who was a Hemingway buff and knew quite a bit about his life, remarked that anyone who drank as much as the writer did for so long a time would go into depression if for no other reason (especially if there had also been manic tendencies). It is a great pity that we did not have, fifteen years ago, the likes of lithium, which has brought so many back from the edge.

And that leads me to express, finally, the hope that I have not seemed disrespectful of a great writer in a period when he was no longer great. If I have so seemed, perhaps I can defuse it a little by pointing out that it is no clearer to you than it is to me that what I have been exhibiting is a Hemingway *critic* in decline—who, like his subject, has taken refuge in autobiography. What I really had to say on the subject of this conference I said a long time ago, thanking whatever gods may be that I have another subject now. I conclude in the realization that after twenty-five years of taking a dim view of the Hemingway hero as Richard Cantwell in *Across the River* . . . I feel at this moment very much at one with the character I have ridiculed. Indeed I retreat as Cantwell does—in both humility and pride, that is—into the position assumed by the superannuated Colonel when suddenly it dawns on him that, quote, "Nobody would give you a penny for your thoughts, he thought. Not this morning. But I've seen them worth a certain amount. . . . when the chips were down." Unquote, and thanks if you remember.

1983

III.

Scholar at Large

10.

The Assumptions of Literature

The questions of the moment as put to me, at least, were such as to give pause if not halt to a man more sensitive and scrupulous than this one. What, no less, are the assumptions of literature? What, further, is its place in this world? And what can the teacher of it best do about teaching it? (Twenty minutes.) Well, you ask impossible questions and you get impossible answers. But this is not news to Professor Leary; he knew I couldn't do it. I take it then that the assignment is to make a brave show of some sort, and I propose to begin (only) by actually taking a direct crack at some answers.

When considering what literature's assumptions might be, the first things that occur to me are these: literature assumes that man is a contemplative and divertible animal, who looks sometimes to books for such order and esthetic experience as his life does not otherwise adequately provide; it assumes that for uniquely human pleasure—that is, intellectual and emotional pleasure—people will go now and again to an art that uses language to build works that are designed to stand in permanent form; it assumes that a precious few human beings can produce by their imaginations, and by the artful use of language, a sort of high-level let's pretend

This paper was read to the National Council of Teachers of English in Philadelphia, November 25, 1961.

that is more deeply real, in certain significant ways, than a lot of what actually is.

It probably follows—or I hope it does—that the place of literature, or its function, is to provide to those who want or need it, through the skilled, artful use of language: order, diversion and esthetic satisfaction—and also vicarious experience in abundance, which is important, since what really happens to us in books really happens to us, and we are the sum of what has happened to us and care, I suppose, about who and what we are.

What the teacher should provide if he can (and it is a very tough dollar) is an introduction—the student is always being introduced, until if ever he begins to make discoveries for himself—an introduction, that is, to the ways in which literature so complexly works. He takes it apart, if he can, and tries to show what goes with what and how it works there. He dissects it while—chiefly through a healthy enthusiasm for it—he leaves it unmurdered (for Wordsworth in this was surely the bunk). Or anyway he leaves it in such condition that in memory, at least, the parts will fall back together and in place again.

Now I could go on indefinitely at this level of banality but not of generality, and anyway I am uncomfortable at it. Further there is at least a sense that we were invited to play a little fast and loose with the questions. It would be better, then, for you anyway, to come down to what I was also invited to consider: as a would-be critic and might-be teacher, what have I been assuming to be important or of special interest in literature?

It's not certain it will be better for the speaker. A man is supposed to look where he's going, know what he's doing, and all that, but it has occurred to me that it could be dangerous, this messing around with one's peaceful, somnolent presuppositions and latent intentions. Suppose you actually found out what you've been up to? It might be that then you'd get self-conscious, and start pointing up nakedly what worked out a lot better when clothed in the various textures of other considerations, and in your own unknown confusions.

I take it that finding out what he was actually doing is one thing that wrecked a really big writer, William Faulkner. As long as Yoknapatawpha County welled out of sources he only partly knew about he was great. But when Malcolm Cowley and others explained that he was miraculously creating a mythical kingdom ("By God," he wrote Cowley, "I didn't know myself what I had tried to do . . .") the jig was up and the author just about finished. This became clearest in *The Town* (1957)—I believe it was Mr. Kazin who pointed this out most effectively—when Faulkner began working up anecdotes about his Snopeses, and the jokes became synthetic, the symbols transparent. He stopped creating Yoknapatawpha and set up shop in it. Similarly, as his peer Ernest Hemingway once protested to me when I was trying to publish a book on him, "The mechanism at the heart of a writer and in the head is as delicate as any electronic device. Then a critic comes along and starts to take that functioning machine to pieces . . . and it helps the writer just as much as though some curious person, not a watch-maker, should take apart his Rolex Oyster Perpetual. It is fine to say it does no harm and anybody has a right to take anyone else's watch apart. But I don't think they have a right while it is still ticking."

Well, I have never flattered myself that I really hurt Mr. Hemingway any—or never felt guilty of it, rather—and I'm already committed to the notion that we don't necessarily "murder to dissect." Further, one doesn't kid himself that his own predilections are so delicate as to be destroyed by even the crudest of analyses (he isn't even sure they are still ticking), and so it is probably quite safe to barge into this thing, which is, hopefully, a sort of tentative answer to this awkward and perhaps gratuitous question: what are my own particular assumptions about literature?

When I first posed myself this question I was nonplussed to draw a sort of semi-blank. I have always plowed, I guess, wherever curiosity led—in American literature, that is, since it is what we call my "field"—and I had to go back and look for clues (fortunately, for present purposes only, the evidence is pretty thin) to see just what the heck it is that I have been assuming.

Aside from all of the standard virtues I mentioned at the beginning, without which really nothing, I think I've been chiefly assuming that literature is valuable in that it offers deep and rewarding insights that are not otherwise readily attainable—insights first into such things as national character and experience, finally into human nature and ourselves, and life itself. There is no need to stop the presses at this point, but I do mean all this in a slightly special sense. (I hope, by the way, that you can forgive this wretched first-person approach, which, given my view of the topic, I appear to be stuck with.) I remember, for example, an exciting few seconds in a dingy graduate-student flat in Iowa City when I discovered

(I think I did) a basic and, as it turned out later, elaborate parallel between *Huckleberry Finn* and Hemingway's work as a whole.* This took a good many pages to work out, but the part of it that I'm now talking about came as an attempt to answer a rude, crude "So what?" (the question put by a tactless and tasteless sociologist who happened to wander in and to whom I am still grateful). As a simple graduate student I had never thought to ask that question in this connection, and had assumed—and had been led to assume—that the sort of demonstration I had made was worth making for its own sake. I still believe it is, but I also think we too seldom ask the question. Our students—and many of our readers, if any—need it answered, and sometimes the answers may be as important as the demonstration that led to the question.

In this case, to go on with the example, it seemed to me that the fact that Americans have so embraced *Huckleberry Finn* and then Hemingway's work (presented so as to point up the basic similarity of the overall story of Hemingway's hero to Huck's experiences) must mean something significant about us as a people. The fact, that is, that an almost identical pattern of events has twice gained an almost universal acceptance suggests certain notions about Americans and their new-world experience that are worth entertaining. It offers rare insights into the story of our vaunted innocence and our expectations in the world, and into the story of what happened to them; it suggests ideas about our essential nature that run counter to more public and more available protestations, and ring somehow truer. Finally something is said about life itself, which in this view of it becomes, plausibly and especially in the formative years, a process of getting yourself rather badly hurt.

This business of a story that has had repeated success over the decades is what led me to my present interest in the whole matter of the long-lived appeal of certain American tales, such as the story of Pocahontas or of Rip Van Winkle. Why is it, exactly, that in one version or another they have been so popular for so long? There are literally hundreds of literary versions of the Pocahontas legend, and there have to be reasons why there are. It seemed to me that if some of those reasons could be learned we might find out not only some things worth knowing about such stories, but also—and perhaps more important in the long run—something new about the audiences that have repeatedly found them compelling; about ourselves, that is.

*"Adventures of Huckleberry Finn," *Ernest Hemingway: A Reconsideration.*

These are the primary concerns of a book I have been working on (and not working on) for a good many years. But there is another important and ultimately related consideration in all this. What attract me as much as anything in literature are the overtones (the suggestions or implications) and undertones (the underlying or background qualities). These present themselves to me at first as faint gongs and subliminal murmurs which every once in a while I hear—way back in my nervous system (which is admittedly a poor one) and nearly inaudible. And I hear them most particularly in these traditional, perennially reappearing works of great general popularity. I don't know exactly the ultimate source of this very special kind of music, nor see any particular justification for believing with Jung—though if right he could account for it—that we racially inherit memories. More likely one responds deeply to certain images and narrative and dramatic situations because they stir memories and associations which trace not to the dawn of the race but to the dawn of our own conscious lives—to buried recollections of childhood fairy-tales and myths, for instances—where they brush chords just as haunting and reverberant as any we could know. But for literary people, at any rate, the problem is not so much where the sounds come from as what they are saying.

The first time I remember hearing this music for sure, and sensed that something big was going on beyond my awareness, was in that novel *Huck Finn*. There is something blurred and dreamlike, as well as epic or mythic about that beautiful river-journey, and I once took the book and tried to identify and establish some symbols, and symbolic processes, and then to decipher and articulate them, in order to attempt an explanation of what I thought the final meanings might be. As the literary world has not perceptibly altered its course since these revelations—and since, as I recall it, Mr. Leary was one of the very few kind enough to approve them in print—I will spare you the details.

Besides, there is at hand a better instance of what I mean. I well remember another occasion when late at night, myself struggling against sleep to read "Rip Van Winkle" for the first time in my adult life (in the usual fond hope of getting through Irving in class, early next morning, unstoned) I encountered that strange scene in the mountain with those strange little men playing a game of bowls. They are, as we all remember, making the sound of thunder, but they are odd-looking and silent and sad as they do it, and the whole business leads, through Rip's partial participation and the drinks he took, to the loss of a generation in his life. I heard bells whanging away that time for sure. The action there was pulsing with overtones. Those little men were speaking, it seemed to me, in signs. But what were the meanings of this pantomime? I didn't figure it out that night, you may be sure. Indeed it took me a whole year to come up with a theory that could be argued. It may of course be an unacceptable one, but if it is right then the overtones many have heard more or less faintly in the tale can be tuned in and amplified. And *that* is the sort of thing I have for some time been up to.

In this case, just to show you, it goes something as follows: The strange little men in that mountain are sad and silent, I claim, because they are dead; they are the highly disguised and remote descendants, that is, of the dead warriors of Odin, collected in Valhalla around their god, who by an ancient confusion is Thor, god of thunder; by bowling they make the sound of thunder, and thus impersonate Thor in his principal activity (rain-making) as a means of worshiping him; this worship, finally, is the secret rite of a cult into which Rip is unknowingly initiated—for which complicity in paganism he is punished by a loss of life. These notions, which by the way I think Irving was almost entirely *un*aware of, and which must seem stupendously and monumentally improbable when unsupported—as they must be here—by an iota of evidence, would seem once again worth establishing, if possible, as a matter of simple or complex interest. But, once more again, the significance of the demonstration is worth investigating, and as it happens something of value concerning Rip himself can be deduced, for by a curious route he slowly appears as a perfectly classic example of what is called "arrested development," an individual who in those little men comes face to face in that mountain with a unique and startling revelation of his own essential nature as a sort of aged child. Further, he soon emerges as the very personification of American innocence, an amiable stereotype of the American male, famous the world over, who has grown old but not up. And lastly some few at least can be brought to see in him a rare image of the child and the primitive in everyone that never grow up and never die in anyone.

Similarly the story of Pocahontas and John Smith, and particularly the well-known rescue scene, which is the heart of it, has produced for me those bells. And by tracing down to the present all the uses of the story in literature—and then discovering that it is also possible to trace it, intact in all parts and unchanged save for the names of the characters, back through medieval literature and finally to ancient—I am able (to my own satisfaction, that is) to account for its popularity and to articulate in fairly plain English what the symbolic action of that story has to say about us as Americans and as human beings. The tale deals always with a young woman who offers herself to a captive knight of some sort; he is always of another country, race, and religion, and the prisoner of her father; she rescues him from her father and is converted to his religion, only to be eventually abandoned by him. I could not possibly fool myself into thinking that a one-sentence statement of what I make of all this would convince even the most gullible that I have an arguable interpretation. But if I had time for a couple of dozen pages a few might become persuaded that the popularity of this tale suggests that the first betrayal—of the father by his daughter—represents a deep-buried desire for a love that transcends, as here, the boundaries of country, creed, and color; and the second betrayal—of the daughter by her lover—exists as a recognition that the first vicariously realized wish is really all too good to be true. It is a sign that we know the difference between what we dream, the coming-together of the lovers, and what we get, their estrangement.

I have the feeling that I have seemed pretty bloody unlikely for quite long enough, and it is time to try to become at least a little less so. The point now to be made, then, is that the considerations I have been talking about can be dealt with only after a lot of other things have taken place. They take the form of answers, to revert to earlier terms, to the so-what? that follows all the digging. What, then, is the nature of the digging? There are many kinds. In the first place, very close and thoughtful and if possible sensitive reading of the primary texts—the kind of reading, in short, that a lot of us learned from the new criticism. (I once thought that if I were ever to be a critic at all I would be a "new" one, and subsequently saw myself described as one of the "new new-critics," which, since the term was never defined, was not very helpful.) Although the interests I am talking about today involve a commitment to "theme" that is devout enough to disqualify me as one (as would the use I make of biography), I think we should all be new critics of one shade or another now and then—but as readers and students, and occasionally as teachers, and not so much as critics. That is, we should read the way they have taught us to, but then digest it, and not put it down, step by step, in print. It's the insights that you get from the method that ought to be published, and not, now that the method is well known, the steps that led to them. (One suspects, by the way, that it was essentially the tedium generated by so many painstaking new-critical analyses, more than any of the inadequacies of the method, that brought about its rather rapid decline from widespread academic favor.)

And other things have to happen first—especially, in the areas that currently interest me, a good deal of perfectly ordinary and traditional research (for some reason now pronounced "ree-search"). If there is real life in him, the scholar—however bitterly he may complain about preferential treatment given to those who have more fashionable tags on—is still honored in his own college. Indeed, and although it is effortlessly penetrated, the disguise I have lately put on for the benefit of colleagues and administrators is more Scholar than Critic. It took a lot of routine blundering about in the library to prove, by checking out as far as could be a number of clues, just who those little men were that Rip watched in that cave, so that what actually happened to him, and what it all might signify, could be argued at all. Similarly it took a lot of ordinary hunting to find all the analogues for the Pocahontas story, so that through the precedents and the offspring some of its meanings and sources of appeal could begin to dawn on one.

In an enterprise of this kind one has, further, need for whatever he can understand (well enough to borrow it) from other disciplines: anthropology, "depth psychology," history, and the study of popular culture, for instances. (Amateur liftings from all four of those areas were necessary in the study of the Rip Van Winkle business alone.) But my point about all this is a little like the one about the new criticism. These things constitute the means, not the end. However interesting in themselves, they should not, in an undertaking of the kind I am trying to describe, be allowed to take over completely.

This thing about the tuning-in and amplifying of faint bells need not of course be restricted to the area of traditional stories. I surely heard the music, some years ago, and to choose but a single and obvious example, in several of Hawthorne's tales—most especially in "My Kinsman, Major Molineux." In this case I was shortly to discover that the explanation had pretty well been made, at least to my satisfaction, with the theory that the story brilliantly celebrates a *rite de passage,* an expertly detailed transformation from youth to manhood, and is also a profound commentary on what happens to all who manage to make that transformation. "Young Goodman Brown," "Alice Doane's Appeal," "Rappacini's Daughter" and other Hawthorne tales are also pregnant with under- and overtones, and although articulating them has become a minor industry the procedure continues to seem profitable.

And so it is with a great deal of the very best fiction (which, since I know it best, is the area I have primarily been thinking of). Because at its best it engages life, which is inexhaustibly rich, at its deepest levels, it has reserves of suggestion and mystery which are themselves inexhaustible. This is the kind of fiction which is most worth teaching, and worth critical attention; and bring all the disciplines to bear on it we will, the essential mysteries remain because of the essential mysteriousness of life. And so the study really becomes the study of life, but—and this is a reason why one prefers it to history or philosophy or other disciplines—it is a study that is enhanced by the rewards that come from the fact that literature is also an art.

Finally, the answers to the so-what? that follow whatever it is that we have been able to demonstrate about a work also bring literature a little out of itself and into the larger world that lies close by but outside books. It is important never—not ever, under any conditions—to get so far from the work itself that you are really talking about something else, to misuse it as a handy route to something that you care about more. But it is not a crime to investigate its largest implications, so long as they are really there. We must never—as an occasional, sceptical student is likely to accuse one of doing—"read things into" works of art. But very much may be read out of them.

1963

11.

The Earlier Psychologists and Poe

Having picked up an "interdisciplinary" degree, I was an instructor at a large Eastern university. My chairman took me aside and told me straight: if I wanted to be an assistant professor I had really better get Published. Soon. (Yes, sir! Yes, sir!) But how? At someone else's instigation my doctor's thesis, which was on Hemingway, was dying out there at some provincial university press and, busy with my teaching overload, I had never even thought about posing as a scholar or critic. (I knew that certain professors "published," but I thought they did it out of some profound irritability, or because they couldn't make it in class.)

As it happened, however, I was at the time reading Poe pretty hard, him with all those beautiful dead or dying ladies, and I'd been wondering what could be the matter with a man that he should write like that. So I went to the New York Public Library to look it up. Survey the field and report the findings, that was the way. And before too long I did have a towering stack of notes on sick-Poe theory. Lest it collapse, I divided it in two piles, labeling one Conceivable, the other Idiotic. Then I shoved all the former into a waste basket. (For all I knew, Princess Marie Bonaparte's Edgar Poe: étude psychoanalytique, *a Conceivable example, was itself demented, whatever Freud really thought about it; easier to handle was a real American book that explained how all Poe's troubles resulted from a lopsided forehead.) So I surveyed* half *the field, wrote it up and mailed it off, and got a prompt acceptance, plus promise of early publication. One for my master! I immediately passed him the news, and two weeks later had his formal letter to the general effect that I was canned.*

From the preface to *Three Bags Full*

I

There never has been much doubt that something was very much the matter with Edgar Allan Poe. A man who by his own admission frequently drank the little more than he was able to handle ("I drank,—God knows how much I drank!") and who experienced periods of actual and well-documented "insanity" late in his life, during which he saw truly terrifying horrors which were not there, and who in the same life wrote strange poems and stories which were and continue to be widely read, could hardly escape the interpretative curiosity of those who came and come after him. Modern theorists would not hesitate long before speculating if nothing were known of his erratic and tortured career, for his work alone urges that something was wrong with its author. His stories, especially, teem with excruciating torture of self and of others, swarm with beautiful dying women who become the more exquisite as the more emaciated, and frankly admit, occasionally, the hyperactive "imp of the perverse" which so often prompted them. Actually, though, a good deal has long been known, or at least believed, about that difficult life and career, and thus a list of those who have published their explanations of the trouble with Poe would take us back to his own lifetime.

This guesswork, rather enlightened at times, and rather oftener not so, has concerned itself generally with the biographical question of what was wrong with him, and the clearly related question, of concern to all serious readers—however wary of genetic fallacies—of the genesis of his work. These are proper questions. The problem of what makes people do what they do is of general and legitimate interest. Moreover, an understanding of what any piece of writing may ultimately "mean" is a thorny but crucial problem. And here an understanding of its author—when one can be gained—is often very useful. Very numerous theories attempting to explain Poe have been put forward in print steadily now for a century, and fall into two groups: those which cannot be called in any meaningful sense "Freudian," and those which can. It is our interest here to look over a selection of explanations of the earlier kind, leaving the psychoanalytic ventures for another day. Some of the earlier attempts are silly, though once in a while charming; some are suggestive. In a rough sort of way most of them illustrate the rise of psychology in nineteenth-century America, in the hands of both amateurs and professionals, from extremely crude beginnings to a little more sophistication and knowledge, but finally to a rather dead-looking end from which a newer psychology was to claim a way out.

Nonpsychoanalytic theories about Poe by no means disappear with the nineteenth century, however, and the mention of a few of the comparatively recent ones suggests the nearly unlimited range the speculator may even now wander in. A most recent attempt to explain the man argues that he was really a frustrated actor, that the theater was a dominating influence in shaping both his personality and his work.[1] Another notion, uttered with supreme conviction a quarter-century ago, is that the original cause of all the poet's trouble lay in an unsatisfactory marriage and home life.[2] Then there is what seems to have been for a long time the traditional French view, dating back to Baudelaire and D'Aurevilly, both of whom enunciated it rather complacently, that the warp in the admired author came at the hands of a strictly utilitarian America not equipped to understand and appreciate him.[3] Though one may be predisposed to sympathy toward this conception, remembering the fact that Poe was often rather badly treated here, it really seems a kind of wishfully chauvinistic view for the French to take, since—to cite but a single instance—Baudelaire (the "French Poe") was himself in trouble with the French law for his poetry. A last example of the diversity of attempts to explain this victim of American folkways—or simply, in this case, the meaning of his work—should be Diana Pittman's breathless revelation of 1941.[4] This was the discovery that just about all of Poe's work is really a coded allegory—of propagandist efforts in connection with British Reform. An account of the true meaning of such a tale as "The Fall of the

1. N. Bryllion Fagin, *The Histrionic Mr. Poe* (Baltimore, 1949).

2. F. D. Bond, "The Problem of Poe," *Open Court* 37 (April 1923), 216–23.

3. Paul Yvon, "Barbey D'Aurevilly et Edgar Poe," *Mémoires de l'Académie nationale de Caen,* n.s. III (1926), 205–21.

4. Diana Pittman, "Key to the Mystery of Edgar Allan Poe," *Southern Literary Messenger,* n.s. III (August–September 1941), 367–77, 418–24; (October–November 1941), 502–9.

This was apparently the fruit of a lifetime of research. Tensely the scholar describes the drama of her pursuit, her trip to England. When the ship on which she was returning to this country with her evidence was stopped by a submarine late in 1939 (in connection with some international difficulty), she responded with alacrity, and cached her notes in a life preserver. The ruse was successful, the article was written, and now "A whole field of gifted writers will be needed to complete what I have been privileged to begin. . . ."

House of Usher" best illustrates the theory in action. "Here is the decline of the British Constitution and the separation of the Church and State symbolized by twin brother and sister. Undoubtedly Poe is picturing the turbulent Parliamentary Reform era which culminated in the passage of the Reform Bill in 1832, in London." The name of Usher symbolizes the British peerage. The "tarn" is the Thames, etc. The articles sparkle with such subtleties as: "Usher improvised 'the last waltz of Von Weber' (WEBer) because he knew it was the last WEB of Tory design his fingers would ever weave."[5]

II

Simpler and in many ways less clodhoppered ingenuities go back into Poe's own day, but begin most significantly with the posthumous first edition of *The Works of the Late Edgar Allan Poe,* with the introductory essays by Lowell, Griswold, and N. P. Willis,—"these three horny-eyed dunces," an early reviewer called them somewhat harshly.[6] It was of course Griswold's notorious "Memoir" which started the trouble, because for many years writers contemplated Poe with nothing more to go on than it and his work, and very few thought to question the likeness it painted. Griswold perceived that Poe's drunkenness was pathological, but he was a stern man and quick to make it clear that the poet's defects were of character, not circumstance—the result, he felt, of too much freedom in the early years. The editor was careful to outline a personality at least part mad, but not so mad that one might not hold him responsible for his behavior, which—as Griswold gave it—needed a lot of explaining.

Thus the article on which was based so much interpretation of Poe as a man—and even of the writing he did—provided plenty of material for people to try to account for, and also offered no very satisfactory theory of its own which might arrest speculation. In the same edition of the Works, moreover, N. P. Willis's "Death of Edgar A. Poe" opened the door by giving what turned out to be a suggestion for an early "theory," which, unlike Griswold's supposition (too much youthful freedom), was to be accepted and extended by others. Willis disclaimed any first-hand experience of the diabolical in Poe, but gathered that he was occasionally insane, and—perhaps without thinking much about it—remarked

5. Ibid., 503.

6. *The Works of the Late Edgar Allan Poe: With Notices of His Life and Genius,* by N. P. Willis, J. R. Lowell, and R. W. Griswold, III (New York, 1850). The vitriolic reviewer has been identified as John Moncure Daniel. See the *Southern Literary Messenger* 16 (March 1850), 172–87.

that he was "inhabited by both a devil and an angel."[7] This conceivably offhand phrase was the first in a series of crude psychologies which we may call "Daemonic," the idea being that Dr. Jekyll contained a Mr. Hyde who was responsible for Jekyll's misbehavior, and for the stranger aspects of his writing.

A Scotch cleric, George Gilfillan, was quick to accept this notion; it was not that Poe was mad, exactly (for this might tend toward apology), but that he was indeed possessed by a "demon." Not that this was so unusual, said Gilfillan, giving it all he had. Poe, a genius, did not differ from other poets in kind, but in degree: "Poets as a tribe have been a rather worthless, wicked set of people; and certainly Edgar A. Poe . . . was probably *the* most worthless and wicked of all his fraternity." Without revealing what it means to be certainly probably something, he snarled: "Poe's heart was as rotten as his conduct was infamous . . . a cool, calculating, deliberate blackguard . . . a swine."[8]

Gilfillan, however forceful, did not have the last word on this theme. Years later Charles F. Briggs explained the poet in Jekyll-Hyde terms,[9] and the prize exhibit of the school did not appear until Oliver Leigh's cleverly written book, a type of phrenological sport, came out in 1906.[10] Leigh started with the observation that few faces are so irregular in each half as was Poe's, and in attempting to get at his mind by examining his face he found the contradictory temperament revealed in its dissimilar halves. By conscientiously manipulating some pictures according to the author's directions, the reader can scrutinize the representations to get a clear perception—whatever he intends to do with it—that the two sides of the poet's head—especially of the forehead—matched very badly indeed. The swelled side was the source of the unbalance, the grotesque and strange, explained Mr. Leigh; the square side housed the builder and technician.

Not all the people who saw a "split" in Poe carried it so far. Back in 1853 R. H. Stoddard found the poet's temperament peculiar and decided it was that the man had brain but no heart. This led to depravity, insanity, and the production of sick and morbid work. But Stoddard was not so complacent about this as to think that such writing had nothing to say to the sane, and in a sentence which sounds remarkably like the psychoana-

7. *Works,* I, xiv.
8. George Gilfillan, *A Third Gallery of Poets* (New York, 1855), 326–27.
9. Charles F. Briggs, "The Personality of Poe," *Independent* 29 (December 1877), 1–2.
10. Oliver Leigh, *Edgar Allan Poe: The Man: The Master: The Martyr* (Chicago, 1906).

lysts who were to come almost three-quarters of a century later he speculated that this kind of literature "mercilessly exposes the depths and secrets of the heart, laying bare to the eyes of all what but few are strong enough to survey unharmed—the black gulfs and chasms of our spiritual nature."[11]

Griswold's "Memoir" received further dignifying from another quarter. In 1857 Andrew Wilson, of the faculty at the University of Edinburgh, rejuvenated the search for an explanation of Poe in his "Infanti Perduti."[12] He had little to add for himself on the subject of Poe's "Insanity," but apparently he stimulated others to speculate anew. One reaction, somewhat delayed, was a loud scoffing. In Ireland, James Purves read Wilson, and termed the notion that Poe was insane "nonsensical," for the somewhat puzzling reason that to call the man this would take his "manliness" from him. Purves became no less confusing as he proceeded with Poe, arguing that, besides, madness "always shows itself in the man's writings, and who will in the wide world be found to assert that he wrote anything which shows signs of such a disease?" The suspicion that Purves might have had Poe confused with some other writer, perhaps Pope, is quickly weakened when he shows himself informed correctly of the author's nationality by claiming more greatness for his poet than for Emerson, Hawthorne, Longfellow, or Lowell. He concluded that Poe is perhaps "the universal American genius,"[13] and thus by making the American writer sane he manages to unsettle all his compatriots, a trade about which many of them may be uncomfortable.

III

From Wilson and Griswold, however, also came the work of a psychologist, Henry Maudsley, and with his notions we move to a group of writers whose speculations may in some loose sense be called "scientific." For the most part they represent rather determined efforts—chiefly of the nineteenth century—to regard mental peculiarities in a rigidly mechanistic way. Maudsley himself was Medical Superintendent of the Manchester Royal Lunatic Hospital, and a famous psychologist, although for him a

11. R. H. Stoddard, "Edgar Allan Poe," *National Magazine* 2 (March, 1853), 200. Stoddard was anticipated here by a line in Lowell's "Fable for Critics" (1848) which remarked of Poe: "the heart somehow seems all squeezed out by the mind. . . ."

12. Andrew Wilson, "Infanti Perduti," *Edinburgh Essays,* by Members of the University (Edinburgh, 1857).

13. James Purves, "Edgar Allan Poe's Works," *Dublin University Magazine* 86 (September 1875), 296–306.

mental disease was a "brain" disease, and the only causes for lunacy he could admit—like overwork or the overexertion of some function—probably sound more physiological than "psychological" today. But such theories are hard to assess, with contemporary scientists often in flat disagreement with each other on such questions as the significance, say, of heredity. One school would flatly deny that insanity, drunkenness, and the like can be inherited; another group flatly denies the denial.[14]

However such questions are eventually decided by medical research, Dr. Maudsley was not hesitant with the facts as he saw them. He was dissatisfied with those who failed to find extenuating circumstances for Poe's character, black as it seemed. These circumstances, he argued, are to be found in his *heredity,* for "infirmities of mind are transmitted from parent to child by a law as sure and constant as any physical infirmity."[15] Moral disease descends from parent to child as surely as does consumption; Maudsley quoted no less an authority than the established scientist Nathaniel Hawthorne, in order to back himself up in this. He also considered the period of Mrs. Poe's gestation, for "before the child is born, it is certain that its after-constitution may be seriously affected by its mother's state of mind." A sudden fright in the mother may become a "permanent and, as it were, a natural constitutional defect in the offspring."[16] Be this as it may (there are medical persons who would support something like this notion today), Dr. Maudsley, after noting one more source of trouble (the lack of a faith in God), considered the matter closed. Many have agreed with him, for the theory that the strange personality which produced the strange writing was the result of a defective heredity has the supreme advantage that it is easy, and seems to stop further troublesome speculation. And thus presumably it is that it has become rather traditional with biographers and critics (Émile Lauvrière and Mary Phillips, to name only two) who wish to write about Poe but who do not really wish to bother with trying to find out what was the matter with him. Such works speak of "innate psycho-neurosis" or "hyper-sensitive nerve heritage," sometimes condescend to mention with a shudder less glib explanations, and rush along. Even John W. Robertson in "A Psychopathic Study" of Poe, published in 1921, can really go no farther than this. Dr. Robertson,

14. See, for example, Amram Scheinfeld, *You and Heredity* (New York, 1939), and George W. Gray, "Brain Storms and Brain Waves," *The Advancing Front of Medicine* (New York, 1941).

15. Henry Maudsley, M.D., "Edgar Allan Poe," *American Journal of Insanity* 17 (October 1860), 167.

16. Ibid., 167–68.

an experienced neurologist, insisted that he had " 'psychologized' many thousands of insane persons" but could himself not go beyond, etiologically, a "bad heredity." This, he felt, led to alcoholism, which finally damaged the brain.[17]

On the problem of alcohol, Poe himself had something to say. One psychiatrist has regretted that Poe did not enter the field of science "where his psychological gifts and uncanny insight might have given us so much sound discovery rather than rich pleasure,"[18] and an earlier writer, Dr. William Lee Howard, credited Poe with a scientific discovery of great value in that he was the first to define the disease, dipsomania, from which he suffered.[19] Actually, what the poet had done was very early to make a distinction which has today become so accepted as to be commonplace. He said, "my enemies referred the insanity to the drink rather than the drink to the insanity"—a perception which waited a long time to be generally recognized as such.

Arvède Barine in her *Essais de littérature pathologique* devoted a chapter to "L'Alcool: Edgar Poe." Citing medical "authority" she regarded the poet's alcoholism as a "simple poisoning," "a particular form of instinctive monomania," whose origin lies in heredity, and which provided Poe with some of his strange effects. She laid part of the blame on uncomprehending compatriots so newly come to intellectual life, but she found the "organic malformation" the chief source of his peculiar genius. When Poe, in refutation of the charge that his work was too much influenced by certain foreign writers, claimed that terror was "not of Germany, but of the soul," "il disait vrai."[20] Norman Douglas has taken a simpler but similar view, thinking it probable that some of Poe's "best writings are the direct result of alcohol";[21] W. C. Brownell thought that alcohol was doubtless responsible for most of the writer's troubles, and also fancied that he saw pronounced effects of its use on the writing.[22]

Brownell, however, protested that aesthetic effects produced by drink

17. John W. Robertson, M.D., *Edgar A. Poe* (San Francisco, 1921).

18. Arthur N. Foxe, M.D., "Poe as Hypnotist," *Psychoanalytic Review* 28 (October 1941), 525.

19. William Lee Howard, M.D., "Poe and His Misunderstood Personality," *Arena* 31 (January 1904), 78.

20. Arvède Barine, "Essais de Littérature Pathologique: L'Alcool: Edgar Poe," *Revue des Deux Mondes* 142 (July 1897), 336–73.

21. Norman Douglas, "Edgar Allan Poe from an English Point of View," *Putnam's Monthly* 5 (January 1909), 436.

22. W. C. Brownell, *American Prose Masters* (New York, 1909), 230.

are quite inferior to those which can be produced by drugs; and despite the fact that there exists no certain evidence that Poe habitually used drugs (and there are reasons to think that he did not), Jeanette Mark's *Genius and Disaster: Studies in Drugs and Genius* traced many of Poe's personal difficulties and much of his work to the habit. "Every paragraph of 'The Fall of the House of Usher' writes itself down as drug work," in her opinion.[23]

Marks attributed the actual insanity, not to drugs alone, but to their impact on the "brain lesion" which Poe's physician, Dr. Mott, diagnosed at his death. Others have accepted this diagnosis (mostly on faith): apparently this is part of an attempt to demolish the last vestiges of the "supernatural," wherever they might be found, by discovering purely tangible, physical causes for all abnormal behavior. It is odd, in this connection, that no one seems to have made very much of the possibility of attributing Poe's trouble to syphilis—perhaps congenital—for the disease could not be diagnosed in his lifetime, and his behavior suggested what we now know as late symptoms of that ailment. Instead, there is the theory of "cerebral" or "psychic" epilepsy.

Francis G. Fairchild was the first to urge this theory, and he attributed both Poe's writing and conduct to it, even to the point of finding his later tales based upon hallucinations incident to that malady. No one could have written "Usher," the theorist felt, without either being subject to the disease, or else anticipating "all the discoveries and observations of the last quarter of a century" since it was written. Anticipating more modern psychologists himself, Fairchild had the idea that if we knew the exact order of production of the poems and stories, it would not be difficult to construct "a kind of psychological biography" of their author. He believed that the disease was inherited, cited a "learned master in psychological medicine," one Dr. Anstie, and let the problem go.[24]

Dr. W. L. Howard called Poe's difficulty "psychic epilepsy," finding the dipsomaniacal attacks "symptoms of disorganized brain cells . . . poisoned at irregular intervals by the bi-products of the physiologic system which are retained in the body through a lack of perfect functioning of

23. Jeanette Marks, *Genius and Disaster: Studies in Drugs and Genius* (New York, 1925), 21. Thomas Dunn English, M.D., may be cited as evidence that Poe did not use drugs habitually. English knew the poet rather well, and did not like him very much, but he thought this charge a "baseless slander." See his "Reminiscences of Poe," *Independent* 48 (October 1896), 1–2.

24. Francis G. Fairchild, "A Mad Man of Letters," *Scribner's Monthly* 10 (October 1875), 690–99.

the nerve cells' faulty metabolism. These toxic materials are accumulative, and when they reach a certain potency, overpower the will . . . and we have temporary insanity. . . ."[25] Phrases like poisonous "bi-products of the physiologic system" are pretty vague, but it may well be that the layman is not competent to judge such a medical hypothesis. And, with such an analysis as this, we enter into a controversy that seems at present to exist over the question of the physiological origins of mental abnormality, for Dr. Howard's words sound very like a primitive statement of a modern theory which argues that there is much evidence to show that a predisposition to epilepsy may indeed be inherited, and that epilepsy itself *is* an effect of disordered body chemistry.[26]

Yet, although the literary man may be incompetent to judge of such matters, he nevertheless might feel with Benjamin Franklin that "this doctrine tho' it might be true, was not very useful"—not useful, that is, for literary purposes. Poe certainly did not write while suffering the kind of attack Howard had in mind, and since Fairchild did not show in any way just how "epileptic hallucinations" are the basis of the later tales, one may remain skeptical. Some theories (alcoholism, drug addiction) might have thrown light on the writing, but in the hands of the theorists did not go past assertion into demonstration; this one also seems not to. And so on such a negative note our search comes here somewhat abruptly to a halt, with the rather discouraging conclusion that no really useful answer to the reader's question of the trouble with Poe may be found in the practitioners of pre-Freudian psychology.

IV

But there is still a way of accounting for Poe's work, at least, which is well within the province of literary people. This way seems at first to say nothing at all about the man's personality, but possibly a great deal about how his poems and tales became what they are. It is concerned primarily with showing the literary forces which influenced the work; the efforts of various scholars in this direction have satisfied many students of Poe. In this connection, for example, Palmer Cobb showed the influence of Hoffmann (and possibly of Ann Radcliffe) on the American.[27] Killis Campbell has found many likely sources for a good deal of Poe's work in

25. Howard, "Poe and His Misunderstood Personality," 79.

26. Gray, "Brain Storms and Brain Waves."

27. Palmer Cobb, "The influence of E. T. A. Hoffmann on the Tales of Edgar Allan Poe," *University of North Carolina Studies in Philology,* III (Chapel Hill, 1908).

the newspapers and magazines which were available to the author.[28] The relevance of such traditional research here is that it provides at least a partial alternative to the purely "psychological" origins given by other writers: perhaps the lover of Berenice pulled all the teeth out of the dead girl's mouth, not because Poe used drugs or alcohol or was possessed of a demon or epilepsy, but because he had read of such an event in a Baltimore newspaper,[29] thought the idea rather horrible—as might any one—and wanted, after the fashion of the time—and to get money—to write a horror story. His own burlesque, "How to Write a Blackwood Article," might be taken to support such a view, and this was substantially the notion of Napier Wilt, who once introduced a little evidence to show that Poe often wrote his stories for the exclusive purpose of making money. "If the use of horror in fiction can be taken as an indication of horror in the mind of the author," he commented, "then most of the tale-writers of the first half of the nineteenth century were verging on insanity."[30]

It is not hard to find flaws in this apparently sobering argument. If we exclude those authors whose use of horror was patently perfunctory and mechanical, and who are now therefore largely forgotten, it would indeed be possible to construct a long list of writers of the period who were "verging on insanity." In addition, Wilt took at full face value Poe's word that he often wrote only to make money; he ignored the rather personal poems without showing why they should be more personal than the stories; he assumed that what a man may have done for money is of necessity not revealing of himself; and he ignored the fact that there *was* horror in Poe's mind, according to his own insistence which was corroborated by others, and that he *was* in his last years at least occasionally "out of" that mind.[31]

However, this general approach can be meaningful, and while still concerning themselves with literary influences other critics have widened it and made it more subtle. Van Wyck Brooks, for example, first mentioned a bad heredity, a bad early environment, and even perhaps a bad

28. Killis Campbell, *The Mind of Poe and Other Studies* (Cambridge, Mass., 1933). See also the first chapter of Margaret Alterton's *Origins of Poe's Critical Theory, University of Iowa Studies,* II (April 1925).

29. There was such an account. See Campbell, *The Mind of Poe,* 167.

30. Napier Wilt, "Poe's Attitude Toward His Tales: A New Document," *Modern Philology* 25 (August 1927), 105.

31. This fact is convincingly documented. See, for example, John Sartain, "Some Reminiscences of Edgar Allan Poe," *Lippincott's Monthly* 43 (March 1889), 411–15.

gestation, as possible causes of the nervous derangement which was to show up in the morbid and obsessive images to be found in the poems and tales of Poe, but he urged that this writing also sprang from a literary mood of the period. "A young woman dying of consumption . . . one might say, was a typical reality of the time. . . . Poe was quite in the tone of the time in presenting 'the death of a beautiful woman' as the most poetic of all themes."[32]

The monumental effort in this direction, however, is Mario Praz's *The Romantic Agony,*[33] that monstrous compendium of curious erudition. To speak here only of the lines devoted off and on in the book to Poe, the burden of Praz's effort can be made to claim that however unlikely it might at first appear, Poe's "terror" was *not* so much of the "soul," but was indeed of Germany—and several other countries. The Italian scholar found the sources for literature in literature, and in the taste of a "Romantic" or "Decadent" period.

A complete list of all the "abnormal tendencies" which a psychologist might leap on in Poe but which Praz shows also to have been epidemic in the period would be very long. The poet's obsession, for instance, with beautiful, dying ladies might seem very personal, possibly tracing back to his own experiences of this event, yet there are heroines before Poe who are admired for—and not despite—their sick bodies. In the same way, beauty tainted with pain, corruption, horror, and death was, as we well know, all over Europe a century ago. The heavy overtone of incest in Roderick Usher's concern for his dying twin sister Madeline may bear some relation to the man who called his sick child-wife (who was his cousin) "Sis," but the subject of incest was everywhere, too; the love of brother and sister was a favorite German theme. Art's imitation of life is reciprocated: "there are some who even go so far as to say that Byron's incest with his half-sister was a plagiarism."[34] Byron, an early favorite of the man who created Roderick, was never so happy, according to Praz, as when he could see shadows of death blighting a love affair, and he could only feel love for one who closely resembled him. Baudelaire wrote, "Chez les Incas on aimait sa soeur; contentez-vous de votre cousine,"[35] almost defining Poe's marriage, from one point of view.

32. Van Wyck Brooks, *The World of Washington Irving* (New York, 1944), 354.

33. Mario Praz, *The Romantic Agony* (London, 1933).

34. Ibid., 69.

35. Quoted by Praz, *The Romantic Agony,* 146. If it should be argued that this all misses the odd "sexlessness" of Poe's writing, then Praz can be called on to show that even this peculiar

And so it goes. The fascination in Poe with what we should call both sadism and masochism might seem to lead to conclusions about his separate human problems, but sadism was the *mal du siècle*; Poe's remark on his own "perversity" (in "The Black Cat") might equally well have been made by any number of people who wrote fiction both before and after him. Poe's persecuted women, perhaps so revealing of his own difficulties, were part of a whole tradition which started with *Clarissa Harlowe,* as Praz effectively demonstrates, and soon went berserk in France. Almost all of Poe can be found not only in many other writers but also even in Delacroix, who had never read Poe until Baudelaire called his attention to the resemblance, whereupon the painter investigated and then agreed that it was a fact.[36]

But however impressive such a thesis may be when supported by a plethora of evidence, there is one problem which such an approach as this can of course not deal with, and that is how it happens that Longfellow, another widely read poet, wrote "Evangeline" instead of "Ulalume," and Cooper, instead of creating Roderick Usher, came up with Natty Bumppo. Praz—speaking of a writer's *predisposition* to receive morbid notions—must have known this, but he cannot say why one man is so "predisposed" when another is not, and thus the question seems ultimately to fall back onto the lap of the psychologist who, ideally, could say why. That this man did not rest comfortably under this burden, however, should be apparent by now. It was not until the interpretation of literature and writers was undertaken by people equipped with newer doctrines than nineteenth-century psychology could avail itself of, that the psychologist—now become psychoanalyst—would be ready to shake the burden from his lap, place it on the couch, and attempt new answers to the old problem of the trouble with Edgar Poe.

1951

mixture of the immediately sexless and yet ultimately lascivious (however sterile) has also many precedents.

36. Ibid., 142.

12.

Hawthorne's Secret: Fathers and Sons and Lovers

In life as in literature, Hawthorne was unique. Aloof, defensive, reserved even with intimates, he could on exceedingly rare occasion be spiritually generous, open, disarmed. Never at any one time were these contradictory and most unequal sides to his nature more deeply felt and clearly articulated than in the letter he wrote his patient fiancée in February of 1842, expressing his willingness for any fully sympathetic person to know everything that was hidden in his heart. But, he warned flatly, such a person—and surely Sophia, above all others, was such—could get no help at all from him.

How iron was the inhibition that prevented Hawthorne from expressing his deepest and most private feelings is never more apparent than in this letter and its resolution. It was here that he at long last agreed to tell his mother and sisters that he was going to marry. But Sophia had no idea, he wrote her, how difficult this was going to be. Directly he acknowledges the "abyss of my nature" and the "cloudy veil" he stretched over it. And completely he denies "any love of secrecy and darkness." It is rather that in his family

> there seems to be a tacit law, that our deepest heart-concernments are not to be spoken of. I cannot gush out in their presence—I

> cannot take my heart in my hand, and show it to them. . . . And they are in the same state as myself.

Characteristic of New England, it may strike some—if for unclear reasons. But for Hawthorne the family "incapacity of free communication" was "meant by Providence as a retribution for something wrong" in early dealings among its members. Whatever the cause, three full months passed and he had still not brought himself to announce his marital plans at home. Sophia finally did it in a letter. Hawthorne's sister Elizabeth responded to the long silence with formal, icy rage.

As Sophia was the first to admit, she never did see into the depths that she knew her husband closed off. And so for those who would like to learn what was there it is fortunate that there was another mortal—enormously sympathetic to the reticent writer, and blessed in Hawthorne's judgment with "a high and noble nature"—who thought he did see into the abyss. When first Mrs. Hawthorne got to know him, Herman Melville impressed her every bit as much as he did her husband. "I am not sure," she wrote her mother, "that he is not a very great man." What struck her most was his "very keen perceptive power":

> Once in a while his animation gives place to a singularly quiet expression . . . an indrawn, dim look, but which at the same time makes you feel that he is at that instant taking deepest note of what is before him. It is a strange, lazy glance, but with a power in it quite unique. He does not seem to penetrate through you, but to take you into himself. I saw him look so at Una yesterday.

It is hard to think he never took Una's father into himself. But it was more than thirty years later that he told her brother Julian, who reported it in print for the first time in 1901, he was "convinced Hawthorne had all his life concealed some great secret, which would, were it known, explain all the mysteries in his career." In saying this, Julian reports, Melville was terribly nervous. Perhaps he was not saying, nor did Julian suspect, that he had long believed he knew the nature of the secret. In fact he had already published a transparent clue to it—without, so far as is known, having attracted any attention whatever.

The literary history, at least, of what Melville thought he had discovered about Hawthorne is simple. In his *Mardi* (1849) he had created and juxtaposed his own dark and fair ladies along conventional though semi-mythic lines. Three years later, shortly after getting to know the Hawthornes, he wrote his deeply troubled *Pierre,* in which he drove the conventions attaching to these figures to the end of the road. He sent a copy to Hawthorne, whose response—unknown—was probably shock. It is a shocking book. Pierre, apparently in love with his mother but engaged to the lovely blonde Lucy, yearns most for the sister he thinks he lacks. Because

> the wife comes later. He who is sisterless is a bachelor before his time. For much that goes to make up the deliciousness of a wife, already lies in the sister.

Soon he discovers that he has one, a half sister, in the darkly beautiful Isabel. Then Melville turns the whole tradition on its head. Pierre rejects his fair fiancée, literally embracing his sibling, and destroys them all. Further, as an unneeded signpost, Melville introduces into his romance, years before Hawthorne, a portrait of Beatrice Cenci. One year before Hawthorne, he had gone to the Barberini Palace to seek out the original of that painting. He bought an engraving of it, which is preserved, noting that "not caught in any copy" was the "expression of suffering about the mouth."

When almost twenty years later he published *Clarel: A Poem and Pilgrimage to the Holy Land* (1876), Melville had Beatrice and Hawthorne together in his mind. In this long and mostly unread work, the young Clarel represents Melville. He is enamored of a middle-aged American artist named Vine, who is clearly Hawthorne: a reclusive, reserved, nonparticipating observer, moralist, and symbolist caught up in the past. Vine rejects a "feminine . . . passionate mood" in Clarel, and while Vine is off guard Clarel has a dramatic insight into the expression on his face—such, perhaps, as Mrs. Hawthorne witnessed in watching Melville. Of Vine, the poet writes

> He wore that nameless look
> About the mouth—so hard to brook—
> That in the Cenci portrait shows,
> Lost in each copy, oil or print;
> Lost, or else slurred, as 'twere a hint
> Which if received, few might sustain:
> A trembling over of small throes

In weak swoll'n lips, which to restrain
Desire is none, nor any rein.

Clarel, according to an English reviewer of the time, is a poem of "about twenty-seven thousand lines, of which we can only say that we do not understand a single word." There is, to be sure, some awkwardness of expression. But what Melville is saying here is that around his mouth Vine had a look, hard either to describe or accept, that appears in the portrait of Beatrice Cenci, though not (as noted in the journal) in copies of it—or else is blurred, as suggesting something few might bear up under if they perceived it: little spasms in indulgent lips that have no strength to hold back desire. There was no need to say more. It was a tell-tale look. The crime symbolized by the Cenci portrait, as Melville's century saw and understood it, was needless to name. Thus Melville had expressed as clearly as he ever chose to—what he took to be the nature of Hawthorne's "great secret."*

Beatrice Cenci, in both Hawthorne and Melville, relates to the figure of the dark lady. And it is generally assumed, thoughtlessly, that the origins of this mysterious female lie in the traditions, chiefly literary, both writers subscribed and contributed to. "Though the celebrated Dark Lady . . . haunts Hawthorne's fiction," a contemporary scholar observes, "she does not appear in his personal legend." That she does not, as it is presently shaped. But what is missing from a modern understanding of this writer is awareness of great gaps in that legend. And of the extent to which his fiction grew out of personal experience, vicarious and direct, which filled those gaps.

In somewhat the same way, the notion of an old, hidden family document, which contains a terrible secret involving an awful crime—still alive in the central character's own day, which the author in his last years could not leave alone—seems a piece of musty Gothic machinery left over from a previous age.† An apparently tired fancy, it is little more

*It is likely that Melville had his deep perception of Hawthorne during their exhilarating relationship in western Massachusetts. His enthusiasm for his older friend was at the time boundless and reckless; his letters to him are electric with it. In the summer of 1851 he was finishing *Moby-Dick* in the same inspired mood; he was about to write *Pierre,* boldest of incest novels. It is conceivable that he mentioned its theme to the man whose "heart beat in my ribs and mine in yours, and both in God's"—as one that might interest them both. If so, this could have been what destroyed the relationship as it had been: the "shock of recognition," a phrase Melville had used in reference to his rapport with Hawthorne, that blew the circuit.

†See Young's "Hawthorne's *Gables* unGarbled" in *Three Bags Full.*

likely to be credited—"believed in"—than the business of an elixir of life immortal which the same writer tried to profit from. So, less conspicuous, the concept of a sibling triangle, which his earliest tale is based on and his final fictions echo, seems an unaccountable invention for a son of the Puritans. But the truth is that neither the triangle nor the hidden document was an actual invention or a matter of literary borrowing.

Truth can be stronger than fiction. And though Melville may not have known it, there really was a Dark Lady of Salem. No part of Hawthorne's legend, she was deep in his life. "You must never expect to see her in the daytime," he cautioned. "I never imagine her in sunshine. . . . I really doubt whether her faculties . . . begin to be exercised till dusk. . . . Their noon is at midnight." He was writing his fair fiancée. Until he married her in middle age—his character formed, career far launched—the shadowy lady was closer to him than anyone.

She loomed large in that isolated household of unmarried Hawthornes on Herbert Street—all through the twelve postgraduate years in the room under the eaves where he said he was shaped, and in turn shaped visions he put before the world. She had been the kindred playmate of his childhood, "my sister E." Eighteen years had passed since she had, as if miraculously, appeared to him a child no more—"a tall handsome young woman," rather, so generally altered he did not know her. When he did, according to his sister L., also present, "he stood transfixed with astonishment."

The exact coloring of Louisa, the younger sister, does not seem to be recorded. But in character and personality she was wholly fair—daytime to Elizabeth's night, domestic as her sister notoriously was not. Cheerful and compliant, she was fond of clothes and dancing. She was "fragile, pale, amiable," according to Julian, and "not very effective." Of Elizabeth, there has been found no likeness, but with long black hair and gray eyes she is said to have inherited her mother's dark beauty. Older, more precocious, individualistic, and forceful than Nathaniel, she paved the paths into which he was drawn: solitary meals and walks, nocturnal reading and writing. Never venturing beyond her tiny sphere, she harbored few illusions as to what was out there. It was "only through books," her brother remarked, but "she knows the world marvelously."

Her own literary career, such as it was, aborted. Only thirteen when she left school, she nevertheless translated the whole of *Bon Jardinier* for her pomologist uncle, and several of Cervantes' tales. What she actually published was unsigned and unrecognized. When he edited *The American*

Magazine she was Nathaniel's only contributor. A Whig who argued politics with her brother, she wrote a eulogy of Alexander Hamilton. *Peter Parley's Universal History* molded American minds for more than half a century, promoting Christian theology and national chauvinism. It made a fortune for its publishers; "It is probable that the writing was entirely hers," according to one who has studied the matter. "Destitute of the ability to earn," as she observed, she was never engaged to review books as she would have liked. But two pages of *American Women Writers* are devoted to her, and an edition of her letters is in preparation.

"For everyday purposes of pot-hooks . . . and flat-irons," Sophia would write her mother, "Elizabeth is not available." If it was up to her to clean a room, it was not cleaned. If there was money, it went for books. Her brother, who so feared her disapproval as a young man, ended calling her "the most sensible woman I ever knew in my life, much superior to me in general talent." Tribute would come as well from both his daughters. "I never remember you to have told me anything twice," Una once wrote her aunt, "and that can be said of very few people; but there are few enough people in the least like you." Yet it was the younger Rose who left the most memorable recollection of "my recluse aunt." By 1897, when she completed her *Memoirs of Hawthorne* in which it appears, Rose had converted to Roman Catholicism, formally taken leave of her alcoholic husband, and was devoting her life to the physical care of terminal patients in cancer wards. She had lived a good deal abroad and had a perspective on the aunt who had lived so long at home alone. The first time Rose saw her, as she recalled it, Ebe was most uncharacteristically knitting. She did not at the moment seem "mysterious" or "romantic." Rose perceived instead the resemblance to her father: it was "magic." She had "the same eloquence in her silences; and when she spoke, it was with a sympathy that played on one's whole perception." Her power was unmistakable, and though she lived in "the utmost monastic retirement" she was "chock-ful of worldly wisdom." She was also, wrote Rose, soon to be Mother Alphonsa, "a good deal unspiritual in everything," and "potentially rather perverse." But she possessed "loving-kindness of a lazy, artistic sort. . . . She was unregenerate, but excellent."

At least as much as Ebe loved books, she loved the woods. Rose remembered her best in them. There she was "quick and ardent," the

> great eyes peering and disappearing again. . . . Her dark brown, long lashes and broadly sweeping eyebrows were distinct against the pal-

> lor of her skin, which was so delicately clear, yet vigorous, that I felt its gleam as one feels the moon.

It was the eyes Rose remembered most powerfully, and not at all as most would recall the eyes of a maiden aunt. "There was nothing which her large, lustrous eyes could not see," said Rose, "and nothing they could not conceal." Ebe was as hostile to the idea of a biography of her brother as he was.

A footnote to the story of Elizabeth Hawthorne is that in her late sixties she took a strong stand on the lurid old rumor of Byron's incest with his half sister Augusta. In two sensational publications, which appeared forty-five years after the poet's death, Harriet Beecher Stowe had zealously undertaken to support Lady Byron in her charge against the reputed lovers. Studying the case with "a lawyer's precision," as someone put it, Ebe vigorously disputed the allegation. Archly dismissing the poet's widow, she remarked that though persons of little imagination ought to be free of idle fancies they are full of them—and always those of an "annoying nature."

Why she found the notion of incest aggravating, rather than disgraceful, repellent, or whatever, is not clear. Perhaps she thought it took genuine imagination, or more knowledge of the world than Lady Byron possessed, to invent such a sin. The intensity of her interest in the whole affair is unexplained, though as something of a dark lady herself and an admirer of "Alice Doane" it does not come, perhaps, as a total surprise. That "the taint of incest" ultimately attaches to the figure of the dark lady in literature has been observed before now. On her first appearance in American fiction—as both dark bride and "Mamma!" to the young hero of Charles Brockden Brown's *Arthur Mervyn* (1800)—the taint is very perceptible.* With the dark bride and half sister of *Pierre* it is the heart of the matter.

In Hawthorne, to be sure, the stain is not generally visible. After Alice Doane, only Miriam of *The Marble Faun* is cloaked in what Nabokov called incest's "subtle perfume," and it evaporates. It has never been argued that Beatrice Rappaccini is related to Giovanni, or Hester Prynne to Dimmesdale, or Zenobia to any man at Blithedale. Timid lovers rejected these women out of sexual fear, perhaps. But if there was anything

*See Young's "Born Decadent: The American Novel and Charles Brockden Brown," *The Southern Review* 17 (Summer 1981), 501–19.

forbidden in their embracing it could only be attributed to the barely perceptible tendency of Hawthorne's young men to see sisters in females everywhere.

This was notably the case in the very beginning, but it is plot, not the symbology of dark and fair, that revealed it. Alice Doane is not physically described at all; it is essential to the story, though it's later contradicted, that she has been seduced by her brother Walter. Though they were potential or imminent lovers in "The Ancestral Footstep," another Alice seems very like a sister to Middleton. Similarly Elsie to Ned in "Etherege" and "Grimshawe." It is only in the most substantial of Hawthorne's posthumous publications, "Septimius Felton," that the dark development in the action matches the symbolic coloring of the heroine. When Alice, later Sybil, of the "large, dark, melancholy eyes" tells Septimius they are closely related, and each shudders to thrill at the touch of the other, nothing could be more plain. The fact that the author again contradicts what he has revealed does nothing to obscure it.

And the final step is inevitable: literature imitates life, literature imitates literature, life imitates literature.

So many things suggest a brother-sister relationship closer than normal, there is reluctance in drawing inferences which seem, paradoxically, too obvious to be valid. Phaedrus announced two thousand years ago that things are not always what they seem. But if they are not, what then is to be made of a sister's open and long-lived admiration for "Alice Doane's Appeal," with its vibrant biographical overtones? (That if they were relevant to her and her brother she would never have mentioned the tale? She was bold: how bold?) How much might be made of her instant, blunt, undying dislike of her brother's wife? Why the vigorous immersion in the details of Byron's relations with his sister, and the ex cathedra rejection of the charges? Closer to home, to what degree can a sister be made out in the shade of that pale beauty who came in sin and desolation to a young man in the bed of his haunted mind, or stood beside it guiltstained as a demon pointed to his breast? If there is nothing of a sister there, is she among the female shadows of "Fancy's Show Box"—a type of sin never perpetrated, only the object of thoughts that pollute the heart? Have these apparitions in a haunted chamber nothing to do with Hawthorne calling his own place under the eaves "squalid"—which still may be defined as "morally repulsive"? In light of a sister's resemblance to a mother, might something more be made of a son's encephalitic reaction (Sophia's diagnosis) to the mother's death? Was the mysteriously injured foot, which as a boy crippled Nathaniel for two years, a Delphic sign that a better name for him than Oberon ("white leprosy") might be Oedipus ("swell-foot")? Fancy's Show Box runs amuck.

But facts, as Winston Churchill once remarked, can baffle the imagination. And they are not all in yet. An extraordinarily large one can be approached, once more, by way of *The Scarlet Letter.*

The court's charge against Hester Prynne in life, as Hawthorne probably knew, would not have been *adultery,* a word he never used either, in her connection, but "a lying together in the same bed," or something of that sort. Nor was punishment for it always the wearing of a symbol. The woman of Boston who came before William Hathorne in 1673 was given a choice. She could leave the colony, as Hester could have, or be whipped, then stand on a stool in the marketplace with a paper on her breast explaining that she was there for her ADULTEROUS AND WHORISH CARRIAGE. But the penalty could be more severe, as at the start of the book the townswomen wished it had been for Hester. In 1644 Mary Latham of Boston, married like Hester to an old man she did not love, lay in bed with "divers young men" and, according to John Winthrop, was executed. Sarah Pore of Salem, who like Hester refused to name the father of her offspring, was whipped, then jailed to be whipped once a month until she confessed him (after a month and a week). A few cases involved the birth of mulatto children to white women; perhaps Hawthorne knew that Martha Cory, that "unhanged witch" of "Young Goodman Brown," was one of them. It is a matter of record that he borrowed Joseph B. Felt's *Annals of Salem,* 1827 (second edition, two volumes, 1849), from the Salem Athenaeum in 1833, and again for three months in 1849 when he was writing *The Scarlet Letter.* Here, it is supposed, he found his symbolic initial, where Felt records that in 1694 a law was passed that those found guilty of adultery

> were to sit an hour on the gallows, with ropes about their necks,—be severely whipt not above 40 stripes; and forever after wear a capital A, two inches long, cut out of cloth coloured differently from their clothes, and sewed on the arms, or back parts of their garments so as always to be seen when they were about.

The situation with the crime of incest was somewhat different. In 1692 Massachusetts made it a capital offense, but in 1695 changed the sentence, as lacking conformity with the law in England. Now the penalty was the same as for adultery, except that the convicted were to wear "a capital I, two inches long of a proportionable bigness, cut in cloth of a contrary colour to their cloathes" and displayed in the province ever after. But incest, the same year, became an especially difficult issue in Massachusetts. So Samuel Sewall indicated in conscientiously borrowing from Increase Mather a little book called ". . . Whether it is Lawful for a Man to Marry his Wives own Sister?" The question was painful, Sewall noted, because "several have married their wives sisters, and the Deputies thought it hard to part them." But a vote of 27 to 24 decided that such alliances did violate the law of God. Close as the tally was, it is hard to see how the deputies could have determined otherwise. In an attempt to be as conservatively Hebraic as possible, New England Puritans defined incest Levitically, thus greatly exceeding the bounds of simple consanguinity. They greatly exceeded Leviticus itself, Chapter 20 of which their law cited, in ruling criminal a man's converse with his "grandfather's wife, wive's grandmother . . . wive's father's sister . . . son's son's wife," and other implausible couplings.

Hawthorne may have known of the act, which was on the books for nearly a hundred years, or not. What he would have known was the most dramatic entry to be found in the tome he twice withdrew from the Athenaeum, Felt's *Annals:*

> 1681, March 29. Two females, for incest, are sentenced to be imprisoned a night, whipped, or pay 5 £, and to stand or sit, during the services of the next lecture day, on a high stool, in the middle alley of Salem meeting-house, having a paper on their heads with their crime written in capital letters.

It was "probably in Felt's Annals," as Hawthorne wrote in "The Custom-House," that he remembered reading of the decease of Jonathan Pue, once like himself Surveyor of Customs for the port of Salem. It was in Pue's hand, in old ink on dingy paper, he says, that he read "a reasonably complete explanation of the whole affair" of Hester Prynne and her legendary letter. In writing his version of it, he admits to having dressed up the account as he liked. But he quickly adds that he still has the original papers, which will be "freely exhibited to whomsoever . . . may desire a sight of them." For posterity, presumably, "I contemplate depositing them with the Essex Historical Society."

That Salem institution had already merged into the Essex Institute, still flourishing. But in pretending to give facts he had in fact invented, Hawthorne was once more—profoundly, and as he knew—concealing a deeper truth. As he could not have known, he was also predicting the final repository of old documents more memorable and significant than Hester's. It was a long-range forecast: they came officially to rest at the Essex Institute on December 10, 1980.

But it is hard to think that Hawthorne had not discovered the real papers, which related most directly to him, some time before he was himself Surveyor of Customs. From the long list of works borrowed—for him, by Ebe—from the Athenaeum, it is clear that he studied his regional past broadly and intensively during his solitary years on Herbert Street. Elizabeth Peabody remarked how he "made himself thoroughly acquainted with the ancient history of Salem." As for his family's past, deep in the town's, he had not one but two older unmarried relatives of the sort that become expert in matters genealogical. He availed himself of both. Old Eben Hathorne, as Nathaniel entered in his notebook, was a forlorn bachelor whose great hobby was "the pride of ancestry." He had "a good many old papers," and an "old book, with the record of the first emigrants (who came over 200 years ago)" in his own hand. (Presumably lost when his house burned shortly after he died.) He "kept telling stories of the family, who seem to have comprised many oddities, eccentric men and women, recluses, &c."—plus "some bastards." Eben also passed it on that "old Susy Ingersoll has a great fund of traditions about the family," which she had got from her mother, Eben's sister. A spinster recluse herself, in a dilapidated old manse one day to be known as the House of the Seven Gables, Susy did not live all alone. "The Duchess," as Nathaniel called her, made her own contribution to family and town gossip by adopting the motherless son of a man who had recently been her gardener.*

The Duchess and Eben were naturally Hathorne specialists. But they knew well that the father of their young relative had married into a family old to Salem and grown more prominent than their own. And if they were up on family scandal along with other local lore, there was nothing to eclipse or match the one that engulfed the children of Nathaniel Haw-

*The boy, educated at Yale, became the Reverend Horace Conolly. He inherited the house, which had by then become the setting for a well-known book, and took the name Ingersoll. In 1837 he told Hawthorne a remarkable story of two Acadians, separated on their wedding day. When the author decided it was "not in my vein," Conolly told it to Longfellow, who then wrote *Evangeline*.

thorne's great-great-great-grandparents, Richard and Anstice Manning. What is most likely is that they would have heard something of the son Nicholas, first Manning in the new world.*

To judge from the record, Nicholas was an adventurer. Born June 23, 1644, the first child of Richard Manning of Dartmouth, Devonshire, and Anstice Calley, he sailed to America at eighteen. The next year in Salem he married the widow Gray, who became first in a line of Elizabeth Mannings that reached Elizabeth Manning Hawthorne, Nathaniel's sister. The eponymous Elizabeth, who had a son but seven years younger than her new husband, promptly bore Nicholas four children, three of whom died as infants. Hawthorne did not inherit the urgency of this passion for matrimony. But he had a maternal ancestor as significant to him as the paternal William Hathorne. This was not his great-great-grandfather Thomas Manning, gunsmith of Ipswich. It was Thomas's older and more conspicuous brother Nicholas.

Nicholas was energetic, enterprising, and above all things family-minded, as might be said. A Salem gunsmith and anchor maker, his rise in the New World was rapid. Received into the church and recognized as one of God's Elect, he was a juryman, constable, and a selectman in company with William Hathorne, next to whose land he purchased ten acres in 1668. At the outbreak of King Philip's War in 1675, he joined up and quickly rose to the rank of captain. Later he commanded the ship *Supply,* with forty men and thirteen guns, and captured the Indians who had made off from Salem harbor with thirteen boats. He was contentious and litigious as well, his name appearing frequently in the Essex County Court records, where he seems to have lost more often than not. He signed his name with a great initial *N,* and a final *g* as bold.

His father had died in England, but Nicholas left a considerable family there. By 1679 he was riding high. He was officially reprimanded for sporting a periwig, and in the spring he chartered the "pink or ship Hannah and Elizabeth," Lot Gourding, Captain, which crossed the Atlantic and returned from Dartmouth with his mother Anstice (frequently Anstis, though Anstice is how her surviving signature reads), his sisters Anstice, Margaret, and Sarah, his brothers Jacob and Thomas, and forty other

*It is also possible that one or more of the many Mannings of Hawthorne's own day would have known about the most unusual event in the family's American history. Hawthorne's maternal grandfather, also Richard Manning, lived in Salem until Nathaniel was eight, and *his* grandfather Thomas, aged seventeen, was in the same town at the time the family name was disgraced.

souls—including a chirurgeon who presented a long bill for compounds such as Histericall Carmanitius suds.

The pink or ship did not put in at Boston until September 14, but only the next year things had become so difficult for the Mannings in Salem that Nicholas left town under something of a cloud. It was not until 1684 that he surfaced at Sheepscot, Maine, as captain of a company that, according to a citizen's complaint to the Governor, "Doth much Obraide & Disturbe vs." It was apparently two years later that he married Mary, daughter of John Mason, who was the largest landholder of the region, having bought twelve thousand acres from the same Robin Hood Major Hathorne had negotiated with. Nicholas acquired an interest in the property, and at about the same time was awarded a judgeship as a supporter of Sir Edmund Andros—recently appointed Governor of the Dominion of New-England. When protorevolutionary Bostonians overthrew Andros in 1689, Judge Manning was arrested for complicity in his maladministration, brought to Boston, and imprisoned. Pleading his record of service he was freed, and seems to have remained in New England until 1697, where there is record of him at Boston—despite the unpleasantness that caused him to flee Salem sixteen years earlier. He must also have returned to military life, for his signature appears on the treaty with the Indians reached at Pemaquid, Maine, in 1693. Long since divorced from Elizabeth, who was awarded his Salem acres next to Hathorne's, his house and two shops and the orchard, he was by 1702 living with Mary as a gunsmith on Staten Island. In 1719 he sold John Manning, his son by Elizabeth, rights to the Maine lands, and was last heard from in Long Island two years later. It is not known if he had offspring by Mary. But in 1768 one Thomas Manning, "Gent^m^ of the province of pennsilvania," petitioned Massachusetts Bay for the quarter share of land along the Sheepscutt River in Lincoln County due him "as heir to John Mason."

It is conceivable that during his researches into Salem's past Hawthorne completely missed Nicholas Manning, though he is mentioned and indexed in the 1829 Felt's *Annals* as captain of a man of war, and more significant facts, along with other old papers—which considerable care had recently been taken to preserve—were close at hand. Conceivably he heard nothing curious of this first-arrived maternal ancestor from friendly Hathorne authorities, though all this seems unlikely. What seems impossible is that, in the early fall of 1833, he could have read without giving the matter further thought, in the same volume of Felt, that on March 29, 1681, two females were sentenced to go on display at the meeting house with the label INCEST on them.* What females? Incest with whom? There was nothing like this anywhere else in the work. As he must also have known, there was only one place where Felt could have discovered such a bit of social history. If he did not, Felt gave it in a note: "Qt Ct.R."

New England Puritans were contentious and litigious in general. A great deal about the vicissitudes of their daily lives can be learned from the primitive account of their experiences with the law: in Salem, its "Quarterly Court Records," Felt's source. The town had a judicial tribunal as early as 1636, when the first sessions of the court of what became Essex County were held there; that is the date of its first surviving document. By 1655 it had some sort of courthouse that needed repair, which stood on what was then called School Street. About twenty years later a new house was erected in the middle of that thoroughfare; in Hawthorne's day the functioning courthouse, completed in 1786, was on the same street, now called Washington. It was a two-story brick building with a cupola on top of the roof and a balustrade on which the Father of His Country had stood. When Nathaniel was a boy, the lower floor was fireproofed for the protection of judicial papers stored there. In 1817 these documents were placed chronologically in ledgers. It was here, very likely, that Hawthorne read how on 24: 9: 1668 Judge Hathorne and others sentenced Hester Craford for fornication with John Wedg. If so, he must have read that on the same day Hester's sister Susana accused Stephen Haskett of fathering the child she murdered. These papers were readily available; in 1836 it was spelled out in print that the clerk of the courts was to maintain them "in good order, and to keep convenient and correct alphabets to the same." The handsome building of Hawthorne's youth was torn down to make way for the railroad. But a larger granite structure opened in 1841, and a brick one beside it twenty years later. It was in the newer building that the early records reposed—out in the open to be handled by anyone, unobserved—until they were prudently removed at last to the Essex Institute.

Even on a fine day, dark red brick against the blue, the joined mid-nineteenth-century museum-like buildings of this establishment on Essex Street are not so appealing as the Custom House, unless to special admirers of Victorian Italian Revival architecture. But unlike the Custom

*It would surely have caught his eye that just below this entry is one that read, "June 28th. Hon. Wm. Hathorne died lately AE 74." An obituary follows.

House this is a busy, thriving institution with large holdings and many treasures—among them the author's desk when he was Surveyor at Salem, and the Charles Osgood portrait of him at thirty-six, every bit as handsome as Elizabeth Peabody said. To examine the recently acquired Records and Files of the Quarterly Courts of Essex County, Massachusetts, the contemporary investigator enters the Institute and turns right on the ground floor into Daland House, which contains the James Duncan Phillips Library. It is a large, airy, pleasant room. He pays two dollars for a yellow card. Close-mouthed, he ignores the nine openly shelved volumes of the court records to 1686: they abstract and print the old documents, he means to see the originals again. Having searched them when they were stored in the brick courthouse where they rested for 120 years, he knows what he wants to copy. He asks the attendant at the reference desk for ledger number 35. She disappears into an area marked "Staff Only," and heads for the fireproof section of the library, where specific items are shelved in locations the Institute does not disclose. Against the walls all around him are works of genealogy and town or county history. She returns with the ledger, which she takes to the table where he is sitting. He remembers from years back that what he is looking for is fixed to page 69.

And so Hawthorne, on some kind of day of some unknown year, must have walked over to Washington Street, and entered the attractive courthouse of his time in search of records he would never so long as he lived forget. His feelings cannot be known—or, perhaps, even plausibly imagined. But the facts are pretty clear. On the first floor were the great ledgers registering some two hundred years of provincial tribulation. After leafing their pages for a while, watching the passing dates, he would eventually have come upon the events of March 29, 1681, which Felt reported. In the middle of page 69 in the thirty-fifth ledger was pasted a piece of old rag paper, of good quality in very good condition—not much stained or "foxed," not "dingy" but lightly tinged yellow. In ink somewhat brownish but very clear, a strong hand that he could make out almost entirely had written, three hundred years ago now:

> Anstis Manning & Margaret Manning now Polfery being brought before the Court at Salem in November 1680 for incestuous carriage with their brother Nicholas Manning who is fled or out of the way, & bound over to this Court at Ipswich March the 29: 81 for farther heareing[.] The delinquents appeared & the evidences being

> read & considered. This Court doth sentence the said Anstis & Margaret to be comitted to prison untill morning & then to be whipt upon the Naked body at Ipswich, & that the next Lecture day at Salem then shall stand or sitt upon an high stoole during the whole time of the Exercise in the open middle ally of the meeting house wth a papper upon each of their heads, written in Capital Letters This is for whorish carriage wth my naturall Brother. And the Constable of Salem is hereby ordered & enjoyned to see that it be performed as to show so appeareing at Salem as above said.*

If he did not know it already, Hawthorne would quickly have learned that the delinquents were the English-born offspring of his direct ancestors. If he read on in the record, and looked a little back, he would have learned more. First he would see that on September 30, 1680, complaint was made against the two women "for lewd carriages wth theire Bro . . . as lying together in y[e] same bed severall times the particulars of which carriage will farther appeare by y[e] Evidences given in to this Court"; they "stand charged with viz: Vehemenent suspicion of committing incest." Just over two months later, Hilliard Veren, clerk of the court,† entered in his distinctive, slightly crabbed hand the first of some striking and specific "Evidences." It was that of Elizabeth Watters, servant and eyewitness, who

> testifieth that sum time the last winter . . . att night there was a quarreilling & disturbance between my master Nicholas manning and his wife whereupon his wife went away out of the house & Lodged att another place & In that very night . . . being a thirst . . . [she] passed thorrough the Roome whear her master and his wife used to Lodge Together & . . . I heard a womans voice which I judged to be Anstis Maning In the bed I heard her say who Is that softly I heard my masters voice In the same bed Answer softly be quiet[.] Then this examinant went up . . . to my felow servants ann

*Immediately beneath this entry on the same piece of paper, a smaller, more difficult hand in different ink has noted that in answer to a petition the court grants that by "paying 5 li [livres (pounds)] in mony shall be remitted 1/4 part of the sentence by whipping . . . the other part . . . to be executed att Salem[.]"

†Veren, or Verin, was officially clerk from 1658 to 1683, when he died. Conceivably Hawthorne encountered the fact that for the same quarter century he was also collector of customs at Salem.

> kelegrew and grace Stiver . . . and tould them . . . upon which we all agreed to Rise Early in the morning to see if we should find them In bed together which we did . . . & we passed thorough the Roome Into the kitchings & left the dore for open that we might see what they further did & . . . saw the offor said Anstis Manning arise out of the bed without her clothes except only an under petticote which we conceived she had then sliped on & presently I saw my master . . . arise out of the same bed without his clothes . . . and put on his clothes siteing by the bed side. . . . Anstis . . . came Into the kitching & s[d] to us . . . are you up already[?] This Examinant further testifieth that she hath severall times since seene her master Afforesaid In bed under the bed clothes with the said Anstice . . . and Like wise his sister margarett . . . severall times [and] that the s[d] nicholas came Into the Room where this examinant was Alone & put his hand under her coats and kist her & attempted to throe her upon the bed but she crieing out he did forbear further actions[.] She further testifieth that the morning above mentioned . . . An Kelegrew called her to Look on the bed when she made it & she saw the bed much stained of a Red colour[.]
>
> Sworne in court at Salem . . .

On the same date, Ann Kelegrew and Grace Stiver (both passengers with the Manning sisters on the *Hannah and Elizabeth*) testified to "the truth of all the above written that Related to theire sight" of both Anstice and Margaret—particularly to "a Red Couler wherewith the bed was much stained." Ann added that her master "hath severall times tempted her to lie with him saying to her Lett me. If I be with Thee an hundred times I will not get thee with child." Two of Manning's daughters-in-law swore on the same date that they feared being alone with the captain, "and Elizabeth saith that one time using some unsivill cariage towards her made her afraid he intended some further eveil [and she] Said to him these words (how can I doe this & sin against God) Where upon he flung awaye very Angry."

Preserved in the court record is the humble petition (in a clerk's hand, but signed E.m.) of Elizabeth Manning, the aggrieved wife, stating that for about half a year, frightened of her husband and his two sisters, and without means, she had lived with one of her daughters. Nor, she went on, did he wish her to return—until the night before the accusations against him were made. Then in her simplicity, as she says, she was overcome with his fair speeches and went back to him, only to find "his intent was to make use of me butt as a cloake (alas I know so much of him & his sisters y[t] hath been a terror to me)." Next Elin Maskoll swore that Mrs. Manning had told her of having several times seen "very wanton cariages betweene her husband manning & his sisters as kissing & tumbling on the bed together" but was afraid to speak. There is also the humbler petition, in her own hand, of the widowed mother of the guilty siblings. It is a large sheet, badly torn, with pieces missing and a good deal that survives indecipherable, but some of its spirit remains:

> . . . into the part of y[e] Earth . . . Affliction . . . desolation . . . my own family . . . fatherless Children . . . my daughters had committed this heinous . . . I should certainly be dum with . . . almost constantly in my Company ever since this cuntry . . . that my son nicholas . . . I hope y[e] Lord will change his hart & . . . merciful to y[e] widow and Strangers as I and my Children are in this land . . . little . . . am capable of
>
> Anstice Manning

Son Nicholas was long fled. His sisters and Margaret's husband petitioned for remission of the fine "which yor honors have Legally sentenced us to"—adding, in an apparent admission of guilt, "the Justice wher of we must acknowlege." (Another section of the record shows that a fine was paid.) Then in 1683 Elizabeth Manning was "freed & released from hir marriage," it having convinced the Court of Assistants of the Colony of Massachusetts Bay, "on perusal of the paper's presented," that her husband was guilty as charged, and declared he would not have "any thing to doe" with his wife. What the record does not show, though there is a reference to her "present condition," is that by the time she was officially on display at the meeting house Margaret Manning Palfrey was seven months with child. The question of paternity was inevitable. There is no known answer to it; a few of her descendants were prominent citizens. She was twenty-four. Her sister Anstice was already thirty, but eventually married a middle-aged widower named Powling. Relatives kept alive for a while her unusual given name. Thomas Manning, Hawthorne's great-great-grandfather, christened his first daughter Anstice.

So tired and contrived seems the whole business of a terrible family secret, recorded in a hidden old document, its very staleness has helped prevent even the suspicion that there might be something alive in it. So extraordinary, then—yet credible and tragic—the actual transcript, that the attempt to find a fictional fascimile for it, which a protagonist contemporary with Hawthorne could somehow be cursed or influenced by, was obviously doomed. But at the end of his career, determined to practice his trade when he had lost the gift of it, Hawthorne clung to materials that were in his vein, even though it was occluded. Having exhausted his paternal ghosts, and laid them to rest, he turned to guiltier, more troubling maternal ones that he could not think how to use.

Not that he had kept them completely out of his work before then, though here much depends on what cannot be definitely established: the time he first learned the Manning secret. According to Ebe, she read what was then called "Alice Doane" in the summer of 1825. If at that early date her brother (and perhaps she) knew the story of Nicholas, Anstice, and Margaret—which was enacted in the same place and period as the story of Leonard, Alice, and Walter—it seems sure that his most unusual tale is a reworking of crucial bits of family history, as suspected with less reason before. Indeed the Manning paradigm would help account for what might otherwise seem redundant, or supererogatory, in his fiction: the incestuous triangle. A single relationship in violation of this taboo is ordinarily dramatic enough to go it alone, having no need for the rivalry that animates a standard threesided affair. Perhaps the precedent explains the recurrence of the pattern. The recurrent name Alice for the young man's sister may also trace to the Manning disaster: Hawthorne could not come any closer to Anstice, which was not particularly serviceable.* He would, then, have taken both Alice and her triangle from the old scandal, simply and plausibly reversing the genders to one sister, two brothers. If, on the other hand, as is quite possible, Hawthorne uncovered the historical facts after having written "Alice Doane," the discovery must have proved an even greater shock. In addition to having come upon a piece of unforgettable bad news from home, as it were, it must have seemed as if he had somehow "forecast" the past—or had all unaware been so in its grip that he had virtually repeated it, at least in fiction. Either way, the facts were indelible, and came near emerging at the end. Less bluntly and less effectively, he reworked the Alice Doane arrangement of sexes in the "Footstep." Following that, he returned to the original one; Septimius Felton has two "sisters," one dark, one fair, and he experiences erotic

*Neither Alice Pyncheon of the *Seven Gables* or Alice Vane of "Edward Randolph's Portrait" has an incestuous role or overtones. But they do share with Anstice the fact that it is as strangers newly from abroad that they play their dramatic parts in early Massachusetts.

sensations with both, as did Nicholas Manning. It is as if the whole "Oedipal tendency" of Hawthorne's fiction had been proclaimed by a Quarterly Court at Salem.

The same court papers also confirm the suspicion raised in the cases of both Felton and Middleton that the guilt of a "first American ancestor" had nothing to do with any Hathorne. A specific and different immigrant is evoked at least once. When Sybil tells Septimius the legend of the bloody footprint, he thinks sharply of "long ago," and "the first known ancestor of his own family, the man with wizard attributes, with the bloody footstep . . . whose sudden disappearance became a myth." The presence, or departure, of "brother Nicholas Manning who is fled" is immediate. Indeed it begins to look as though the Ancestral Footstep of Hawthorne's last works was in his mind everywhere implanted by Nicholas—who never in the fiction disappeared without leaving the permanent mark of his crime, the nature of which is finally plain. So the hale and manly blacksmiths in the fiction—notably Danforth and Hollingsworth—must have been associated in Hawthorne's mind with Mannings, who were metalworkers from Nicholas down to Nathaniel's grandfather Manning.

Far more to the point, however, is the realization that the testimony of the Manning maidservants to the forbidden behavior of their master with his sisters—and the indelible, homely, scarlet evidence of it they adduced—make transcendently clear that for the author the bloody footprint was the very symbol and sign of Nicholas, the mark of his consanguine guilt. To carry the matter to the heart of things, Hawthorne regularly associated, or even equated, blood and guilt. It has already been argued that his essential vision of the world, diabolically revealed to him as young Goodman Brown, was "to behold the whole earth one stain of guilt, one mighty bloodspot." Now it appears that the dutiful servants uncovered the source not only of that distinctive imagery but of the vision itself, Hawthorne's apocalypse. The sentence of the Quarterly Court made the dreadful truth final and formal, but with the prior testimony the dye was cast.

Such observations are not made casually, but they relate in the end to an even more serious matter that cannot be avoided. Since Hawthorne's ancestral secret turns out to be of a piece with Clarel's startling insight into Vine's, and since he admitted to having inherited "strong traits" from forebears that are not to be found in those he draws attention to, but might be in the ancestors he kept hidden, and since the ultimate secret of dark ladies is said to be of the same nature, there does not appear to be any way around the question of the relationship between Nathaniel and Elizabeth Hawthorne. The least that must reluctantly be suggested, and the most that can be responsibly intimated, is that it looks as if Something Happened. Just what that may have been—and the range of possibility is broad—it would be as fruitless as vulgar to guess. A very conservative position could call on the argument of "Fancy's Show Box." It could have been something inward, nothing overt. Guilt can arise from deeds which, physically, "never had existence." All alone in a "midnight chamber . . . the soul can pollute itself"*—with the "ghosts of . . . never perpetrated sins." It would follow that the guilty female shades, which elsewhere haunt that chamber, were all in the mind of Oberon. The lustful heart has sinned already, as the Gospel according to Saint Matthew announced.

Guilty thoughts, however, are common to practically everyone, and the deep blue region of Hawthorne's guilt seems peculiarly his. It stretches credulity to think that his nature contained such an area of culpability as a result of nothing more than imagination or longing. Nor does it seem likely that something other than self-knowledge gave him the idea that "moral diseases which lead to crime" are passed down the generations—or that he was thinking of an infirmity not connected with the earliest Mannings. Hawthorne felt himself freed, or rescued, or saved by marriage, but in his last work seems returned to his dungeon—the darkest corner of it. Perhaps he felt that if he could master in fiction what once again bothered him it would cease to do so. "If he wrote it he could get rid of it" is a thought that has found its way into Bartlett's *Familiar Quotations*. So in the past Hawthorne had exorcised matters that appear to have troubled him: boyhood submission, in a couple of early tales, to his Uncle Robert; phantom visitors to his solitary room; even, perhaps, by way of flashback in "Alice Doane's Appeal," the guilt-charged shock of his father's sudden death. Surely the vivid specters of compromised females in the Show Box of Fancy, in Dimmesdale's private quarters, as well as in the Haunted Chamber, reflect something that had burdened him—which in some way had "happened."

But where Hawthorne came closest to dealing with the weight he would most like to get rid of, "secretly confessing" his own secret, as it

**Self-pollution* was commonly conveyed by the term in Hawthorne's time. *Webster's Third New International Dictionary* still gives "emission of semen at other times than in coition" as a definition of *pollution*.

were, and where he came very near doing what he said he could not do—lead the sympathetic mortal across the veiled abyss of his nature and into his depths—is in *The Scarlet Letter.* Failure to hear his confession has resulted from his own success: first in putting readers in mind of the wrong ancestors in "The Custom-House," and then of the wrong symbol throughout the romance. The clearest account of Hawthorne's un-told tale is the buried story of the minister and Hester.

It had seemed improbable that Hawthorne could have conveyed so eloquently the force of Place in Hester's life—how a dark event that colored it rooted her to the region of its occurrence—without having experienced at Salem something of the kind himself, or without knowing of any shame that attached to his deep roots there. Knowing these hidden roots, and of the crime that clung to them, remarkably increases a reader's sense of the immediacy of the author's relation to his book. This is striking on Hester's first appearance—in "The Market-Place," where "her sentence bore, that she should stand a certain time" and did, "fully revealed before the crowd" to show her letter under the weight of a thousand eyes. Impossible, in visualizing this scene, that Hawthorne could have erased from his mind the image of Anstice and Margaret standing, or sitting upon a high stool,* before the congregation during the whole time of the exercise at the meeting house, wearing letters grimmer than Hester's. Perhaps they thought wistfully, as she does, back to their native village in Old England, and their "paternal home . . . of antique gentility." Very likely it was of them he thought first, then of Hester. But it is doubtful, as he pictured things, that they wore on their heads the wordy indictment the court dictated. On their breasts, rather, the capital *I* two inches long of a color contrasting to their clothing that the law would very soon prescribe for Salem. And as Hester stood with her infant in her arms before the staring women—uppermost in whose minds was the "riddle" of its paternity—Hawthorne must have been aware of the darker riddle that pressed on those who stared at Margaret "Polfery" and her imminent expectation. The guilty Dimmesdale, who is fled for the time, will hide an *A* on his chest until he confesses it and dies; it is unlikely that Nicholas Manning felt any need to confess the invisible *I* he took to the grave. But more than once the breasts of the author's afflicted heroes were lacerated with guilt, and in this book, in his own way, the author will confess it.

*Originally the "stool of repentance" placed in Scottish churches for the display of offenders, especially against chastity.

His way is partly through establishing recognizable relationships to the characters in it. In a limited but real sense, he is represented as Arthur Dimmesdale, author of powerful sermons, the chief literary genre of his time and place—in the line of Oberon, another writer and another guilty witness of female ghosts. As for Dimmesdale's daughter, all who have read Hawthorne's descriptions of his child Una as a youngster have recognized Pearl's origins in his life. Una was born in Concord to "The New Adam and Eve"; Pearl was "worthy to have been brought forth in Eden." But the marked resemblance of Hester Prynne to Elizabeth Hawthorne—another dark lady, eventually rejected—seems to have gone quite unnoticed.

It adds up. Both women were distinctive for independence of mind and spirit. Both were intellectually and morally bold. As Ebe was "a good deal unspiritual," indeed "unregenerate," Hester is so uninterested in the spiritual and religious matters that are life itself to her lover it is a wonder that the author does not remark or account for the fact. She tries to persuade her minister that they should simply sail off into the broad world from their narrow province. Her sin has effectively ostracized her, but she does not even believe in it. "What we did," she pointedly tells Dimmesdale, "had a consecration of its own." (This romantic position so frightened the author of it he is quick to remark that Shame, Despair, and Solitude "had made her strong, but taught her much amiss.") Both women were dark, isolated beauties, knowing little of the world but not innocents; both were "sensible," strong, unafraid, decisive, frank, shockproof. In defiantly embroidering her *A,* Hester is even "rather perverse." Aside from accidental motherhood, needlework is her only sign of domesticity, as knitting was Ebe's. Both women are "at home outdoors"—Hester in chapters called "A Forest Walk," ". . . at the Brook-Side," and "A Flood of Sunshine," where the "whole richness of her beauty came back." She is the only really effective dark lady in Hawthorne. Like Ebe, she is "excellent," and possessed of loving-kindness. And by the time Hawthorne wrote his book, Ebe was in a retirement more secluded than Hester's even after Pearl was grown and gone, Dimmesdale and Chillingworth dead.

Chillingworth, the husband, is not of this family—but essential to a related one. A misshapen, diabolical figure with an evil eye, he is roughly equivalent to the wizard who was responsible for the incest in "Alice Doane's Appeal"—and not unconnected to that "first ancestor" with "wizard attributes" who echoed Nicholas Manning. This is to say that like the wizard in the early tale, Chillingworth in *The Scarlet Letter* takes responsibility for the sexual transgression that ruined everyone but Pearl, the product of it. A man "already in decay," he admits to Hester, it was his folly in marrying a young and beautiful woman that led straight to her "blazing letter." Thus in a special but very real way, Dimmesdale is Hawthorne, Hester stands for his sister, and Pearl is his daughter. Chillingworth represents the controlling force of "witchcraft"—which, as Hawthorne told Longfellow, had made him captive in the dungeon of his own chamber (where his Fame, and maybe his Infamy, was won).

But in that "blazing" letter there is a serious problem. And the solution to it solves whatever mysteries are left in "The Custom-House." Despite its power and penetration and durability, there is a weakness at the heart of *The Scarlet Letter*. It is the awkward disproportion between the reality of adultery and the unreal horror with which it is regarded in the book. Puritans took adultery seriously, and punished it in several ways—severely. Yet in Hawthorne's romance they do not react to it as to a sin against the sanctity and vows of marriage, but as something more obnoxious, repulsive. It is somewhat as if, turning to life, Hester Craford's crime, which was fornication, was as revolting as her sister Susana's when she killed her child. Hawthorne's view is as extreme as the community's, and he becomes increasingly insistent on it. As noted before, he claimed that his book was "positively hell-fired" without ever explaining how. So, apparently, was the *A* itself; long after Hester he put it on his own breast and felt its "burning heat"—his own experience of sensations several tortured characters had suffered in that region. So superstitious townspeople claimed Hester's letter was "red-hot with infernal fire." It does indeed appear that something about his symbol was eluding his grasp, and some deep meaning to his story escaping with it.

The hellfire burns in the missing elements. In this case, at least, D. H. Lawrence was absolutely right: if he is to get to the heart of the matter the reader must look through the surface, and discover "the inner diabolism of the secret meaning" of *The Scarlet Letter*. It far evaded Lawrence, but nothing Hawthorne wrote makes the point as firmly. He saw through the surface of his symbol well enough, and no aspect of it got past him. It is readers who fail to see, since he covered it over so thoroughly, that in Hawthorne's mind Hester's *A* is an *I*. His book really deals, as he said it did, with "the taint of deepest sin in the most sacred quality of human life." Adultery cannot compete for that title.

What is actually going on becomes clearer and clearer as the story approaches its end, by which time the *A* is completely unsuited to the way people view it. In "The Procession" which leads to the close, a "rude and boorish" crowd acts out the point. It thronged about Hester, and then "stood, fixed . . . by the centrifugal force of the repugnance which the mystic symbol inspired." If the symbol is an *A,* as the reader has been relentlessly reminded, it is absurd now to call it mystic. It is equally unreasonable to think that the letter could immobilize with repulsion an assembly of country folk—or city. And then, underlining this implausibility, Dimmesdale speaks out to destroy completely the *A*'s credibility. He takes the occasion of his farewell address to "People of New England!" to redirect their attention to the object that has already transfixed them. "It hath cast a lurid gleam," he cries, "of awe and horrible repugnance" about Hester. "Ye have all shuddered at it!" The same mark has been on his breast, he confesses, and the devil—once more the familiar image—"fretted it continually with the touch of his burning finger." And finally, as if this were not already more than enough, at his death hour, Dimmesdale incredibly

> "bids you look again at Hester's scarlet letter . . . with all its mysterious horror."

The only thing mysterious about the *A* is why he and the New Englanders found it revolting. As if in a desperate last charade, author and minister are straining frantically to make the people see what diabolical letter—sin, crime—lies just beneath the surface.

It has not worked. People have not understood. But when in "Conclusion" Hawthorne points a single moral from his tragic tale, he feels he has done all he could. And the message is remarkably applicable to him:

> Be true! Be true! Be true! Show freely to the world, if not your worst, yet some trait whereby the worst may be inferred!

He was probably satisfied that this is what he had himself just done. The "trait" he mentions is an "essential" one, such as he invited readers to look for in fictitious characters like Dimmesdale; it is a "strong trait" of his ancestors, such as he said had intertwined with his own nature. And now from it, perhaps, the "worst" has been inferred. When he broke down in trying to read the newly finished ending of his book to Sophia, he must have felt that at last he had been true, though she did not understand either. Having stood with Dimmesdale—having become Dimmesdale, struggling to publish his letter before he died—he had got it off his chest. It might also be that there was an obscure family relation between the emotional upheaval in reading the passage to his wife and the one that attended the death of his mother.

With Dimmesdale, Hester, Pearl, and Chillingworth the principals on stage at the finale, and the crowd behind them become a chorus, in voices of "awe and wonder," the last scene of *The Scarlet Letter* brings to a climax the book's remarkably operatic quality. All eyes are on Dimmesdale in his redemptive agony. But as much as Hawthorne had invested in the minister, he was very likely conscious too of another figure standing obscure and motionless in the wings. This would be the dim, improbable, hulking presence of Samuel Johnson, transported ghostlike from Uttoxeter, where in eloquent silence he had like Hawthorne expressed his guilt. Hawthorne was powerfully drawn to the tale, which he told three times, of how Samuel Johnson, having once refused to tend his sick father's bookstall in the marketplace of that town, returned to it fifty years later to stand, bareheaded in the rain for an hour, where it had stood. On his fifty-first birthday Hawthorne recorded in his notebook his "pilgrimage" to that "holy site." He searched there for the right location, which is unrecorded. Presumably he wanted to stand a moment himself.

Penance, too, is good for the soul. On finishing his book, Hawthorne thought he might feel better. Having thrown, he says, all the light he can on the letter imprinted in Dimmesdale's flesh, he hopes to "erase its deep print out of [his] own brain," where "long meditation has fixed it in very undesirable distinctness." Having written it, he hoped to get rid of it; he had dealt with many things by writing them. And then, in the last line of the book, he invokes yet once more the appearance of an *A,* still glowing red in the gloom. But this does not mean he had failed to exorcise the image that had become oppressive. For that was of an *I*—worn and bleached, very likely, until it had faded white. So, fulfilling his name, may Oberon have blanched on first exposure to the old record that spelled the letter out. Now in his own way, so far as he was able, Hawthorne had spelled it out in his romance. And still kept "the inmost Me behind its veil," as he announced he would do in "The Custom-House." Under the triple cover of persona, symbol, and substitute ancestry, he had confessed his secret and kept it too.

1984

13.

In Search of a Lost Generation

If America ever really had a "Lost Generation," it is probably to be found in a group of cultivated, successful men and women who were truly exiled—expelled from their homes, their properties confiscated, their lives threatened till they could book passage. This was no trickle of writers and other artists, though there were a few among them. In all they were 100,000 people, and that at a time when Philadelphia, the second largest city in the British empire, was smaller than the Pennsylvania small town where this is written. They were, of course, the American-born Loyalists of our Revolution, who lost just about everything—all because they did their duty as they had learned it, and opposed the idea of colonial Independence, as did at the start virtually all Patriots, and as some Patriot leaders continued to do even after its Declaration was signed. The people born, say, during the years somewhere around 1750 really made up a generation—people in the same boat, as they took off for England, Canada, and Nova Scotia. They were not a particularly artistic group, except for a couple of painters; there were a few poets and essayists. It was not a literary age on either side. Yet where Gertrude Stein could say "America is my country, Paris my home," she was clearly found. This generation died thinking of America as its country too, but not of London or Halifax as home. They had lost both.

But "Lost Generation" means to us another group, and since the term is so widely used, at least in some circles, it might not be a bad idea to consider if there ever was such a thing. I was recently asked to do exactly that, and thought I'd best go to the library and find out. The results were mixed. There is no card in the catalogue. As for encyclopedias: the *Britannica,* old and new, no. *Grolier, Collier's, World Book,* no. *International* yes, but too skimpy to register. *Encyclopedia Americana* aha!—one column of solid information: authoritative, probably definitive, the Word:

> A common but misleading designation . . . Origin is something Stein told Hemingway in Paris that he used as epigraph for *Sun Also Rises* and made famous. Born of experience of literate young Americans in World War I . . . Uprooted by war, disillusioned with ideals and traditions of own upbringing. Reaction: philosophic despair, personal hedonism. Expatriation and art to compensate. Dislike of America (Prohibition), Paris antithetical (also cheap). Pioneers: Stein and Pound. Presence of Joyce. Names of American poets and novelists in Montparnasse . . . Crash of the Market in '29 . . . Henry Miller rings down curtain, only Gertrude left. Irony of tag in that Hemingway thought it nonsense; Stein got it from proprietor of a garage. Hemingway right: Renaissance of American letters in 1920s by people known as lost.

But that doesn't answer the question. The term is there, but called a tag, misleading and with a disreputable past. Worse, I had not read through the first sentence before a sense of déjà vu began hailing down: for me to say there was a Lost Generation because it's entered here means only that I said there was; fatal to the argument that those paragraphs weren't written by someone else.* But it was on the same trip to the library that I made a momentous, uncatalogued discovery. There has got to be a Lost Generation because there is a *Lost Generation Journal.* Originally out of Tulsa, Oklahoma, then moved to Carbondale, Illinois, it is edited by a professor of journalism who kept his Lost Generation Archives, like Hemingway's manuscripts, in the vault of a bank. The existence of this periodical nails down the concept; you can't have a magazine devoted to the study of something that never was.

*What might have been added is that but for a most belated act we might never have had the term. *The Sun Also Rises* was professionally typed and ready for the printer before Hemingway pencilled in Miss Stein's remark.

Or can you? In his maiden issue the editor leads off with a standard discussion of the term in question, which arrives, however, at a clear conclusion: unless we mean by it a Literary Generation, the Lost one "doesn't exist"—contains "virtually no one." I never thought we meant anything else, but the editor didn't get away with his argument anyhow, and in the next issue prints a rejoinder to it by a minor member of the Generation. There was *too* a Lost Generation, he says, which "consisted entirely of Harold Stearns," who with a book to his credit arrived in Paris and became a "souse." Stearns' autobiography, originally *A Street I Know* (1935), was reissued as *The Confessions of a Harvard Man* (Paget Press, 1984), which I reviewed for *The New Criterion* (December, 1984). Stearns was not in the War, but was genuinely, totally, and willfully *lost* in Paris. Asked about his drunken, sloppy-hilarious appearance as Harvey Stone in *The Sun Also Rises,* he approved it. And so the editor of the *Journal* and his enormous staff continued bringing out a periodical that was not sure of its subject.

Just another sign of the continuing interest in the American Twenties, the nation's favorite decade. Serious concern with its writers, which began over fifty years ago with a book by Malcolm Cowley, got virtually out of control. Minor members of an alleged group became object of massive scrutiny. A recent book on Robert McAlmon is excellent. One on Harry Crosby (*Black Sun,* 1976) is brilliant. (I wrote a jacket blurb for its author, Geoffrey Wolff: "utterly engrossing . . . A frequently exciting, wholly satisfying book. Beautiful.") Clearly this would continue until there is nobody left to write about. *But,* I asked in 1975, were there no women in that generation—no American female writers living and loving and writing in Paris? There certainly were. The biggest development since 1975 in the subject at hand has been the outpouring of books about them. (These books underline what I have always thought the secret appeal of Paris in those years: sexual freedom.)

But to return to those writers we have long called a "generation." Were they? And were they "lost"? And what do we mean by these words? In 1973 Malcolm Cowley published a second book on the subject called *A Second Flowering: Works and Days of the Lost Generation.* On this occasion *The Southern Review* asked me to do a full-scale piece on its author and his career.* This seemed a happy thought. I had been admirer of his since 1940 when I began subscribing to *The New Republic.* He is

*"For Malcolm Cowley: Critic, Poet, 1898—," *Southern Review* 9 (Autumn 1973), 778–96.

the Generation's spokesman and historian; he writes well himself. *Exile's Return* (1934) had recorded and interpreted his generation and bequeathed it to mine, twenty years later. Further, when I looked for previous works on Cowley from which I might do a little academic shoplifting I discovered there were precisely none. I was on my own.

I began by rereading that famous book, and got the idea that there was indeed a Lost Generation, though it would be unfair to stick him with that label, since he writes it with misgivings, never having found a better one. He uses the life of Harry Crosby to sum up the "themes" he'd developed, which tied his exiles together:

> The separation from home, the effects of service in the ambulance corps, the exile in France, then other themes, bohemianism, the religion of art, the escape from society, the effort to defend one's originality . . . then the whole final period of demoralization when the whole philosophical structure crumbled from within . . .

The philosophical structure that crumbled had never been put together, in my opinion, but let it go. It is a fine book (and in its revised, 1951, edition even better); both participant and diarist, its author happily shared what he long ago called Fitzgerald's "double vision": he was both a drinker at the long party and the sober observer of it. I then read or reread all his other books, and finally got to the new one. It is a series of essays—some marked with brilliance, others with an over-familiarity that is simply stunning—on eight writers, to wit Hart Crane, Cummings, Dos Passos, Faulkner, Fitzgerald, Hemingway, Thorton Wilder and Thomas Wolfe. Their Works and Days make up, this time, his Lost Generation. Along the way I had bestowed a good deal of praise, along with a few digs, but toward the end I voiced an objection:

> My final quibble with this book is not so much with the idea of a lost generation as with the notion of a "generation"—so far as this suggests a "group"—at all. The "sense of group identity" that Cowley imputes to his gathering of writers strikes me as mostly a myth. Beyond their contemporaneity the only thing they had absolutely in common was talent and a passionate dedication to writing, which practically all good writers have. The critic tries to attribute a considerable amount of common historical experience to them as well, but the thing that is supposed to have done most to "lose" them

> was the War, and of his eight writers five were never in it. Some of these people read some of the others, but by and large they did not—except by reputation—know each other well enough to nod. They had no real consciousness of any group; only Fitzgerald, the most generous, seems ever to have thought about "My Generation" at all. What had Faulkner and Hemingway to do with Cummings, Wilder, and Crane?

And so on. I did admit the fact that Hemingway and Crane were both born on July 21, 1899, and had died of their own volition—even conceded that Hemingway had a theory about Crane's suicide ("picked up the wrong sailor"). And I held off saying that some of these writers—Faulkner and Wolfe, for two—did not strike me as Lost Generation writers at all. But I did suggest that the critic had spent so much time compiling lists of American writers born between 1891 and 1905—which he began in 1951 with 224 names, and extends in this book to 385—because listing and counting obscure the fact that something else is missing: the sense of identity that makes a group a group. I dodged the question of "lost" as hopelessly vague.

Malcolm responded to me in a letter of some length. He was not as pleased as I wanted him to be with what I had intended overall as a tribute (it appeared right beside Austin Warren's "Homage to Allen Tate"; some of Cowley's friends, however, were pleased). He was, he said, in mild disgruntlement, and his main objection was right here: even if they seldom met together the writers of his Second Flowering (which he now refers to as "wartime" generation, despite his subtitle) really did make a group. Some of them were old college chums, but more they thought of themselves as brothers in arms, up the establishment. Where, he wanted to know, did I get the idea that five of his eight were never in the war?

Well, from history, or biography—specifically from Cowley. Fitzgerald and Faulkner, he goes on, were in uniform even if they didn't get overseas, and both imagined themselves dead on the battlefield. Wolfe and Crane were too young to be drafted; but they and Kenneth Burke and Matty Josephson worked in shipyards. Well again, I was never too young to be drafted, and have never worked in a shipyard, but I think things go on there that are different from war. I am committed to the importance and validity of vicarious experience, so I have to credit the combat fantasies of Fitzgerald and Faulkner as meaningful, but I don't have to consider them the same as being there in the vulnerable flesh.

Mr. Cowley concludes this part of the letter, the only relevant part, by saying that he could go on and on defending his concept, and that in his book he was really thinking of a larger group, and most of *them* were soldiers.

I'm not sure that is valid, though to be sure it was Cowley himself who earlier pointed out the remarkable number of writers-to-be who drove ambulances or camions in World War I; Dos Passos, Cummings, Hemingway, Julian Green, Harry Crosby, John Howard Lawson, Louis Bromfield, Dashiell Hammett (and Cowley), among others. Thus as I pondered these matters I was slow in recognizing something more obvious: the old problem of a writer having some essays that could appear together in a book, and a publisher willing to issue it, and then through the title, and preface or introduction, writer or publisher or both trying to impose more unity on the pieces than they actually have. Thus what Malcolm is saying to me is that there *was* a Generation, but that its members were not the people he put under the heading of one this time. Without the subtitle, and the concept that is supposed to inform the book and help hold it together (and the overfamiliar material) there was nothing basically the matter.

And perhaps the trouble with me, among others, is literal-or narrow-mindedness. But it does seem to me that to qualify for membership in this group a writer should 1) have had experience of World War I—at least osmotic from having been on the scene of some of it, and 2) have spent some bohemian period in Paris. If we accept that, then of the writers in Cowley's recent collection exactly three qualify: Cummings, Dos Passos, and Hemingway. Some generation. If we ease up a little and require only one of these criteria we still eliminate Faulkner and Wolfe as a minimum.

To appreciate the importance of that war to those who were in it, most of us have to read, study. There is nothing in our personal histories that would allow us to understand intuitively. A well known novelist who *was* too young for World War II has often told me how he envies my experience of it; I would hand it to him gratis if I could, on a worn silver platter. I do not believe that my long involvement in that fracas had *any* lasting effect on me; even my hatred of the military diminishes as the years go by. All I wanted was to get out of uniform and on with other matters. My war was no watershed; there was no orgy of pleasure or relief at its passing. No Jazz Age: new problems, A Bomb, Cold War. No crash of the stock market to terminate a tidy period like the Twenties. I can't even remember any parties. The first war was very different in its effect on people, and the great esthetic exile that followed it was based on the previous experience of Europe, even though in most cases that had been unpleasant. Those young men were fantastically eager to get in it; I've forgotten how many times Hemingway flunked his physical (such a dream in my day!) before the Red Cross finally took him. And it was the War that did most to "disengage" them from society, and make them restless for more adventures abroad. But for the war there would have been no Twenties as we know them, and no expatriation on the scale we measure. It was a new world, which Fitzgerald with his Princeton commission and Brooks Brothers uniform described rather well: "this thing, knocked to pieces, leaky, red hot, threatening to blow up . . ."

Paris, my second criterion, made a difference—first of all because it was not America. I have seen a letter Hemingway wrote up in Michigan shortly after the war in which he says he was willing to die for this country but would be damned if he'd live in it. It is ironic that America should remember so warmly those who only wanted to get out. And it is seldom remarked how little they knew about their country and its cultural past. Cowley confessed for them all some time ago their ignorance of virtually all American literature before 1910, his date. There is a lot they would have liked, as many of them eventually did, in Melville, Whitman, and even Emerson, Thoreau, and Hawthorne. As late as 1935 Hemingway could dismiss *Moby-Dick* out of hand (later on he rectified that), pronounce Thoreau (whose prose he failed to surpass) "unreadable," and lump together Emerson, Hawthorne, and Whittier. I doubt that he had read one of them. A man who can claim as he did that Emerson did not know that a new classic bears no relation to old classics could not have read even "The American Scholar," most famous of the essays, which says exactly that but much better.

But, if they were getting out, why Paris? Anyone who reads books at all knows the answers to that; a single one, Hemingway's *Moveable Feast*—very minor, very beautiful—will provide many of them. But I like to think of the man who came after the ball was over, swept up the debris, and wrote the American expatriate epitaph. Henry Miller didn't arrive until 1930, and was already 38. It was a different Paris now—Quasimodo's Paris, he called it—and a different sort of American in it. The streets were cancerous to his view; he once went five days with nothing to eat. For some reason I always remember the line: "Irene [a Russian princess] has the clap, Osborn has bronchitis, and I have the piles." His adventures burlesqued the expatriate romance, the potentially tragic hero of it was now a clown. Time was that no literate American came back from Paris without an illegal *Tropic of Cancer* smuggled away in his luggage. Miller had penetrated deepest into the city and established a quite different vision of it, at once comic, anguished, and corrosive. But even he, looking back later, would remember a city whose atmosphere was "saturated with creation"; of a miserable place where he had lived for years would say "the whole street is given up to quiet, joyous work . . . men and women devoted to things of the spirit." If Miller could remember it that way, anyone could.

But if the experience of a particular war and of a particularly attractive city were extremely important in the lives of at least a few young American writers that does not make them automatically a "generation," nor mean that they were a "lost" one. In his *After the Lost Generation,* John Aldridge called it a generation in the "purest sense." But what makes a "generation"? First, I should think, its members should have been born at about the same time. So does Mr. Cowley, and to demonstrate that the writers of his generation were so born he worked up his list of 385 names of American writers. There is nothing objectionable about this as a hobby; it is not a bad way to keep busy without actually working. But I think the list has almost no significance. In the first place, to get it that long he has to come up with some very remarkable writers. Mathilde Eiker, Margarete Leech, and Charles Merz, all born in 1893: identify two out of three. In the second place, to get so many names he has to let the period of birth run from 1891 to 1905. It does not seem to me that anyone born fourteen years before or after I was would belong to my generation—if there were one. Further: if we took the years 1930–1944, and really scraped the barrel, would it be so hard to come up with as many names? No, it wouldn't.

For a number of people to constitute a recognizable generation, in the second place, there has to be some sense of affinity among them, a consciousness of self as part of a group, a feeling of things shared. Perhaps Cowley thinks as he does about his writers because he, at least, has exactly what it takes to belong—not just the war and Paris, but this very awareness: his first literary essay, written in 1921, was called "This Youngest Generation." Fitzgerald, too well fixed financially to live the bohemian life in France and never in the war, also felt himself part of a larger whole. But this requires a magnanimity of spirit and a degree of humility— a willingness to recognize that one is not all that unique—that these two men were blessed with and a lot of other writers lacked.

"Hemingway had no feeling for the group," Malcolm wrote me. I believe it. Faulkner, Wolfe—one could make his own list of those who didn't.

As for Lost, that is a big little word, and far from clear in the present connection. If I understood *Exile's Return,* Cowley meant by it that the people he was writing about were uprooted, unattached to any region or tradition; were educated for a different world than they graduated into, and accepted no older guides to conduct. All this makes an uncertain amount of sense. But if the same observations may be made of the Beat Generation, or the nameless one of the American Sixties, then what? John Aldridge remarked that the same expatriate writers felt themselves "the specially doomed and forsaken"; this is the Poor Little Lamb-Kipling-Wiffenpoof concept. It might be found in the likes of a very early Dos Passos novel called *One Man's Initiation,* but that is lost too. Lost has many meanings, few of which apply here. "Lacking in confidence"? No. As in "no longer visible"? Scarcely. "Ruined or destroyed"? Harry Crosby, and if you include him perhaps Hart Crane. "Spiritually or morally ruined or destroyed"? In the eyes of some of their elders, it may be, or the devout. Art was the religion, morality was subject to redefinition. They were not ruined in their own eyes.

The point might be not they *were* lost but *had* lost—such things as the values of pre-war, middle class America, the virtues of their upbringing. There certainly was a Generation Gap: Hemingway and his parents presented a bottomless case, and he was not alone. Yet that things had *been* lost is still misleading, since the values had been intentionally discarded. Lost as meaning "inaccessible to good influence" expresses what the *patron* of Gertrude Stein's garage meant about his mechanic *perdue* and little else.

In fact, there is news on that score. The definitive account of how "Une Génération Perdue" came about was given for all time by Hemingway in *A Moveable Feast,* and so was his contempt for the term. The *patron* told Miss Stein's mechanic "You are all a *génération perdue.*" Then she applied it to Hemingway. "That's what you all are. All of you young people who served in the war. You are a lost génération." He then dismisses "her lost generation talk and all the dirty, easy labels." But this story has now been independently annihilated by James R. Mellow in his book on Stein, and by revelations taken from the Hemingway manuscripts at the Kennedy Library by Jacqueline Tavernier-Courbin. The plain facts are that "The Lost Generation—A Novel" was the author's original title for his *Sun Also Rises,* and that when he first wrote the tale of the lost mechanic it had nothing whatsoever to do with war. Neither the *patron* nor Hemingway mentions the war. I think we should speak of "the so-called Lost Generation," or at the very least put the term in quotes.

As for the *Lost Generation Journal,* I regret having predicted in 1975 that it was about to expire. As of 1988, it has not done so, though its last issued is dated 1986. I bring you the latest word. If you'd like to subscribe the editor is Thomas W. Wood, Jr., and home plate is Box 167-D, Route 1, St. James, MO 65559.

1975; 1990

14.

The Lost Generation and Yours

Except for nature, it's been a long time since things have looked good in the spring. Here you go—Out into the World, as they say—with your country in the grip of unpardonable war, racial crisis, urban crisis, and so forth—and all of us still existing in the shadow of a great bomb that may yet wipe us out before our time. You'll forgive me, I think, if I recall the day 31 years ago when I sat out there, never dreaming I'd ever stand up here: no way. The only thing I remember about the address at my commencement (except for the length of it) is that I didn't listen, so I shouldn't expect you to. (I'm told it's parents who pay attention on these occasions.) I attended many of my professors in those days, but the characters that got brought in from outside were usually something else instead. We didn't have the word Establishment for them yet—an import from Great Britain. But that's who they were, and what they were beginning to peddle was World War II, about which my mind was Made Up; we should stay out of it. During the days immediately surrounding my graduation, look what happened. Germany and Italy invaded France, the Allied armies were driven clean off the continent of Europe, the Germans took Paris without a fight (unbelievable!), and France surrendered. My isolationist position was to be shot down with a lot of others at Pearl Harbor, and I spent 4½ years in the Field Artillery. Do you mind if I wish you better luck?

A commencement address delivered at Westminster College, May 30, 1971

I have often thought that I should have been born just short of a generation before I was: too young for World War I, but old enough to get good and Lost for a few years. The "Lost Generation" was really not a bad one to be in, especially if you were a literary-minded fellow and could have lived it up with all those writers and artists in Paris in the Twenties. Never before or since such a sense that life and letters were being born anew as then and there, never such exhilaration at having escaped this country. The food was cheap and more than good; wine was nearly free; you could live extremely well in that then-finest and most beautiful of cities on $25 per week—that's for two.

I have undertaken to talk about that generation and yours because they are probably the two most significant, publicized and distinct of identifiable generations of this century in America. Yours is still nameless, I think. I have been reading about it in a couple of "authoritative" books: Theodore Roszak's *Making a Counter Culture,* and Charles Reich's *Greening of America,* which is currently the bestselling hardback in America. Here is announced the start of a new culture in our country—a culture which is the product of the young, for the basis of the argument is that "most of what is presently happening that is new, provocative and engaging in politics, education, the arts, and social relations . . . is the creation of youth." Raised permissively by Dr. Spock, and in parental affluence (so prosperity is simply assumed), young people rebel not just against their parents but society at large, which is now a "technocracy." The new culture involves a new way of looking at things, as first conceived by Allen Ginsberg's poem "Howl"—which, we are told, was written in an afternoon. It protests "I am a human being: do not mutilate, spindle or tear" (and the motto, of course, is Make Love Not War). Anti-scientific, anti-materialistic, anti-cerebral, it is just not interested in the prodigious economic and technological feats of our time; it is dedicated instead to the "non-intellective" aspects of life; it subjugates "things" and celebrates human life and well-being. Science built the technocracy, but is no longer the route to knowledge, for science "negates or subordinates visionary experience" and thus "commits the sin of diminishing our existence." The focus of consciousness shifts to the Far East—oriental religion and mysticism, for the question is no longer "How shall we know?" but "How shall we live?" To find that out we must reinstate the magical world-view from which human creativity and community derived.

Reich's book announces that this counter-culture is about to produce a revolution against the technocracy (which he calls the Corporate

State)—an elevation to a "higher reason" and a more human community of "liberated individuals." Rock, pot, acid, bell-bottoms—these are not "passing fads" but the sign of something really significant: we have moved into "Consciousness III." Consciousness I was the early, American, pioneering, self-sufficient (or "inner directed") moralistic spirit that in time gave way to Consciousness II, the cooperative, organization-minded (or "other directed") moralistic spirit that sacrificed itself and its immediate interests for the good of the whole. Consciousness III is "greening America" with its spirit: wide-eyed, open to experience, innocent, anti-consumptionist, radically subjective, less "moral" than loving. And the revolution is surely coming, because its foe, the machine called the Corporate State, has begun to self-destruct (as when the commercial on TV demands a hedonistic consumption of goods and the news program it pays for exposes the murderous reality of Viet Nam). All this got started in the late Sixties when, united by a revulsion against that war, the young showed (by letting their hair grow, putting on costumes, blaring rock music, taking "trips," and so on) that they were disaffiliating from parents, schools, the drift and draft of our society, competition, discrimination, and all the rest—even logic and reason—to affiliate with their own generation. They've liberated their minds to "wonder and awe," and they proclaim in the face of society "Myself I Sing." Science, technology, the State will soon play but a subordinate, marginal part in our lives; a new heaven, a new earth are at hand.

I did not make any of that up: it's for real. But I did not come here this afternoon without a reaction to it, either—a thesis, indeed, which I can put into a sentence. The Lost Generation, in my opinion, was not lost, and yours isn't found. The irony of the lost generation as a tag is that the man who did most to popularize it had himself rejected it from the start. Thinking it a piece of "splendid bombast," Hemingway in his posthumously published memoirs of the Paris days recalled how he had disputed Miss Stein, who had got the phrase from the proprietor of a garage that had been slow in fixing her car. His disavowal was prophetic. The Twenties were to see the richest flowering of American letters since the so-called "American Renaissance" of our mid-19th century—a great part of it written by people who knew exactly what they were up to.

My misgivings about the green or counter culture will take longer to describe. I would first point out that a great deal—indeed most—of what's supposed to be "new, provocative, and engaging" in all this may provoke and engage some, but is not new at all. A lot of it is simply carried over from the Beat Generation, which flourished from say, 1956 till 1960; much of it is a repeat of the lost generation, 1919–1929; most of it was said (although a great deal better) during the "American Renaissance," 1850–1855, which I mentioned a moment ago. The Beats were also rebels from society, who decided that the way down is the way out. Voluntarily poor, anti-materialistic, anti-rationalistic, anarchic, individualistic, freaked out, they clustered in their communities, or wandered the country, celebrating joy, illumination, drugs, sex, mysticism—anything that makes one receptive to life. And so, like the present generation, were the Losts alienated from their country by a war; they rejected their parents and middle-class American culture for the same reasons as today: materialism, prudery, inhibition, hypocrisy. Substitute alcohol for drugs, jazz for rock, and most of it will fit. The Losts like the Beats knew what fun was to be found in poverty, bohemia, anarchy; the ideas and "life style" of Henry Miller, perhaps the sole transitional figure, are a very close precedent for what we are hearing about today. Even the form of rejecting traditional philosophy—the question is now not "How shall we know?" but "How shall we live?"—can be located in *The Sun Also Rises,* the lost generation's manifesto, where Hemingway writes "I did not care what it was all about. All I wanted to know was how to live in it."

More audible still, in the New Consciousness, are the echoes of mid-19th century American Romanticism: Emerson, Thoreau, Whitman—all three of whom preached non-conformity, anti-materialism, and joy. The archetypal American anti-materialist was Ralph Waldo Emerson ("Things are in the saddle/And ride mankind. . . . Things are of the snake.") He was also our first prominent student of oriental mysticism. But for present purposes he is most important for the influence he exerted in different ways on Thoreau and Whitman, neither of whom could have existed as we know them without him. Thoreau simply put Emerson's theories into practice, and—at Walden Pond—Thoreau became the great-grandfather of all American drop outs—living on almost nothing (but health foods, which he raised himself). A mystic, wide-open to nature, he was also an anarchist, and the originator of the idea of passive resistance. His masterpiece is *Walden,* and its announced subject is "How shall we live?"

Whitman, too, was visionary, and the true patron saint of America's "greening." "Myself I Sing" *is* Whitman, and it was Whitman who first proposed "A Passage to India"—the name of his poem urging a merger with oriental thought. The poem "Howl" comes directly out of him with an assist from Henry Miller; indeed on reading it, I wonder what *else*

Ginsberg did on the afternoon he wrote it. Whitman with his rough clothes and beard, his absolute democracy, his refusal to discriminate among persons or even in nature—before it hits the road the counter culture should have his "Song of Myself" by heart, and *Walden* in the knapsack.

In short it seems to me that the current rebellion against American culture in general is not only not new but is a perennial American growth, with roots deep in our tradition, that blossoms forth with pretty much the same flowers every so-many years on a schedule that may one day be charted. I have, however, more serious reservations about it—for example to the drug bit, a bad scene if I ever saw one. Quite apart from the obvious and terrible dangers in it, I tend to doubt the advisability of expanding minds that have as yet so little in them. Another thing: I find it hard to see how the new consciousness can express itself in a political manner, and how can you have a revolution without politics? An uneasy alliance with the New Left does not seem to have worked, and the anarchy implied or explicit in the movement would seem to make political organization impossible. Consciousness I and II took definite political forms (Republican and Democrat, very crudely), and III seems to be building a life style for a society it cannot bring about.

Most appalling to me is the fact that nowhere in what I've been reading is there an awareness of the vast area of choice that exists between the extremes of the counter culture and the technocracy. It's as though the whole infield and outfield of a baseball diamond were suddenly out-of-bounds—and nothing fair but far left and right. Disqualified without mention are all those who have *not* abandoned reason and the intellect but (1) do not embrace technology or the State, (2) care little about the Gross National Product or the Dow Jones, (3) oppose all forms of pollution, (4) never thought (with President Nixon) that the moonlanding was "the greatest event since the creation," (5) never thought that any part of the war in Viet Nam represented "America's finest hour," and so on. Of all positions that a thoughtful person might take, these books ignore all but two at the extremes; in between, where most of the people I know are living, you would think there is nobody.

There are lots of bodies there, and I live with them. Personally, I am not *about* to knock reason; it has obvious limits, but has—you know?—solved many problems in human history. I'm not even against science: do you think Zen Buddhism is going to come up with a cure for cancer? To be truthful, I'm not even against materialism—not when I remember that one-third of the world's people are starving to death while we sit here (many of them in countries far-advanced in non-scientific thought). But none of this means that I am implacably opposed to the youth movement, especially when I return to your graduating class—much of which, I realize, isn't very far into the counter culture. The largest class in the nation's history, it is moving into the leanest job market of recent memory—but without, so far as I have seen, much bitterness or panic. The old Puritan or Protestant "work ethic" (work hard, save, don't ease up, nose to the grindstone, don't look around) is clearly weakening as its limitations become obvious. Instead of letting the job determine what they are going to become, some graduates are determined to find what they are first. Some are going into "alternate vocations," which can be very rewarding. Despite the long-term trend to specialization, a new social orientation has been widely detected among those headed for the professions—law students interested in social change, medical students headed for the public health service, graduate students in my own areas less concerned with "scholarship" than with teaching the young. Started with the Peace Corps, a generous concern for the well-being of others now pervades the country, and *it* says "My Unself I Sing."

I don't know what will happen with all the *anti*-social energy that's recently been generated too (except I know that one thing which always happens to youth is middle age). Nor do I suppose I have answers to the thorny problems that sharply face us—unless an impossible one. But I do know that we had all of us better keep the channels open—eyes, ears, minds, hearts. (It was for listening to his kids that Secretary Hickel got bounced out of the Nixon administration, and how, my friends would ask, can you improve on that?) The mistake of young people, if I may pontificate for a moment, is a failure to know or appreciate the massive and subtle pressures that have molded their parents (and are just as surely if differently molding them). And the mistake of age is to let those deep-sea pressures fracture the ear-drum until it doesn't hear what the young are saying. The result is rage on both sides: the kid who bites the hand that fed him right up to the shoulder, the parent who tells her Kent State child "they should have shot you too."

In drawing to a close I would remind that Christian lady of a saying: "a society that hates its young has no future." To deny the young is to deny tomorrow, and unless we believe in tomorrow what are we doing here today? Faith, hope, charity—we need all we can get of each (though I sometimes doubt that I have enough of any). I spoke a moment ago of an "impossible solution," by which I meant an answer that I despair of our ever getting to in time. You know it too; it is a very old one. But for me the poet Auden put it best for our age when he wrote, in the dark days just before *my* graduation from college, "We must love one another or die." To that I would only add that I told you I wasn't against you: if any generation—mine, the lost, or yours—has or ever had a head-start in the direction Auden points to, it is assuredly yours.

Written in 1971, previously unpublished

15.

Scott Fitzgerald's Waste Land

"To T. S. Eliot, the master of us all." Thus Fitzgerald in the front of his *Great Gatsby* when first it appeared in 1925. Eliot, whose long poem *The Waste Land* of three years earlier Fitzgerald had particularly revered, read the novel, and paid its author a tribute in return. But as for any basic similarity between the books, which might in some small way help account for the mutual admiration of two rather dissimilar writers—no one seems to have clearly seen one. Fitzgerald himself is not known to have done so, and Eliot has said, in a letter to the present writer, that although he retains his high opinion of the novel he sees no connection between it and his poem. The notion that the two works have some vague resemblance is not highly original, but as far as is known they have never been really compared.

There is nothing especially surprising about that, for to the casual eye they do not seem to have much in common save their rough contemporaneity, their deserved status as modern "classics" and a severe compression in the writing. Eliot's poem on the civilization of our time, seen in terms of a sort of mythic dust bowl, and Fitzgerald's novel about a young man of suspicious money who is destroyed while mixing with the wealthy of Long Island in the Twenties, look, even perhaps to the more careful eye, very unlike.

In several ways, they are. Long thought of by many people as a book about "wild parties," Gatsby has at the very least three serious general points to make—one for each of the three principal men in the novel: Jay Gatsby, the murdered parvenu; Tom Buchanan, who is indirectly responsible for Gatsby's death; and Nick Carraway, the narrator, and commentator on the action. And two of these themes have nothing whatever to do with Eliot.

Fitzgerald's point about Gatsby is not difficult to see: he has composed for him a peculiarly American tragedy. Sponsored as a boy by a type of 19th-century pioneer, appropriately named Dan Cody, Gatsby has worked his way up to becoming a kind of 20th century version of his benefactor (his great wealth is probably the wages of bootlegging). The result of a near-realization of his own Platonic—one could just as well say Emersonian—conception of himself, but dedicated to meretricious ends which cannot get him what he wants (among other things, Tom Buchanan's wife, Daisy), Gatsby could have existed in no other country. A man of "corruption . . . concealing his incorruptible dream," a man with a "heightened sensitivity to the promises of life," a "gift for hope, a romantic readiness," and even a romantic conception of love—all go to introduce this emphasis on Gatsby's American-ness. Several other touches establish and clinch it: his father's notion, "he'd of been a great man . . . like James J. Hill," a comparison which Nick uncomfortably recognizes as valid; the beat-up boyhood copy of "Hopalong Cassidy"; and the adolescent "Schedule," taken straight from America's true prototype, Benjamin Franklin ("Study electricity, etc . . . 7.15–8.15 A.M. . . . Study needed invention . . . 7.00–9.00 P.M."), as well as the "General Resolves" which follow ("Read one improving book or magazine per week. Save $5.00 [crossed out] $3 per week . . ."). "It just shows you," as his father said. Thus when all the information is in, and Gatsby is dead, at the hands of a crazed Mr. Wilson who thinks Gatsby, and not Daisy Buchanan (as was the case) has killed Mrs. Wilson in a hit-and-run accident, it becomes clear that what Fitzgerald has sketched is a tragedy as essentially American in its nature as any Dreiser ever wrote.

Tom Buchanan's part in all this goes to establish that "the very rich are different from you and me"—as Fitzgerald had said in an earlier story. To this famous remark, Ernest Hemingway famously rejoined, "Yes, they have more money." On this occasion Hemingway may be said to have had the wit, but Fitzgerald the truth; his treatment of the Buchanans is a deft incision to the heart of the difference, and one no other American writer has been able to make so knowingly.

This is the element of the novel that connects the other two themes: if the very rich were not different, Gatsby would not have been killed and Nick would not have so soon soured on these people and walked out of their lives, registering Fitzgerald's moral disapproval and final point. The scene in which the idea is put across is very quick: it is simply an image glimpsed through a rift in a drawn blind. Tom is talking intently to his wife; he covers her hand with his and she nods in agreement. But the picture is a revelation, and it does not take much ingenuity to figure out what was said—and what it did not need saying; for Daisy need only be reminded of certain fundamental truths—that we did not hear. Gatsby is willing to take the blame for the accident, and the Buchanans are going to let him. Out of an hysterical sense of their own crucial importance and special worth, Tom and Daisy must reaffirm a marriage that had fallen apart, close ranks, and accept without a word Gatsby's foolish gesture as one properly due them. Their wealth, in short, has marked them off from ordinary, traditional standards of behavior as profoundly as if they were gangsters. What the sociologists might call an "in-group" feeling permits them to override decency and morality in the very name of these virtues. Later, when the conspiracy has come off successfully, Nick confirms this view of Tom's behavior:

> I saw that what he had done was, to him, entirely justified. . . . They were careless people, Tom and Daisy—they smashed up things and creatures and then retreated back into their money or their vast carelessness, or whatever it was that kept them together, and let other people clean up the mess they had made . . .

And here Nick takes his leave, ridding them of "my provincial squeamishness forever."

In many ways it is Nick, at times apparently only the man telling the story, who is the central figure in this novel. Before it is easiest to see what his scruples and judgments mean, however, it is necessary to consider Mr. Eliot's *Waste Land.* And for the purpose of refreshing memories of that enormously complex work it may be legitimate to mutilate it a little by extracting such of its features as are relevant here.

As is well known, Eliot based his poem on some ancient fertility myths, reputedly the origins of the Grail legend, and principally concerned with a wasted land, a blighted place where vegetation fails and animals are unable to reproduce themselves. A Fisher King, ruler of this unhappy region, has suffered a genital wound or disease; his impotence is thus appropriate to his realm. Eliot's conception of the spiritual sterility of the contemporary world is his reason for seeing it in the terms of the legends. With the loss of the knowledge of good and evil, on which our very difference from the animals depends, human experience has simply lost its meaning.

Part I of the poem includes, among several other things, many allusions to other writings, which either hint at the superiority of the past, or find past precedents for the unhappy vision, as in an echo from Ecclesiastes—a "heap of broken images, where the sun beats, / And the dead tree gives no shelter . . . / And the dry stone no sound of water,"—where desire fails and all is vanity.

The second section presents two instances, upper and lower class, of contemporary life without faith, and thus without hope or meaning. Surrounded by reminders of the magnificence of the past the wealthy have no part in it. In an ornate setting, a couple plays chess, a mechanical activity of those who have nothing to do. The lady's "nerves are bad." She asks what she shall do: "What shall we do tomorrow? What shall we ever do?" And at the opposite social pole two women in a pub, speaking vulgarly of abortion and promiscuous adultery, are overheard. Eliot, murky in the background, is giving us our choice.

It is in the third part that Tiresias, legendary expert on sexual matters, appears to witness what happens now at "the violet hour"—that crucial time of promise at the end of the working day "when the eyes and back / Turn upward from the desk, when the human engine waits / Like a taxi throbbing waiting . . ." A shopgirl, betraying the moment, goes home to a solitary supper taken out of tins, and then on her divan indifferently accepts the pleasureless, pointless assault of an objectionable young man.

Other loveless-affairs follow, to a similar effect, and finally, in the concluding fifth part, the death of contemporary civilization is envisaged, the waste land is sketched again, and the poem approaches its end with the Fisher King wondering: "Shall I at least set my lands in order?" He then speaks of the "fragments I have shored against my ruins," and on this note, among others, the poem closes.

An interesting series of parallels between this poem and Ernest Hemingway's *The Sun Also Rises* (1926) has been established, most elaborately by Richard P. Adams, but the affinity between it and *Gatsby* is every bit as remarkable. Hemingway had in common with the poet principally a protagonist who was literally emasculated, and whose land had gone figuratively sterile as a result. With Fitzgerald the situation is reversed; he starts with a literally sterile section of land, an ash dump, and makes it both a severe comment on the people who live near it, and a kind of "cause" of the impotence of the character, Mr. Wilson, who ultimately destroys Gatsby.

This "waste land"—Fitzgerald's own phrase, and an ominous symbol—is very specifically described. Bounded on one side by "a foul river," it is

> a valley of ashes—a fantastic farm where ashes grow like wheat into ridges and hills and grotesque gardens; where ashes take the forms of houses and chimneys and rising smoke and, finally, with a transcendent effort, of ash-gray men, who move dimly and already crumbling through the powdery air.

Halfway between Manhattan and the Long Island homes of Jay Gatsby, Daisy and Tom Buchanan, and Nick Carraway, this area (it fittingly "hasn't got any name") is the dead center of the book. It is the scene of the climax of the plot, the auto-accident; and Gatsby's estate, around which the action might at first glance seem to revolve, is really but an ornate façade to this terrible place. The symbol has another side to it, though, for "brooding over the solemn dumping ground," "dimmed a little by many paintless days," are the eyes of Dr. T. J. Eckleburg's sign:

> . . . blue and gigantic—their retinas are one yard high. They look out of no face, but, instead, from a pair of enormous yellow spectacles which pass over a non-existent nose. Evidently some wild wag of an oculist . . .

Eventually we see this scene as the essence of Fitzgerald's judgment on the whole picture of society his story describes: blindness extending out over the totally barren remains of the past. We might also note that the symbol is extremely like Eliot in its second half, as well as its first, for as the poet remarked of a later waste land of his, which The Hollow Men inhabit: "There are no eyes here / In this valley of dying stars / In this hollow valley / This broken jaw of our lost kingdoms . . . Sightless . . ."

Living above a garage, and right beside the ash-land ("contiguous to absolutely nothing") are Mr. and Mrs. Wilson, married twelve years and childless. It is strongly implied that the "spiritless" Mr. Wilson, as Fitzgerald calls him, is at "fault" here; he is "that ashen fantastic figure" as though the land had taken his own fertility from him. Mrs. Wilson, to complicate matters, has a "panting vitality," and although thoroughly vulgar is satisfactory to Tom Buchanan. The relationships of Tom, aristocratic husband of the aristocratic Daisy, thus introduce life on an upper and lower class level, as the narrator accompanies him from wife to mistress and back. In both classes this life, as revealed again mainly by women, is equally hopeless. Alcohol does no better than chess, and echoing the lady who played that game in the poem ("What shall we do tomorrow? What shall we ever do?"), Daisy asks for help: "What'll we plan? . . . What do people plan?" And when an unbearable heat (where the sun beats, and the dead tree gives no shelter) intensifies her desperation, she cries "What'll we do with ourselves this afternoon? And the day after that, and the next thirty years?"

When Tom gives a party with Mrs. Wilson and her friends (where a little dog looking on "with blind eyes through the smoke" serves as a telling reminder of Eckleburg's eyes and the ash dump), we witness the same inadequacy of life among the lowly. In its messy and oppressive tone the party is more reminiscent of "Sweeney among the Nightingales" than of Eliot's cockney pub, but again Fitzgerald's point is exactly the same: life on Manhattan Island among the "people" is no more fruitful or meaningful than life on Long Island among their "superiors."

As in the earlier waste land, one telling symptom of general chaos in *Gatsby* is that most traditions are broken or lost. There is no religious faith; God's functions are taken over by an advertisement for eyeglasses. Tom, a decayed survival of what may once have been a competent aristocracy, is reduced to corruption and the vicious ignorant speeches he makes. Gatsby's fabulous parties—the perfect examples of collapsed traditions—are attended by uninvited people who are unknown to a host they do not bother to meet. Surrounded by the magnificence of the past as provided in Gatsby's mansion, no one participates in it; the really remarkable thing about the Gothic library is that the books in it are real—"have pages and everything." Soon Gatsby, standing guard over Daisy outside her house while she betrays and deserts him, is at one with Dr. Eckleburg's eyes, and the poor dog at the party—"blindly watching over nothing," as Fitzgerald puts it. And when he is dead no one indebted to him but Nick attends his funeral. Nick, that is, and Gatsby's pathetic father, and the "owl-eyed" man who made the remark about the books. He is owl-eyed because of the thickness of his glasses, and rain at the burial makes it even harder for him to see. But in contrast to Dr. Eckleburg's pervasive blindness, and the blindness of all the others, he—holding to the old forms, admiring the books and bothering to come to the funeral—does just barely "see."

Nick, who clearly speaks for Fitzgerald, sees a little too, and his final perception is to be Eliot's. But first, prematurely old and tired, he is Tiresias (as was also, incidentally, the hero of *The Sun Also Rises*). He is the passive witness, that is, to adultery in which he does not participate and on which he is commentator. Eliot's "I Tiresias," we recall, waits "at the violet hour, when the eyes and back / Turn upward from the desk, when the human engine waits / Like a taxi throbbing waiting," and then observes only a waste of time—the lonely canned-dinner of the typist and the fatuous ministrations of the clerk. Fitzgerald's Tiresias, at the same hour, sometimes (in his mind) also follows anonymous women home to their flats. And he says, immediately following this admission,

> At the enchanted metropolitan twilight I felt a haunting loneliness . . . poor young clerks who loitered in front of windows waiting until it was time for a solitary restaurant dinner—young clerks in the dusk, wasting the most poignant moments of night and life.
>
> Again at eight o'clock, when the dark lanes of the Forties were lined five deep with throbbing taxicabs . . . I felt a sinking in my heart.

After his final disenchantment with his corrupted friends, a sobered Nick Carraway finds himself (like the protagonist of Eliot's poem) brooding on the superiority of the past, and appealing to certain traditions of an earlier era. He justly perceives in himself the strength of an honesty and decency which the others have lacked. He has learned the merit of his own background which taught him such values, and at the end of the novel, pondering how much better a place Long Island had been long ago before it was spoiled, he withdraws a thousand miles to his home: "a little complacent from growing up in the Carraway house in a city where dwellings are still called through the decades by a family's name"—the opposites, clearly, of Gatsby's estate, which was a luxurious counterpart to the furnished rooms and one-night cheap hotels of Eliot's transient, uprooted civilization. In the end, in short, the protagonist, very like Eliot's, feeling that the world has lost sight of his tradition, longs to reclaim it. Can he at least set his lands in order? These fragments he shores against his ruins.

We have by no means exhausted the possibilities of this parallelism. A hotel Metropole, the odd sound "jug-jug," and "death-by-water," for instances, figure in both works. A case might be made for saying that Mrs. Buchanan, Daisy, is a species of "hyacinth girl," Meyer Wolfshiem a sort of Mr. Eugenides; and something might be done with the fact that Gatsby himself is said to be committed "to the following of a grail."

In such an undertaking as this one, however, it is important to know when to put on the brakes; perhaps we should stop here, and investigate instead a question that would come up of its own accord: how much of all this did Fitzgerald know? It is not possible, really, to answer that question with any assurance, or in a sentence. Some of these similarities are probably to be charged to coincidence—the similar use of "eyes," for instance, blind over a valley of ashing stars: "The Hollow Men" and *Gatsby* were written about the same time, and published in the same year. (Besides, as Arthur Mizener has explained in his biography of the novelist, Fitzgerald probably got that idea from an illustrated dust-jacket he had seen). As for *The Waste Land,* surely certain aspects of it had made a deep impression on the young novelist (on one extraordinary occasion, some years later, he went so far as to read a section of it to its author, to show him how it should go). It would be rather difficult to believe, therefore, that he was not aware of the precedent for his significant ash dump, and he might well have conceded, if ever asked, that Eliot had provided the model for several other things. On the other hand, the very closeness of the passages that approach paraphrase could be used to argue that at these points Fitzgerald was quite unaware of the real source of his thoughts and images, or else—an honest man—he would have changed what he wrote. What we would have here, then, would be a striking case of "unconscious influence."

In the end it is best to urge only what contributes to the present purpose, which is to suggest unremarked subtleties in Fitzgerald's remarkable book. Here the question of indebtedness is to be put aside, and the point would be simply the notion that to establish certain parallels between *The Great Gatsby* and *The Waste Land* is to throw new light on the richness and depth of that already widely admired novel.

1956; 1964

16.

Iowa City, and After

> *. . . for men's normal growth in virtue and wisdom comes from the imitations of their heroes: their history is that of their friendships and their admirations.*—AUSTIN WARREN

I can only tell how it was with me then, hoping that since Austin was so large a part of how it was, a little will emerge of how *he* was. "Then" was just before the Second War—University of Iowa, he a professor and I a graduate student of English. Commonplace enough, but the situation was anything but that, for my rather literal and hopelessly secular mind found itself suddenly churched—by someone who not only inhabited this world with an intensity that had no precedent in my experience, but also another world, "a universe whose reality is not mechanical or sensible but personal and miraculous." The Spiritual Life had been mostly a term to me; here was a man living one—dramatic, jagged, genuine. I thought Baroque was a style of architecture or music; here it was (I have just given a Warren definition) in the flesh.

Intense, and every bit as complex. His words came at you in quotation marks, or quotes within quotes; you had to be on your toes. Everything vibrated. He did conversational appoggiaturas, and could go off like a cadenza. He was witty, doubting, dedicated. Walled in by his passionate concerns (he once demanded of me to know why they were still playing baseball when football had begun; World Series was an inscrutable concept), he seemed a chain of firecrackers, a perpetual explosion of being. Or, such was the effect on me, an implosion.

I think our encounters then had no effect on him whatever. They permanently opened to me, however, a possibility of existence which I could never realize, but without the vision of which I doubt I'd have persisted in the vicissitudes of getting into this profession. I saw almost at once that "life" and "art" were both richer and more charged than ever suspected, and that the academy was not at all a bad place for either.

And, in a sense, I do not know him well. As he wrote recently, our relationship has been "unique: never intimates, we have intuitively understood, and evaluated, one another with more warmth, and more rigor, than the literal extent of our shared experience would seem to warrant." Exactly so. But after all these years he does recall certain "hours spent together," particularly at the house on Summit Avenue when Eleanor Blake Warren was still alive. I do, too.

Iowa City, when I arrived there in the sunny steam of September, 1941, was to my surprise full of excitement: around the clock graduate-student *bohème,* intrigue of various sorts, personality clashes and professional rivalries at high temperatures, music, painting, literary sophistication (the in-book was *Nightwood*). It took only days to discover that the nucleus of the little galaxy in which I found myself orbited was, like me, a small, energetic man from Massachusetts for whom the Hub was Home. "In his classroom," Austin has written, "Babbitt was an experience not before encountered nor ever to be forgotten." I will say the same of Warren. The classroom in this case was his office, where a few bright young people had at "New England Poetry" (somewhat ecumenically defined so as to include an Anglican from St. Louis). It was hypnotic. Our mentor performed such gyrations—twitched, grimaced, shot his jaw up and out so as surely to imperil his neck, tortured unlit cigarettes into tiny shreds—you'd have thought it hard to follow the words. But he fired questions, usually rhetorical, proposed comic absurdities or whimsical speculations, boomed with laughter, made sudden penetrations, and I missed nothing. Afterward the acolytes would sometimes go drink beer; I think we felt vaguely blessed.

Less vaguely when invited backstage, to the house on Summit. One cocktail party comes back remarkably clear. It ended with Austin (always

Mr. Warren in those days) playing strenuous hymns on the organ—he knew the good ones—and all of us singing (him with that unexpected baritone), and singing the best of all, "Let All Mortal Flesh Keep Silence," the loudest. (Other sounds echo: the stentorian tones in which he violated the pious hush of the university library; the startling crack in his own library of the spine of a new book—he broke its back to exalt its spirit, I believe.)

That strain once more; it bids remembrance rise. Especially of the evening when I was invited for dinner—not to have dinner but to take it—with Eleanor. Mrs. Warren is also vivid still, a striking, dignified, gracious woman with a considerable intellectual life of her own (years later a friend told me of discussing Plato with her while she was dying), who was very kind to the sole guest. With religious objects and pictures all about, the house was a rectory of indeterminable denomination. We took roast lamb, and the image of Austin pouring the wine as if he had consecrated it—with a fresh, folded white towel and mischievous eyes—is after thirty-five years indelible, an epiphany.

The bell on this charmed world began tolling at Pearl Harbor, and before long I enlisted—in a sort of mild exasperation that people did not seem to have grasped the fact that a war was on and an age had ended. Perhaps Austin knew; we never discussed it. Whatever he was he was not draftable.

Nor, in my case, much of a prophet. His prognosis, friends told me, was that during the war I would find myself and not return to the university. Wrong on both counts; over four years later, astonished to find me a live civilian again, and mainly on the strength of things past, I went back to Iowa City. Where things past were truly past. An age had indeed ended, and to some extent there was a reversal of roles. Now Austin was single and less settled, while most of us were married and digging in—older and more "responsible" if no smarter, more professional if less interesting. No more *agnus dei;* Mr. Warren, as it appeared to my chance view, was living on cornflakes—variously, unceremoniously dished up—and, I believe, gin. (He would consent to eat fowl, an indulgence born of a hilarious hatred of chickens.)

The house was, physically, as I had pictured it. I lived in it over one Christmas vacation when he had gone to Boston—by Greyhound, as I recall, to "do penance." The point of my residence was chiefly to service a coal-burning monster by a process which he demonstrated to the accompaniment of such a dazzling prescription ("re*cal*citrant clinkers . . .

one THRUSTS . . .") that I retained nothing but the style and had to summon a repairman after the first ministration. This grieved Austin on his return; all things considered I think I disappointed him in many ways. I was full of complaints about how things were "run" in my program; he did not think that people of our calling should be expected to *run* anything. My new grey overcoat appalled him: "you look like a *Calvert* salesman." Most of all he wondered if I were truly *sérieux,* and to be sure I was more intent on seizing the degree and getting back East than anything else. (I suspect that question dogged him, though he never spoke it; twenty years later he wrote me—apropos of something sassy I had written—"you are as serious 'underneath' as anyone need be.")

On the other hand we often drank wine in his living room while listening to music over a giant mushroom of a speaker turned loud enough to panic the dead, not to speak of the neighbors (the brasses of Gabrieli's "In Ecclesiis" ring yet in the ears). And he told me once, beaming, "you always wince at the right places." In that room there was also one night a select party for "the other Warren." I was halfway through *All the King's Men,* just out, and very excited: "you just go on home and finish it," Robert Penn W. told me. But I stayed, and we did away with a remarkable amount of bourbon; I seemed the only one it affected much. And then that period ended.

Bound for Michigan, Austin left Iowa before I did, first having blown effectively on my spark of an idea for a Hemingway dissertation. And in the quarter century that has elapsed I have seen him only twice. We correspond sporadically, the lapses all on my end (he is a conscientious epistolarian, who writes the kind of letters you keep). We have sketched our similarly precipitous downs and ups, and discussed what we have been reading of each other's—virtually everything. In 1957 the *Sewanee Review* gave me the opportunity to pay public homage, in what was disguised as a review of *New England Saints,* his favorite among his books, and mine. (I realize I cannot capture him; look there.)* Even today, with my own books on the shelf, and despite our cosmic differences—can you, for instance, think of a writer less to his taste than the one I am most associated with, the one who grandly announced "the Baroque is dead"?—I still feel discipled.

I last saw him, as I hope to again, where he belongs—in Providence. (I won't be the only one to remark that.) Both of us widowers blessed—

*"A New England Hagiography," *Sewanee Review* 65 (Spring 1957), 321–31.

deae ex machina—with miraculous second marriages, I found him in a Warren peace: ruddy, reposed, physically reassembled; alcohol and tobacco strictly moderated; mind and spirit intact, reconciled, luminous. It was April, 1972. We sat talking, he and I, Toni and Katherine, each in an assigned chair with the drink he had made us. Outside there was snow on the spring. So much to cover, so little time! The phone rang and rang and no one made a move. Here was the fragile exile—infinitely vulnerable, unpredictably resilient—finally at home; it hit me like a benediction. And when he took us up the winding staircase to his study I knew an austere shrine: a plain crucifix, a plainer writing table, a bookcase made from an apple box when he went to college, a few icons—but also (epiphany revisited!) a little fridge for beer. It came over me that he was still as I thought in the beginning unique but, as well, one at last with his spiritual ancestors, the same New English poet-scholar-priests he memorialized.

1976

17.

American Poetry in the Twentieth Century

It is perhaps an unfortunate fact that even in America the achievements of American poets in the 20th century are being obscured by the considerable success of the American novel. Four of our novelists have won the Nobel Prize for Literature: Sinclair Lewis, Pearl Buck, William Faulkner and Ernest Hemingway. But only one of our poets has been so honoured, T. S. Eliot, and although we still count him an American, because of his having been born in and shaped by the United States, he has been a British subject since the Twenties. Nevertheless, poetry has flourished in America—with those who care about it—for 45 years now. A surprising number of people write it, and a surprising number of them are competent at their craft. We count at least two "great" or near-great poets, T.S. Eliot and Robert Frost, and a dozen or more poets who deserve the attention of people anywhere who care about the arts.

Twentieth-century American poetry does not really begin, as it ought, in 1900 but in 1912. Before that time, our poets, mostly very poor ones, were writing just as they would have been writing had they been living in the 19th century. Between Emily Dickinson, who died a couple of decades before 1900, and the year of 1912 which saw a poetic renaissance, the only poet who need be considered is E.A. Robinson who had a new and distinctive way of writing for which, chiefly, we remember him. He

An address to Indian students at the University of New Delhi, 1957 believed that poetry should be written in the natural language of speech, that there should be no twisting of word-order for the sake of rhyme, no structure to the sentences of verse that would not come naturally to the ordinary speaking voice. Robinson also had a distinctive subject matter—the people of a small New England town called, in his poems about them, "Tilbury Town" (it is actually the town of his birth and upbringing, Gardiner, in the state of Maine). He wrote a great many poems, mostly short ones, about these people; although the poems are impeccably rhymed and metred in traditional verse forms, they sound so natural to the ear, so simple, straightforward and unembellished with traditional poetic "effects" that Robinson eventually became famous for them, and his reputation has come to seem secure.

We say he "eventually" became famous because for many long years the poet, determined to stick to poetry in a country that seemed to want none of the sort he wrote, suffered severe deprivation. He was poor, obscure, alone. But over the years he managed to hold on, mainly in New York City, and he finally came into his own. One thing that kept him going was the fact that the saloons of the time used to give free food with the drinks one bought and paid for; another was the building of the New York subway system, which afforded him a job as a manual laborer for some time. But the big day for Robinson was the 27th of March, 1905, when he, one of the most obscure men in America, came home to his miserable lodging place and found a letter from the President of the United States, Theodore Roosevelt, who had seen a few poems of Robinson's in the magazines, had much admired them, and wondered how the poet was getting along. The President later got the poet a decent job, and wrote and published an essay on his work.

Ideologically, Robinson was a pessimist, but also an idealist and an anti-materialist. But it is for neither his ideas, which are not especially original, nor his most popular long poems, for which he is best remembered. It is for the clear, simple, dramatic portraits of the characters of Tilbury Town.

However, as I said before, Robinson is not a beginning; the year 1912 is the start of the so-called Poetic Renaissance in American literature. In this year a magazine called *Poetry* was founded in Chicago by an astute lady, Harriet Monroe, and from then until about 1922, when the style and ideas of T.S. Eliot began to predominate, the new poetry coming out of Chicago was the center of literate attention. It was, on the whole, a realistic, democratic, distinctively American kind of verse. It could be crude, and proudly crude (it had no faith in gentility and the more cultivated Eastern part of the country); it was a new thing, and self-consciously mid-western in mood. More specifically, it was a revolt from the dead hand of the later Victorian poets, and our equivalent to the brilliant Irish Renaissance that just preceded it. The poet felt much as the great Irishman Yeats had felt about Tennyson: we are "weary of all this"—weary, that is, of rhetoric, poetic diction, and everything artificial in verse. Poetry should be simple as the simplest prose, as Robinson had felt (but for which reason he was not much looked to).

In this movement we think most readily of three poets who were connected with *Poetry* magazine and who had a good deal in common: Edgar Lee Masters, Vachel Lindsay, and Carl Sandburg. Masters became well known for a book of poems called *Spoon River Anthology*—short, dramatic monologues spoken by the residents of the graveyard of a small mid-western town, who tell of their lives there—of brief joys, long griefs, frustrated ambitions. It was not a happy book, and its hard-headed, realistic attitudes contrasted effectively with the sort of sentimental verse that at the time was so popular with the general reader, and so unpopular with serious readers and poets themselves.

Vachel Lindsay was a better poet than Masters, and he was a great deal more colorful as a man. For many years he travelled the United States as a hobo, trading his rhymes for bread (with such as would buy), and chanting his strange verses on lecture platforms, preaching forever the cause of Beauty—ridiculed, oftener than not, and finally a suicide, but a memorable poet and an original. He wrote good poems on many American public figures, his insight into the country was deep, and it was Lindsay who did so much to elevate certain legendary Americans like Pocahontas and Huckleberry Finn to their present status as significant figures of American mythology.

But of these three Carl Sandburg has long been the best known—ever since his poem "Chicago" was published in 1914 and made a minor sensation. He was also the most influential of the poets writing in those days when, as Yeats said, "the fiddles were tuning up all over America." Sandburg's poems are very simple and very prosaic. They are usually like little editorials, or "human interest stories," and often marked with criticism of social evils from a passionately democratic spokesman. They are full of slang, and the flavor of the times, but perhaps most important they are "prosey"—that is to say they sound very much as if they were prose, and indeed many people will argue that except for the typography, the way they are set up on the page, some of them are prose. This is, of course, what is called "free verse"—a style of poetry started chiefly by a 19th-century American poet, Walt Whitman in his *Leaves of Grass*.

Shortly after this outburst of new voices another trio of poets—but these were women—came to the foreground of attention, and because of their similarity we can again speak of them together. These are Sara Teasdale, Edna St. Vincent Millay, and Elinor Wylie, and they are grouped together not only because of their contemporaneity but also because they were all poets of lyrical sensibility and, put together, their limited talents added up to a sort of modern renaissance of Romanticism in America. It was an emotional, individualistic, lyrical and self-expressive interlude, quite apart from the other main trends of the period.

Sara Teasdale was a poet of love, which she made into a kind of religion, and as such she was a forerunner of a great social movement of the American Twenties: the emancipation of women. Women who were seeking total equality with men, and completely equal freedom, found in her an apostle of self-revelation and freedom of expression. But she herself was far too reticent to accept such a role (when "whole schools of woman poets," it has been said, were proudly announcing that they were "with child," married or no). This position was saved for Edna St. Vincent Millay, who became the poet of feminine revolt and self-expression, chiefly by shocking the middle class with frank revelations of her feelings until it got used to them. Miss Millay announced that "What lips my lips have kissed, and where, and why, I have forgotten, and what arms have lain under my head till morning . . . In my heart . . . a quiet pain for unremembered lads that not again will turn to me at midnight with a cry . . ." Even more famously she announced, to such critics as deplored the reckless way she lived, or said she lived, that it was true:

My candle burns at both ends,
It will not last the night.
But oh my friends and ah my foes
It gives a lovely light!

More reserved, like Sara Teasdale, was Elinor Wylie, a refined, fastidious poet, elegant, polished, but also warm, sensitive, romantic. She wrote several poems which have no title. They are traditional in style, feminine in feeling, and therefore typify well enough the work of this group.

At about the same time as the poetic renaissance and with a similar insistence on the new simplicity of language, the doing-away with poetic verbiage, came the most widely read and praised of all serious 20th-century American poets, Robert Frost. Frost is above all things the poet of rural New England, writing of that section of the nation, and writing in the rhythms and with the diction of New England speech—the distinctive way the language is spoken there. His subject matter broadens to universal themes and what he writes about is ultimately the human condition, but it is still New England that we think of when we think of him, for most immediately he is the poet of the farms, farmers, fields, crops, and woods of that section. It is the freshness of his language, a kind of wisdom that he has acquired, and a deep, communicated joy in the life of rural, natural simplicity that have brought him eminence. Ideologically, he is a kind of modern classicist, a noble Roman, as it were, most resembling Horace, but transplanted to New England. He endorses the old Emersonian, New England ideal of self-reliance, of independence and standing on your own two feet, as we say: and in other ways he is reminiscent of Emerson, for Frost's is not a truly 20th-century mind. He's as untouched by the great new ideological forces that have swept over the world in our time as Emerson was. But it is not ideas as such that interest Frost in his poetry. All the fun, he has said many times, is in how you say a thing, and it is Frost's intention to say it the way the people of his section would say it—colloquially. The pleasure of recognition is strong in his work—the pleasure of seeing in print what one has heard many times but never seen on the page before what he calls the "common in experience, uncommon in writing." He gets the flavor of talk, and that is the poetry in him.

Some of Frost's little poems are only deceptively simple, and it is clear that he sometimes is saying more than at first glance he seems to be saying. This is true of what is probably his most famous poem—one which has been called the finest lyric poem in 20th-century English. It is called "Stopping by Woods on a Snowy Evening," and it is apparently only a description of a man, the poet presumably, who stops in a horse and buggy by the side of a wood to watch the snow fall peacefully, beautifully in it. He says it is the "darkest evening of the year," this night—and since a snowy night is not a dark one, objectively, we feel that he must mean it is dark for him. The little horse is nervous about his sitting there and soon we see that the man is tempted to something—tempted perhaps to enter the woods himself, or just to lie down somewhere and sleep—perhaps for ever. And that is what he is thinking of when he resists the impulse, remembers his obligations, and tells himself that he has a long way to go before he can be free of this life.

Now none of the poets we have mentioned so far would be considered really "modern" poets by sophisticated American readers, despite the fact that Sandburg and Frost, at least, are still alive. "Modern" American poetry—that is to say poetry that reflects the difficulties and complexities of the modern world—begins in America with the publication of the earliest poems of T.S. Eliot. Eliot ranks, at the very least, as one of the great minor poets in the history of English literature; he is one of the two greatest American poets (in my opinion, Emily Dickinson is the other), and when recently I heard him introduced as the greatest living man of letters I don't think there was a person among the many in the room who doubted that claim. His influence on other poets, and on readers, has been nearly incalculable; literary taste and critical taste have, in our time, been swayed profoundly in the direction of his taste—most directly by the poetry and the criticism of poetry he has written. "Let us go then, you and I . . ." Modern poetry has never for a moment been the same since those lines—written while this poet was a student at Harvard—were published.

Eliot has long been important for both his ideas and his style. Ideologically he is very conservative; stylistically he has been radical. Born and raised in the American Middle West of an old and distinguished American family, Eliot came east to Harvard College, where he published his first revolutionary poems; then he went east farther still—to England, where in 1927 he became a British subject and a communicant, also, of the Anglo-Catholic church; much of his poetry since that time has been religious and philosophical. This seemed a very strange evolution to many of his intellectual admirers. In his early poems he had written a brilliant indictment of modern society. In what is perhaps the greatest poem of the century in English (it is certainly the most influential), *The Waste Land,* he compared the contemporary world to a sort of desert where nothing could grow or bear fruit, where everything, including the people, is sterile, and wasting away. Shortly after that he further described the inhabitants of such a world as "Hollow Men." Eliot led his followers to the very brink of absolute despair, and just when it looked as if suicide were the only answer he backed away from the cliff they thought he was standing on and joined the church—to many of his followers the very institution that seemed deader than the rest he had described as dead. In addition it was a relatively narrow and orthodox view of Anglicanism that the poet took, and relatively few of his followers followed him into it. And so he became, in his famous pronouncement, an Anglican in religion, a classicist in literature, a royalist in politics; and it is probably safe to say that the majority of his admirers continued to admire his verse while they struggled to stay free of the ideas it expressed. But it has been a struggle and, as we have already said, his influence has been profound—almost unprecedented.

The most important single idea which Eliot has expounded is probably the notion that modern life is without meaning—is pointless, futile and sterile—unless one has religious faith. Without the knowledge of good and evil, which depends on religious faith, mankind does not truly exist. Roughly speaking his poems, from the famous study of "J. Alfred Prufrock" up through "Gerontion," *The Waste Land* and "The Hollow Men," depict individuals existing without gods, and in this meaningless state. After his conversion, and in the poems called "Ash Wednesday" and the "Four Quartets," the accent is religious and philosophical.

But whatever the ideas, the technique is always brilliant and original. Eliot has many devices, and one must understand them all if one is to begin to understand him—often a very difficult thing to do. For one thing, there are no transitions, as such, in Eliot. One thought, or image, suggests another and we leap to the other without pause or explanation—just as the mind jumps about. Then there is the "objective correlative"—a theory and practice that comes from the poet's perception that to state an emotion is not to evoke it, that to say with the Romantics "I fell upon the thorns of life" is not to arouse a painful sensation in the reader—unless it be one directed against the poet. What the poet must do instead and what Eliot tries to do, is to find an objective correlative for the emotion, a set of objects, a chain of events, a situation, which is the formula of the emotion, and which when evoked by the poet will provoke the emotion in the reader himself. And then there are, for the highly literate, all the allusions that he makes—references to past literature (sometimes to suggest the superiority of the past) which greatly enrich the meaning of what he is saying by adding another "level" to the undertaking. His imagery was once also new. The very opening lines of his first poem, "The Love Song of J. Alfred Prufrock," established this:

> Let us go then, you and I
> When the evening is stretched out against the sky
> Like a patient etherized upon a table . . .

Truly it is not too much to say that English verse, including its American side, has never for a moment been the same since those lines were published.

Eliot is a difficult poet. Unless one is willing to work on him, to study, re-read, read perhaps other books he has used, and then go back and re-read again, one will not get much from him. But the simple fact is that readers by the thousands have found that all this effort is very much worthwhile. Indeed it is probably safe to say that very few literary experiences of our time have been more rewarding.

It doubtless follows from what I have said that it is hard to find a piece of Eliot's work that will mean anything if it is just read to you; it is hard to make much out of any of his poems on one reading, let alone one listening. But I think you might get some notion of Eliot, if you don't already have one, from listening to "The Hollow Men." These are the sort of men whom Eliot sees inhabiting the contemporary world—lacking the knowledge of God and of spiritual reality—meaningless, empty. To these, in the poem, he contrasts people with "eyes"—that is spiritual eyes, people who can see contrasts. They are the eyes of spiritual reality. We are sightless, he says, "unless the eyes reappear as the . . . multifoliate rose" (a traditional emblem of Christ, also of the Virgin Mary)—and this is

> The hope only
> Of empty men.

In the end, parodying an old English nursery rhyme ("Here we go round the mulberry bush"), he ridicules the pointlessness of modern life, breaks into fragments of the Lord's Prayer and finishes by saying, famously, that this world, the contemporary world, will not end with a great explosion but—befitting us, the Hollow Men, with a "Whimper," a tiny, insignificant squeak of pain and complaint.

Let us now turn to another highly influential modern American poet who has also been critical of the modern world, Ezra Pound. Pound, like Eliot, long disassociated himself from the country of his birth, and the irony of his position is that although there are many parallels between the work and ideas of both men, Eliot has achieved enormous fame while Pound has fallen deep into official disrepute. Never so widely followed as Eliot, Pound was nevertheless for years a leader in the campaign for the "new poetry," and dozens of literary ideas emerged from his iconoclastic and fertile intelligence. He also became, like Eliot, enormously learned in the literatures of the world, and a large part of his contribution has been the introduction of writers hitherto little known to western civilization—Tagore, for one, among them, and several Chinese and Japanese poets; but also old and forgotten French and Italian writers. From the work of these "discovered" writers Pound produced what seemed a sort of pastiche, or paste-up, in his own poetry, which is tremendously learned, bookish, and difficult for the general reader—indeed, often, for the trained reader. He has long considered his *Cantos* his major work, and he once defined their subject as "the presentness of the past"—an attempt, that is, to write about the modern world in such a way as to show how alive the past is to one who knows about it, and to create a new poetry out of the living remains of earlier literatures. Eliot has of course also done a certain amount of this, most notably in his *The Waste Land* and indeed Eliot dedicated *The Waste Land* to Pound as "il miglior fabbro" (that is, the better maker, or fabricator—an ambiguous compliment). But Pound also edited, and radically, the manuscript of that great work before it appeared and Eliot has freely given the impression that Pound's suggestions, chiefly for cutting, were followed.

The problem with Pound, then, is why he does not enjoy a reputation comparable to Eliot's, and the answer to that question is complex. One obvious reason has to do with the difficulty of Pound's work—the plain and ordinary difficulty of trying to follow a mind saturated with learning and full of allusions to poets of whom most people have never heard (and often in languages, including, importantly, the Chinese, which almost no westerners are equipped to read). The other chief reason has been the course of his ideological and political career. This began when, back before the first world war, Pound left his native land for Europe; America was, for him, a land of idiots and money-changers dedicated to the destruction of the culture to which he intended to dedicate his life. For many years he harangued such countrymen as would listen to him from abroad—often with wit and great skill, but often, too, with great monotony, for two things were beginning to obsess Ezra Pound. One was that usury, excessive interest charged on borrowed money, was ruining the world; the other, related, obsession was a hatred of the Jews. Just before the second war, Pound, living now in Rapallo on the Italian Riviera, came to the public support of the Italian dictator Mussolini, and during that war he is alleged to have made treasonable broadcasts to American troops over the Italian radio. Finally, at the end of the war he was brought to the United States to face the charge of treason. This situation became fantastically complex when the Library of Congress, a government agency, but acting through a completely free and independent committee, awarded the imprisoned poet a prize for his long service to the literary arts. This, as might be imagined, caused a considerable uproar, and a bitter and lively debate was waged as to whether or not it is legitimate to approve or honor the poems while detesting the ideas the poems express—or, indeed, if it is possible to distinguish, ultimately, between how a thing is said and what it says. That argument died out rather inconclusively and it appeared that another one, every bit as troublesome, would take its place when Pound came to trial. Pound was declared legally insane, and he still resides, as a prisoner-patient, in a government hospital in Washington. But the trouble is by no means over, and will not end when he dies (he is now a fairly old man), because he is still writing and publishing his *Cantos,* and the question is now whether this poetry, incomprehensible always to the average reader, is itself insane. His supporters emphatically deny that it is, but if it isn't should he then be tried for his alleged crimes (in which case many people who have studied the record believe he would be found innocent of actual treason)? Or, as others believe, should he be released? None of these questions is easy to answer, and the best way to leave this topic is to say that it will be many, many years before the works, poetic and otherwise, of Ezra Pound are placed in their proper perspective and are properly evaluated.

An outstanding characteristic of modern American (and English) poetry is its difficulty for average readers—it must be studied, worked on—and the next poet to be discussed here, Hart Crane, is also a difficult one. Crane's work can best be seen as an improbable blending of the technique of T. S. Eliot with the all-embracing faith of the great 19th-century American poet, so unlike Eliot, Walt Whitman. In 1922 Crane, a very young but promising writer, was deeply and lastingly impressed with Eliot's *The Waste Land.* He endorsed the symbolic, compressed method whole-heartedly, but he felt that "after this perfection of death nothing is possible but a motion of some kind"—he felt, in short, that it was impossible to go further in the direction of disillusion and despair. What he aimed to do was to wed the technique that expressed that despair with Whitman's optimism and faith in a new world.

At this time Crane was living in Brooklyn, New York, and every day, as Whitman had done before him, he crossed the East River to New York City. But now there was a great bridge where Whitman had gone by ferryboat, and the idea of that bridge as a symbol began to grow in Crane's mind. Finally he decided on his ambitious plan: he would write a long poem that would recreate the major positive forces in the development of America's civilization, of which, it seemed to him, that great bridge was the newest. He wanted in his poem, called "The Bridge," to write a poem of affirmation, not despair, and to create a sweeping synthesis of American values as he saw them established by certain key figures in our development—Columbus, Pocahontas, Rip Van Winkle, and so on. Unifying all men, in his mind, was man's power to create, and the symbol of this power was the bridge, which was also a symbol of time and space, of various planes of American life, and of the oneness of the past with the present. This was a tremendous load even for so splendid a bridge, and the truth is that Crane never truly realized his ambitions for this poem. His biggest troubles, technically, were obscurity and a failure to firmly establish some of his myths—grandiose and elaborate—as myths. He had other troubles of a less literary kind. Neurotic and difficult himself, his personal life was a tragic mess, and on April 26th, 1932, about noon, he leapt off a ship on which he was returning from Mexico; his body was never recovered.

And so Crane's life, like his work, was technically a failure. But although his poems are marred by a kind of private logic and symbolism, they are in moments of clarity and vision very impressive for lyrical intensity and a great variety of powerful imagery. His epic and synthetic aims were too large for his talent—perhaps for any talent—but his failures count much higher in the scale of American literary values than the successes of countless minor poets.

After Crane, the problem of selection here becomes very hard. We have had since his time so many good poets, but so few truly outstanding ones, as it now appears, that no two critics would, I think, mention or discuss the same figures. My problem, then, is to choose a few from the many poets who deserve to be discussed. And first I would like to mention, at least, three poets whom I do not feel I have time to go into, but whose names you should know, at least, if you do not already know them. These are the sometimes-associated names of Allen Tate, John Crowe Ransom and Robert Penn Warren. We often associate these names in America because these men are friends, their work and their literary opinions (which have been very influential) have many things in common, and they are all Southerners, who in association with each other began to emerge on the literary scene at about the same time. They are all good poets, and good critics as well, and they have, particularly in their criticism, helped to bring about a small revolution in American literary taste, especially as it filters through the universities where their influence has been most marked. Instead of these, however, I have chosen three other poets of approximately the same generation—chiefly because they are somewhat better known as poets in America and their names are more likely to be mentioned in discussions of American poetry because of their slightly greater popularity. These men are E. E. Cummings, Wallace Stevens, and Robinson Jeffers.

Cummings is a sort of 20th-century, highly individualistic, Romantic; and a rather pleasant, amusing and ingratiating snob (the word is a little too harsh) who takes his pleasure in mocking vulgar middle-class democracy in a kind of last-ditch stand for Art for Art's Sake. He at least pretends to despise order, and to promote chaos (one of his books is called, significantly, *is 5*—meaning that in poetry, anyway, two and two is five); he thumbs his nose irreverently at anything common, ordinary, or usual. He is, however, a very amusing and likeable poet.

Cummings is most notorious in America for his very curious typography—for the way his poems are set up on the page—the most obvious manifestation of his joy in thumbing his nose. In Cumming's poetry it is not at all unusual to come across a parenthetical mark that falls in the middle of a word or a capital letter; he always prints the first-person singular "i" in lower case, as a small letter (also God is never capitalized). And these things look very strange on the page. But they are supposed to add meaning—the "i", and the "g" in god are small to suggest the relative unimportance of these things in the modern world, for instance. Cummings is brilliant, naughty, perverse, and most of his work falls into one of two categories. His poems are either (on the whole) satirical—poems mocking the American love of Home, Country, and such venerated institutions—or they are curiously love poems—love poems of great lyrical and sensuous beauty. Indeed, in an age when love poetry of any value is rare (since the lady poets of the Twenties, anyhow) Cummings rates now as the best (for he is still alive and writing).

Wallace Stevens has for years rated in America as the poet's poet—that is the poet who, par excellence, is admired by other poets even though his popular reputation is not so great as, say, Frost's or Eliot's. Stevens is, or was until his recent death, a curious figure—as pure and disinterested a poet as we had and also an important businessman and lawyer, the vice-president of the very sizeable Hartford Accident and Indemnity Company. Stevens is known for his rich imagery and musical rhythms, in which he plays with dreams of romantic love and beauty while his ironic mind mocks these very things. His poems exploit the boredom of a world in which spiritual intensities are largely missing. In his later work he developed a profoundly philosophic interest, and puzzled over the problem of reality. Which reality stimulates the artist and brings about creation? Is it the actual world that the material of poetry is drawn from, or is it the dream world that he sees in opposition to the imperfections of life that supplies him? This separation, which is that between art and life, and the reasons for the separation, and the philosophic problem of reality—which of these worlds is ultimately real?—these problems make up the subject matter of his later verse, subtle, vivid and polished.

Robinson Jeffers is as different from Cummings and Stevens as they are from each other, and since 1925 he has had an audience for the type of long, narrative poem that he published first in his book *Roan Stallion,* which concerns a woman and a horse. He is the poet, then, of strange stories which mix Freudian themes and symbols with a type of primitivism and a lot of violent action. In about the same year Jeffers settled in a place that has become a good symbol for him—a gray stone house on a cliff overlooking the Pacific, with a 30-feet tower of ocean boulders enclosing his studio, which he built himself. Jeffers lives and writes there; he has repudiated our commercial, industrial civilization, turned to isolation, and written of primitive backwoods Californians of his own invention. But these people and their stories seem to come more directly from the bloodiest and grimmest of Greek Tragedies—but colored with modern, that is to say Freudian, psychology. Jeffers portrays man struggling to free himself from a contaminated humanity, rejecting society and God (that is the god of love) for some nature god of violence, and reaching for a freedom that overrides law, morality and the banalities of ordinary ways of living. His poems aim at a tragic terror, and high-pitched emotion, which intends to cleanse us of contamination and bring us to a higher realm of existence.

We have covered now as best as we can American poetry in the 20th century as far as the Second World War; during the war years and since then we have had so many promising young poets that the problem of selection for a short Paper has become impossible. The best I can do, then, is to choose two young poets as chiefly representative of what has been going on in recent years; I have chosen Karl Shapiro and, as my most recent specimen, Richard Wilbur. Mr. Shapiro, I am told, was last year in India on a visit similar to this one I am on (so was Allen Tate, whom I mentioned earlier); he attained most of his reputation in the years just preceding the war. It is his distinction, it seems to me, that he combines a considerable facility with traditional forms of verse-making and a strikingly modern, or contemporary, subject matter and view of the world. He is significant if only as a spokesman for his age, though he is more—a poet.

Since the Second War American poetry has shown a tendency away from obscurity, and toward a certain elegance and formalism—indirectly indicative, perhaps, of the country's prosperity and the absence of overriding domestic problems. Typical of this trend, and in my view the best of what have been called (without sarcasm or bitterness) the "Court Poets," is Richard Wilbur, who though still a young man has published three mature, polished, graceful and thoughtful volumes, and has won many prizes for his verse. I should like, in particular, to refer to his poem, called "The Juggler," simply because it shows the concern for form—not only in its style, but in its open admiration for form, grace, elegance and order in quite another realm than poetry—that is in juggling. And, as he shows, it is a meaningful admiration, for the poet admires not just the skill that can juggle the balls, and balance the table, the broom and the plate, but also what this triumph represents, a victory not only over disorder and over the force of gravity but a victory too over those forces that keep us emotionally and spiritually earth-bound, a victory over the "world's weight."

I am afraid that by way of conclusion I must end this paper much as I began—that is with mainly the same generalizations. America does not reward its writers, especially its poets, very richly; most American poets have very small audiences, relative to the population of the country, and it is shocking that only a handful of them—three or four at best—can make a living by writing poetry. But thousands of Americans write poetry. It is my unsupported but considered opinion that there are as many people writing poetry in America as reading it. And so we have this confusion, that if we judge the country's interest in poetry by the cash value of poetry—what the people will pay for it—the results are very discouraging to those who care for poetry; whereas if we judge that interest by the numbers of people engaged in writing verse the result is the opposite of discouraging. In addition it should be pointed out that if America does not reward its poets richly, it does allow them a great deal of freedom;

American poets may take the most unpopular of stands and maintain them; if they are good poets they will eventually find an audience, and—short, perhaps, of actual treason—they will not be interfered with; they can speak their minds whatever they think.

But the success of American poetry in the 20th century has not, I think, been chiefly ideological, it has been stylistic. Our poets as a whole, although by no means lacking in ideas, have been most concerned with new ways of expressing them, and I would say that their greatest success has been in the field of technical competence, in a few cases, technical brilliance. It is our novel that has brought most attention to American literature in recent years, but it is my conviction that as the world comes to know our poets better it will feel, as I do, the irony that lies in the fact that this great nation, by reputation so vulgar, materialistic and commercial, should produce so much good poetry.

1957

18.

One Man's Apple

I have been asked to say what it has been like, over the years, to write in central Pennsylvania, "remote from any Big Apple." I had thought there was no other mecca, and its nickname badly bruised. No matter; the question was clear, and my first thought simple. If one has something to write about, plus the strength, ability, and will to do the writing (very big ifs, in case you've never tried), practically anywhere will do, including cluttered, ill-lighted places. Books have been written on ice boxes (Thomas Wolfe), beds of hotel rooms too small to hold anything else (John O'Hara), and on somebody else's time (Faulkner among many). On drugs, alcohol, caffeine, nothing. In prisons, army barracks, and the presence of small children; in libraries, writers' colonies, and well-appointed studies. Name it, someone wrote a book there. There's not even need for "time" to write, which can always be stolen from job, family, sleep, something. It is said that if you need a job done in a hurry give it to the busiest man you know. The academic antithesis of that is give a scholar "time off" in which to write, and often the scholar gets nothing written. My first book was composed under a Four-Course Load—large classes, no help, and a commute of an hour each way, during which I graded papers while dangling from a subway strap. Then my employer dumped me on the grounds of insufficient publication.

It is rumored that writers differ, which may be so. A few have to go romantic distances to get in the mood, achieve perspective, have experiences, or absorb atmosphere. Many don't. It was in nearby residential Pine Grove Mills that John Barth, who said he'd never been anywhere at the time, or done anything, wrote the novels that made him famous. On the other hand, Melville was already famous when he moved into a handsome farmhouse in the scenic Berkshires, wrote a masterpiece, and pretty much wrecked himself in the process. It can go lots of ways.

I was thinking along these lines longer than you'd believe before it dawned on me that if you count Queens, it was in New York City that *I* first wrote a book. All right, I can say that where one lived at the time had nothing to do with it. But the truth is that I think it did. New York is supposed to be where things are at. There's something in the air. Lots of people—in finance, the arts, publishing, Yankee uniforms, whatever—have claimed that just being there, plugged in to some piece of the action, gives them extra energy, and a sense of belonging. Even the cops and cabbies feel like this; I too, all during the time I was doing the book. And during the protracted period, well-punctuated by lunches with my editor, of getting it in print. A single, distinctly metropolitan moment stands out indelibly. It came one evening on the subway. I was sitting down—no rush hour, no papers to grade (no job)—skimming a column in the *Post* (it was Leonard Lyons), and my name caught my eye in an item which reported that Hemingway had not authorized the book I'd written on him. (Correct.) Nobody took my picture, or begged an autograph. But this was an end to solipsism: concrete evidence that there was a world out there, to which one was connected. Incredible.

You wouldn't want to count on that some Monday in middle Pennsylvania. Or, at publication, on partying with friends one had made at Rinehart, the publisher. Or on becoming in the Village a temporary hero to astonished denizens of the Cedar Street Tavern, some of whom may have doubted you could read a book. It is not that I wish I could have stayed indefinitely in the city, which is an exciting place, and difficult. Or could not have gone back. Rather that to everything there is a season, as the Preacher said, and I am glad to have had that one. I took the business of getting fired along with other business, not to worry over much. If the career was on hold, the book was selling, and still does. It was recently pirated in Japan, a handsome job.

I survived the year during which Hemingway did what he could, which was ample, to stop my book on a grant from the American Council of Learned Societies. That was 1952. There were *no* jobs in my line of work, not that I heard of. Then, under such pressure as I could exert, the author relented, the book appeared, traveled well, and I had an offer from Kansas State. During World War II I had spent two full years in the worst of Texas and Oklahoma with the field artillery, pockmarking the countryside, and didn't think of Kansas as a big step up. But I had the pleasure of accepting an associate professorship without ever having achieved genuine assistant professorhood, and besides, no one in his right mind turned down $5,400 a year.

In my Washington Square days, New York University proved too big, anonymous, and fragmented to give any sense of intellectual community—at least to its instructors, who earned only a little less than its elevator operators. Hence I didn't yet know that a university can provide faculty with some sense of belonging to a bigger world, such as I tapped in Manhattan. Nor did I learn it in Manhattan, Kansas. There I did have bright, impressive friends and colleagues. But for reasons unknown to me they were by and large unproductive. Ability was held in reserve, talent exceeded ambition. (Something in the water maybe, though it was scarce.)

What I discovered in Kansas was a gift for adaptability. Without ever deciding to, I went along with things much as they were. While based there I did make a longish lecture tour of Indian universities. And, jumping from the frier into the freezer, spent a "visiting" academic year at Minnesota. Nor, as a writer, was I wholly inactive. I published a few essays and three of my India lectures. I also stole from my Hemingway book a 48-page pamphlet, which has long been translated into languages I'd never heard of—even into English (Basic). But mostly I remember teaching my classes, fighting the environment, and trying to live as well as possible with congenial associates. The notes from strenuous research on what I call American "literary myth," done in New York on my ACLS year, gathered local dust.

Something akin to the adrenaline I felt in New York I felt at Minnesota. It was a lively English department, from Allen Tate at the top to young Murray Krieger, rapidly ascendant. The corridors bustled; the city was alive. Before long I found myself sneaking over to the office weekends. "Studies in American Literary Myth" was reactivated, and parts of it made progress. But there had never been a regular slot for me in Folwell Hall, and after my three quarters I returned to Kansas to confront my parched, outlandish fate by embracing it. I bought a house in town, my first, joined the country club, and began playing erratic golf.

Settled in, I immediately had from Penn State what is called a Feeler.

The letter felt good. I made the visit east; the offer was good; I accepted. Having never been seriously tempted by opportunities to take a job elsewhere, I now have the 25-year rocker (but don't know how to affix the little brass plaque).

Why has this place worked out for me? First, the move proved tonic. This was escape from a section of the country that is to me alien and underprivileged. And there was return; an Easterner born and raised, I saw it as home country, though I'd prefer it nearer ocean. Town and campus were green when they were supposed to be, colorful in the fall. (The only place to live winters is in your head.) Within limits, I was not broke. Improved spirits paid other dividends. Seeds, planted in years past had grown, and it was near time for plucking. I finally got my paper on Rip Van Winkle, in off-and-on progress for seven years, the way I wanted it, and after initial publication it began appearing in anthologies. Then I finished a similar study of Pocahontas, begun even further back. Now I began contribution regularly to *The Kenyon Review,* where the essays first appeared. By now the change to inner direction was obvious, and the Pennsylvania season was ripe.

Writing has been a large part of this development. For many years I have not been comfortable unless meanwhile, back at the office, something is under way, slow as it goes. The University has conspired to keep me at it, by providing conducive conditions. Pattee Library has been a continuing surprise, time and again coming up with what I did not expect to find. One naturally has to visit other libraries, sites and cities, but this would be true wherever one lived. I've had very productive colleagues, and direct help from them; I've been encouraged to teach what I like. Meanwhile, back at home, I've been blessed with a happy second marriage, an expanding/contracting family, and a niftier house, ideally situated, than I ever thought to occupy on a professor's salary. If one cannot write under such conditions one cannot write.

Somewhere (probably in Hotchner) Hemingway said that all his novels had begun as short stories; he'd never actually planned on writing a novel. This is surely untrue, but I can parallel it. After having brought out however many volumes (the number depends on how you count), I had never yet sat down to write a book. The first *Hemingway* was a complete *re*write of my doctor's thesis, which was *not* a book. The *Reconsideration* was an expansion and updating; *Three Bags Full* was a compilation of things already written and printed. For a long time the Hemingway *Inventory* was a long list for the benefit of the lady who owned the manuscripts, now in the J. F. Kennedy Library—where, on the occasion of their acquisition, I had a marvelous chat with the President's widow. The idea of a book was Mary's. My most recent book got to be one when it refused to confine itself to the chapter I was writing for a larger book. The exception is *Revolutionary Ladies,* which was a book in my mind as soon as the topic crossed it. This one grew out of the discovery that at the time of our Revolution there was a small group of American girls—beautiful, aristocratic, Loyalist, Anglican—who got caught up in the double jeopardy of sexual scandal and war. As like-minded free spirits in a circumscribed world, they were unrecognized. I thought I had a gathering of some amazing stories. And it did win a prize in American History (Knopf, the publisher, and I thought it somewhat more artful). But it did little else. Many people, including reviewers, couldn't handle it. Perhaps I shouldn't figure out what I'm doing until I'm pretty well on my way.

So *Hawthorne's Secret,* my latest, was supposed to be a single part of something to be called *Dark Lady of the Republic.** But the Hawthorne thesis is radical, and if accepted changes traditional views of the author and, notably, of *The Scarlet Letter.* My new perception of him brings us back, as it happens, to where I began with Hemingway: convinced once more that writers are more profoundly in their fictions or nonfictions than is generally agreed. If it can be sensitively discovered where they hurt, perhaps one can learn why and how they hurt, and how in their work they handle it, overcome it. This, possibly, is a route to the whole heart and art of many writers. But it was certainly unrecommended when I got started. T. S. Eliot had laid it down for everyone: art is *im*personal; it *transforms* the artist's private agonies. I never thought it transformed them out of sight. And was happy, along with 13,999 other people, to hear Eliot say it in person, in a (well-attended) 1956 lecture at Minnesota. He spoke of the critic's need—obligation—to know the biography of his poet—going well out of his way to specify *dead* poet as I winced, Hemingway being much alive.

Now I work on Melville, also Cooper, both dead. It is not, of course, never has been, all roses. Healthy gardens grow vigorous weeds. I have logged more time in hospitals than one would wish for, have lost the pleasure I once took in travel. But this has been a good place to work,

*Two essays—"Born Decadent: The American Novel and Charles Brockden Brown," *The Southern Review* (Summer 1981), 501–19, and "First American Novel: *The Power of Sympathy,* In Place," *College Literature* (May 1984), 115–24—were intended as chapters in this uncompleted project.

and to live. (I am reminded that the Youngs once thought of moving to Newport, Rhode Island, when I retired.) Here we remain, ocean or no. Our second growth roots are here. You can only do so much transplanting.

1985

19.

American Fiction, American Life

I would like to approach my topic with a bit of autobiography, if you'll excuse it, for I have had a slightly strange experience which has a sort of relevance for you.

A few years ago I read a paper about literary criticism at one of the meetings of the Modern Language Association (the English professor's equivalent of a plumber's convention), held that year in Washington, D.C. When I was done there was the customary polite applause, and a couple of dumb questions; that, I thought, was the customary end of that (and just as well, too, by the way). But it turned out that a kind of spy for the State Department had sneaked into the Statler, and a few months later I found myself in India—not deported, exactly, but giving lectures on American literature to the faculties of a series of Indian universities. The idea, as I understood it, was to encourage them to see that there *is* an American literature, and to initiate courses in it. Behind this idea was the notion, I believe, that a wider knowledge and a deeper understanding of our writing would work toward a better understanding of us, and thus, in an honorable way, promote our interests in the Orient. And behind that was the notion—at least in my mind—that I was implying, though

A talk presented to members of the Peace Corps in training at The Pennsylvania State University in the summer of 1962.

never stating, a message, which was: Don't judge us by Hollywood, and *Life* magazine (which Indians detested, incidentally); look for the true America in our serious writers; more specifically, look for at least a part of modern America in modern American fiction—in our best novels, which, I should add now lest you doubt it later, I very much admire.

It is obvious that I was bringing American literature to foreigners, which is not what you are about to be up to. But a part of my point is that if one doesn't bring it to them they will bring it to you. Intellectuals, that is, of all grades of competence and sophistication the world over, are intensely interested in the likes of Hemingway and Faulkner, and many of them are feverish to discuss the matter with a live educated American. Now this can be a curious—possibly an unnerving—experience for the likes of you and me, knowing as we do so many people who do not honor intellectuals in the first place, and couldn't tell William Faulkner from William Cullen Bryant and care less in the second.

Well, it was a rough trip, punctuated inauspiciously by Little Rock at the start and Sputnik I toward the end, with two weeks of Communist Kerala in between, and endless curry, constant traveling, unbelievably uninteresting hotels, and prohibition, and condiments that can take the top of your head off. Indeed, I ended in the hospital with nurses around the clock. But although I would gladly supply you with some colorful details about intestines, liver, and other parts in distress, my story has less to do with how *I* fared than with how an idea made out—the idea, that is that non-Americans can learn a good deal that is true and valuable about twentieth-century American life by reading the best twentieth-century American literature. In short, does our literature reflect our life? More specifically, does our novel reflect it?

As it happens, this isn't a bad question to discuss, either. It has a highly significant history in this country, it is full of complexity, occasionally of irony, and it raises very large questions, both about the nature of literature (not to mention art itself) and about the nature of the country which *you* will soon be reflecting and representing.

Now the twentieth-century American novel began very conveniently, and precisely on time—with the publication in 1900 of a book by Theodore Dreiser called *Sister Carrie.* We say it "began" with this novel because there are attitudes in it which, though they had deep roots, came to a sort of American fruition in this work. Very loosely speaking, these attitudes are "Naturalistic." Naturalism is a pessimistic form of determinism which holds that there is nothing above or beyond nature (like a God), that man is essentially an animal (who does not possess free will), and that his life is a pointless struggle (in which morals are meaningless) against blind forces that pitilessly overwhelm him.

As for the novel itself, it tells the story, as many of you know, of an ordinary girl, Carrie, who comes to the big city, Chicago, has an affair with a salesman and then with the unhappily married manager of a fashionable restaurant. He, Hurstwood, steals money from his employers and he and Carrie run away together, are caught, released, and then he tries for a new career in New York. He is unsuccessful, eventually becomes a beggar, and then kills himself. Meanwhile Carrie, although she has no great ability, becomes a famous actress, remaining however as unhappy at the end of the book as she was at the start. She goes up in the world, then, as Hurstwood goes down, and there is no real accounting for that fact; she is not remarkable or talented or worthy. Nor despite the theft—a momentary lapse of judgment, and freakish—is there any real explaining why Hurstwood goes into such a desperate decline. This, I think Dreiser is saying, is life. That is: there is no particular connection between virtue and reward. What you get has very little to do with what you deserve. In his other, best-known novel, *An American Tragedy,* Dreiser tells the story of a poor boy who, on his way up the social scale, somewhat passively murders his pregnant girl friend, is tried, and condemned to death—though, as the author persuasively argues and his title suggest, it was really America that was to "blame."

By the mid-Twenties, when Dreiser wrote his *American Tragedy,* two other important writers were intensively examining the national scene: Sherwood Anderson and Sinclair Lewis, who have been referred to, respectively, as the Village Mystic and the Village Atheist. Anderson is best remembered for his studies of what he called "grotesques": small-town Americans who have been thwarted in love, and terribly warped by the lack of it. Lewis, the first American to win world-wide recognition with a Nobel Prize, was a kind of iconoclast who denounced by satire the homely norm of American life as dull, stupid, narrow, and fatuous. One after another, and to vast applause, our small towns and their citizens, our businessmen and social workers, the ministry, the medical profession, and other aspects of our society, came in for his amusing but withering ridicule.

It is not so much of Lewis and Anderson, however, that most of us think today when we think of the Twenties, but more of a slightly younger group whose careers were beginning in that decade: Hemingway, Faulkner, John Dos Passos, and Scott Fitzgerald. Hemingway's best novels of this period (many would say his best novels, period) were *The Sun Also Rises* and *A Farewell to Arms*. The first told the story of the aimless, dissolute, expatriated members of a "lost generation" in general, and in particular the bitter, hopeless story of a man who had been emasculated in the war. The second is even more disillusioned and pessimistic. It deals with the war itself—with a man who is forced to desert the army in which he has been fighting, and who loses his mistress as well, when she dies bearing his child. Faulkner we recognize chiefly as the author of a many-volumed saga of the Deep South, a bitter comic-tragedy of the abysmal decadence of its old aristocrats, and the hilarious but horrifying rise of the absolutely unscrupulous newcomers who displace them. A violent, macabre, and Gothic saga of a land cursed by slavery and ravaged by the Civil War, the mansions are inhabited by the drunken, impotent, and helpless remains of the once-proud, and the rats are overrunning the mansions. "Hemingway's world," as one of his critics has pointed out, "is one in which things do not grow and bear fruit, but explode, break, decompose, or are eaten away. . . . [His] characters do not 'mature' in the ordinary sense, do not become 'adult.' It is impossible to picture them in a family circle, going to the polls to vote, or making out their income tax returns. . . . It is a world seen through a crack in the wall by a man who is pinned down by gunfire." And Faulkner's world is even more garishly populated.

> If one were to make a prolonged visit to a hospital for the insane, talking at length to its inmates, one would have as balanced a view of a cross section of humanity as one receives from the fiction of Faulkner. . . . You may search his novels from end to end without finding a single family in which the relationships are not twisted either by perversion or insanity.

Now this is a very hostile (and a very inferior) critic speaking (one J. Donald Adams by name), but he is within smelling-distance of a point, and if a long-established and well-known American critic is unable to see what Faulkner is doing, what are non-Americans to make of him? At the center of his stage are a famous woman who lives for many years with the corpse of her lover ("A Rose for Emily"); a degenerate criminal who rapes a college girl with a corncob (*Sanctuary*—she enters a brothel where she and a new lover put on sexual exhibitions for his vicarious pleasure);

a boy who elopes with a cow, and a young man who desires above all women his sister (a girl who gives herself to any man who wants her, and also desires her brother—*The Sound and the Fury*); a man who lets his daughter die in childbirth, a white nymphomaniac who gets herself into a delirium because she thinks of her sexual partner as a Negro (he later cuts her head nearly off, and then is lynched, and emasculated with a butcher's knife—*Light in August*).

I could go on like that, but there is less sensational business to attend to. The fact is, however, that when we turn to the other two most prominent novelists of this era in America, John Dos Passos and Scott Fitzgerald, the situation is not a whole lot more cheerful. Dos Passos' best work appears, of course, in his trilogy, *USA*. *USA* is an epic of monumental, national failure, is the tragedy of a modern industrial society in which the individual is simply wrecked. A flat, sour drabness pervades all three volumes. There is no joy, no happiness; success is empty and failure is pregnant; all the lives are toneless and dismal. But the whole thing seems intensely real, and so it follows that the indictment is overwhelming.

At first glance Fitzgerald presents a more attractive picture, but second glances into his better novels, *The Great Gatsby* and *Tender Is the Night,* begin to penetrate the superficial party atmosphere, and to correct that picture. Gatsby is an amiable, decent man of suspicious wealth who is murdered through the absolutely unscrupulous plotting of some self-important decadent aristocrats, while a giant ash dump serves as an eloquent commentary on the meaning of the lives of the characters. The latter novel reveals the appalling disintegration of a few apparently glamorous, expatriated aristocrats; the heroine is periodically insane as the result of an incestuous girlhood relationship with her father, and the hero is destroyed by his patient.

Nor is the picture much more pleasing when we trace the story of our fiction past this halcyon period and into the present—through Thomas Wolfe and John Steinbeck to the really brutal war novels like *The Naked and the Dead* and *From Here to Eternity,* or to the truly poisonous imagination of the likes of Truman Capote, or finally to the work of the most widely known young American writer, J. D. Salinger, in whose fiction the most appropriate response to the world his really worthwhile protagonists are forced to inhabit seems to be a nervous breakdown.

Now I would argue that I have given a fair—however sketchy—picture of what the ordinary non-American reader would find in the best fiction of our best twentieth-century novelists. Have I given a picture of life in America that is more valid than our trashy movies and our lady's magazines will give? "What," says the astonished foreign reader of our better novels, "is life so utterly grim and pointless in America as I read in Dreiser? Are people so isolated and misshapen as in Anderson? Such ridiculous and stupid hicks as in Lewis? So bitter, so desperate as in Hemingway? So depraved as in Faulkner? So depressed and depressing as Dos Passos presents them? Is it as disheartening as Fitzgerald has it? Are there *really* no families in the United States? No homes? No heterosexual parents who love each other and their children? Not even any passably happy and decent citizens? No religion? No culture? No hope? I don't think I understand this country very well."

Just before I went to India a lot of people were pretty stirred up about this state of affairs—about the picture of life in America they have, as compared to the picture they fear others will get from reading our best books. Many of the foremost journals in the country—*The New York Times, Harper's, Life,* for instance—opened their columns to this discussion. What will the world think of us? It is bad for our prestige abroad. Here we are relatively happy, and the most prosperous nation in the history of the world, wishing for both political and psychological reasons to be liked abroad everywhere. And what do you find in our books? Misery, degradation, despair. "Is it right," one sympathetic foreign observer wanted to know, "that the great *flowering* of the American novel should hamper America's leadership of the free world?" Or let us consider the way the point is put by *Life* magazine, whose editorial committees do on occasion and however misguidedly concern themselves with important questions:

> Ours is the most powerful nation in the world. It has had a decade of unparalleled prosperity. It has gone further than any other society in the history of man toward creating a truly classless society. Yet it is still producing a literature which sounds sometimes as if it were written by an unemployed homosexual living in a packing-box shanty on the city dump. . . .

And, after coming out strong for a novel by Herman Wouk called *Marjorie Morningstar,* they cap the argument with the impression that a French critic got of us by reading our fiction: "A hypocritical society based on the power of money, racial prejudice, sexual taboos. Exile, alcohol, suicide seem the only escape."

The notion here is, of course, that if our literature does not reflect the beneficent and bountiful facts of our life it is false, untrue to the country of its origin, and dangerous.

If we had time I think I could trace this argument back at the very least to Thomas Jefferson for you—back, that is, to his agrarian view of the country as the world's healthy answer to the decadence of urban Europe. But in our literature the argument classically begins with a man named William Dean Howells. Himself a novelist, Howells once reviewed a translation of Dostoevski's *Crime and Punishment,* and in the course of it he remarked that "whoever struck a note so profoundly tragic in American fiction would do a false and mistaken thing. . . ." Life is not so bad here: "Our novelists, therefore, concern themselves with the more smiling aspects of life, which are the more American. . . ." It is "the large, cheerful average of health and success and happy life" which is "peculiarly American."

Later Robert Frost reinforced this opinion in verse:

> It makes the guild of novel writers sick
> To be expected to be Dostoievskis
> On nothing worse than too muck luck and comfort.

Just before this Frost had asked:

> . . . How are we to write
> The Russian novel in America
> As long as life goes so unterribly?

And I recall that more recently, during an investigation of Communist activity in Hollywood, Mrs. Leila Rogers (the estimable mother of Ginger Rogers) testified that a certain movie was unAmerican because it was "gloomy."

Precisely Howells' point, if in a vulgar reduction; nor is the Howells view of American experience the ignorant error it is often taken for; it is a half- or partial truth. But most serious fiction in our century is not exactly "smiling."

It is a happy fact for whatever coherence this discussion may pretend to that Theodore Dreiser springs directly out of, and in direct antagonism to, the Howells view. Modern American fiction was conceived—not born yet, but conceived—on the very day (somewhere in the mid-1890's) when Dreiser sat down and began "examining the current magazines." They *did* reflect the smiling aspects of American life, and his dissatisfaction with them was epochal:

> I was never more confounded than by the discrepancy existing between my own observations and those displayed here, the beauty and peace and charm to be found in everything, the almost complete absence of any reference to the coarse and vulgar and the cruel and the terrible. . . . Love was almost invariably rewarded . . . dreams came true . . . with such an air of assurance, omniscience and condescension, that I was quite put out by my own lacks and defects. They . . . wrote of nobility of character and sacrifice and the greatness of ideals and joy in simple things. . . . I had no such tales to tell, and however much I tried, I could not think of any.

And so he wrote *Sister Carrie,* which was a tale he *had* to tell. And what happened? Although he did find a firm to print it, for a long time the book was not effectively distributed because the wife of one of his publishers, a lady somewhat like Howells, named Doubleday, stopped it.* And when it did get out and was generally read, one of the most distinguished professors in America, Stuart Pratt Sherman, put his stern magisterial seal of disapproval on it: the book was unacceptable because it was "outside American life." More recently William Faulkner wrote *Sanctuary,* a wild and horrifying melodrama apparently far more open to that charge. Indeed Faulkner told us in a preface to that novel that in a deliberate attempt to make a quick dollar he had invented "the most horrific tale I could imagine." (A highly successful attempt, one might add, since this is the best-selling of his books; and a successful statement, too, since the professors and critics took him at his word, which is a bad habit they have when dealing with writers and what they say about their own books.)

But what of the truth? One thing we may say with confidence is that Professor Sherman didn't know as much as he might have about American life, which Dreiser's story was very much a part of. Sister Carrie was Dreiser's own sister, and her unhappy story was substantially true; indeed

*This "myth" has recently been corrected by Donald Pizer in his critical edition of the novel (New York: Norton, 1970), but the basic point—the publisher's dire objections to the book—remains unchanged.

where Dreiser changed things he brightened the picture, for in "real life" the tale was more depressing, sordid, and "Russian." In the same way, Faulkner did not "invent" a wild and horrifying tale in *Sanctuary:* substantially it, too, happened in America, and he knew the story well. His rapist was an actual Memphis gangster named Pumphrey; his coed was a real Ole Miss coed; and I am told by an expert on Faulkner that the almost incredibly offensive object in the book was in life "worse than" the one specified. These things are not at all "outside American life," though some professors are. But are they representative of it? Do they reflect it? Even to ask the question points up its absurdity.

Let me read to you a passage in which Robert Penn Warren, himself a novelist, confronts our problem. He starts this way, by backing off a little:

> Once upon a time there was a nation, which we shall call X. At the time of which we write this nation stood at a moment of great power and great promise. A few generations earlier it had concluded a long and bloody civil war to achieve unity. More recently, in that unity, it had won a crashing victory over foreign foes. It had undergone, and was undergoing, a social revolution; there was unparalleled prosperity, a relaxing of old sanctions and prejudices, a widening of opportunity for all classes, great rewards for energy and intelligence. Its flag was on strange seas; its power was felt in the world. It was, even, producing a famous literature.
>
> But—and here is the strange thing in that moment of energy and optimism—a large part, the most famous part, of that literature exhibited violence, degradation and despair as part of the human condition: tales of the old time of the civil war, tales of lust and horror, brother pimping for sister, father lusting for daughter, a head of the state doting on a fair youth, an old man's eyes plucked out, another old man killed in his sleep, friendship betrayed, obligations forgone, good men cursing the gods, and the whole scene drenched in blood. Foreigners encountering this literature might well conclude that the Land of X was peopled by degenerates sadly lacking in taste, manners and principle.

And then Mr. Warren came to the point. He was not, as some of you have guessed, talking about the situation in modern America. X is England in the great age of Elizabeth, the age that produced perhaps the greatest literature the world has ever seen. The idea that since America is enjoying a period of great prosperity our literature should reflect this success has obviously got something wrong with it. Indeed it is drowned in confusion.

Since it is entirely possible that some of you will one day be faced with a foreign friend of this country, who in order to learn more about us once made his way very painfully through, say, a Faulkner novel (for Faulkner is difficult reading even for Americans), and emerged wide-eyed with dismay, it might be useful if I tried to spell out what some of the chief misconceptions about the relationship of art and life seem to me to be. If you should happen to see any sense in what I say now, and happen to remember some of it then, you just might find opportunity to use it. For clarity and simplicity I shall enumerate my points in a one, two, three fashion. (Or so I tell my classes: the real reason is that this way I don't have to compose any transitions.)

I. Serious literature is never a reflection of life. If people want to employ this sort of terminology they should change the language: literature is a refraction of life, and it cannot do without that distinction. The good writer does not mirror what is around him. He presents what he has encountered in one way or another—if only in his dreams or nightmares—as its rays have been deflected through his own, individual eyes. It is the angle of refraction, which distinguishes the quality of his vision, that we reject or esteem. (I am simplifying wildly, but a certain amount of that is necessary for present purposes, and I am not done yet.)

II. Art is not life, but an ordering and an intensification of it. Nobody really wants "life" in literature, for life as we all know is a mess, an affair of utter disorder and sprawl, and for long and frequent stretches is so stupifyingly tedious that to read about it as it "really is" would shortly drive us mad. This cliché, "Art imitates Life," handed me and perhaps you in high school, is generally pinned on Aristotle (who will survive it). His thesis was not unguarded, however; he did allow for the artist eliminating the accidental (which I called ordering) and for heightening the essential (intensification) so as to get at the significant. But this still may play down the role the imagination enjoys in art, for as someone said a long time ago, "Imitation will fashion what it has seen, but imagination will go on to what it has not seen." The "pleasure of recognition" in literature—seeing on the printed page what we have often seen in life, but seldom or never before seen written down—can be very rewarding and is quite generally available to readers. But the pleasures of vision are deeper and more rewarding and enduring.

The fact that life is frequently boring and takes a lot of working on before it becomes literature explains among other things why literature is a form of escape. I know that "escape literature" is a dirty term, but the fact is that in a sense all literature is escape literature. It varies enormously to be sure in quality, seriousness, and so forth, and it matters more what we escape to than from, but there is that point again: nobody really wants to read about life precisely and exactly as he knows it. This helps to explain as well why tragedy is perhaps the greatest of all forms of literature. It may seem odd that we should relish tragedy in our books as we assuredly do not in our lives, but it is the most exhilarating, and the most ennobling, of all literary experiences, and it requires a very high degree of ordering and intensification. At a low level there is the shop-girl's well-known preference for a teary ending at the movies, or the housewife's addiction to the absolutely desperate situations of soap opera, but at the other end there is Ahab, in the stupendous tragedy of *Moby-Dick,* who cries out "My topmost greatness lies in my topmost grief." It is a remark worth pondering, if you never have. But to get on:

III. Serious fiction in America has generally operated, at least since Hawthorne, Melville, and Poe, as a reaction against the facile optimisms our country periodically produces. These important writers all are saying, as Melville said that Hawthorne did, "No! in thunder" to the cheerful, affirmative, and often commercial popular views of their times. As we have seen, Dreiser began both his career and modern American fiction in the identical reaction, and it still goes on. However obvious, it is too often forgotten that our writers live in a society where a kind of idiot optimism is popularly and commercially insisted on. Surrounded as they are by magazine fiction and movies, "family" television, Madison Avenue, and all the rest, they are incessantly driven to try to right the balance—driven by a completely human perversity that reacts in disgust from the piety and cant of an inescapable diet of fake satisfactions and sentimental sorrows. This is an important and often ignored partial accounting for all the misery and sickness you find in our best writers today. How can they do other?

IV. America is too big, too paradoxical, complex, diverse, and heterogeneous to be reflected *or* refracted in any single work, or group of works, or even perhaps in the whole of serious contemporary literature. There are a dozen, or a hundred, or a thousand Americas! And from what point of view, or angle of refraction, should any one of these be seen? The intellectual's? The man in the street's? The woman of the street's? Or the home? The poet's? When you multiply the number of possible Americas by the number of possible approaches you come up in that region where figures begin to cease to convey much, at least to me.

V. The people who bewail the fact that our fiction does not now reflect the large, cheerful average of health and success in American life seem invariably to forget that there is nothing especially new about this situation. Writing about the American novel from its start to the present, one of the best critics of our fiction, Richard Chase, has pointed out, "The imagination that produced much of the best and most characteristic American fiction has been shaped by the contradictions and not by the unities and harmonies of our culture." Mr. Chase does not do much to explain why this is so, and he is forced to leave out of his discussion a good many books I would think it necessary to include, presumably because they do not fit his thesis very well. But he is on to something. Our novel is not the English novel, which "has followed a middle way. It is notable for its great practical sanity, its powerful engrossing composition of wide ranges of experience into a moral centrality and equability of judgment. . . . The profound poetry of disorder we find in the American novel is missing, with rare exceptions, from the English." The American novel "has been stirred, rather, by the aesthetic possibilities of radical forms of alienation, contradiction, and disorder." I suspect that this is essentially true, and that people who attack our modern fiction for being unreflective of the country that produced it are dodging a deeper question (which for present purposes I, too, must dodge), which is, why has this been basically true from the very beginning?

VI. This is the last one, and in the nature of a very narrow concession. I suppose that in a way a writer like Hemingway or Faulkner does, in some highly subtle fashion, speak profoundly of the American experience, and thus, by a very difficult route, give a picture of us that rings of truth. But it takes real effort, real understanding, and even vision, as well as a great deal of experience of this country, to see how and why this is so. Very few Americans have what it takes. Then how can we expect someone who is not an American to see the point? We cannot. (And it is very easy, by the way, to expect more of foreign intellectuals than they can produce; a sense of cultural and intellectual inferiority has afflicted almost all of us ever since Sinclair Lewis—or maybe Mark Twain; some of you will be discovering before long, I will venture to predict, that you are a lot smarter than you thought you were. It is easy, too, to expect more knowledge of your country abroad than one will find; I will predict further that the number and the depths of plain misconceptions some of you will encounter will take your wind away.)

Let me lift a little something more from Robert Penn Warren—this time a sort of anecdote he told. He once talked, he says, with an Italian Fascist who had deserted Mussolini in the Second World War and had come over to fight on our side. Why? Warren asked him. Because of the American novelists, the man answered. "The Fascists used to let us read American fiction because it gave, they thought, a picture of a decadent America. They thought it was good propaganda for fascism to let us read Dreiser, Faulkner, Sinclair Lewis. But you know, it suddenly occurred to me that if democracy could allow that kind of criticism of itself, it must be very strong and good. So I took to the mountains."

Well, I think that is very fine indeed. But note that this soldier was a highly perceptive fellow—and besides, he couldn't have had much of a picture of America yet, either, though he was on the right track.

Really to begin to find America in its modern books you would need to realize all the things I have mentioned, I think, plus a good many things I am not taking time to mention (fortunately for you), and a good many more I haven't the wit to mention (unfortunately for me). It happens that there are valuable and essential insights to be got from such nineteenth-century writers as Whitman and Twain, and you will be hearing about that later in this series of lectures. But as for finding us where we have been looking tonight, I doubt it.

Where then is America to be found? Perhaps because the country is so complex and huge, there have been very few attempts to capture it whole. Indeed only two of our really notable modern novelists have had the intention: Thomas Wolfe and John Dos Passos. And both attempts were seriously vitiated—Wolfe's by his failures of discipline, and by the fact that by the time he had truly discovered his purpose he was soon to die, Dos Passos' by the fact that *USA* was written out of the depths of a depression, and by a bitter man, and therefore presents a more sour, or jaundiced view of the country than most people are willing to accept.

Dos Passos did, however, try impressionistically to capture the country. For instance:

> U.S.A. is the slice of a continent. U.S.A. is a group of holding companies, some aggregations of trade unions, a set of laws bound

> in calf, a radio network, a chain of moving picture theatres, a column of stock-quotations rubbed out and written in by a Western Union boy on a blackboard, a public-library full of old newspapers and dogeared history-books with protests scrawled on the margins in pencil. U.S.A. is the world's greatest rivervalley fringed with mountains and hills. U.S.A. is a set of bigmouthed officials with too many bankaccounts. U.S.A. is a lot of men buried in their uniforms in Arlington Cemetery. U.S.A. is the letters at the end of an address when you are away from home. But mostly U.S.A. is the speech of the people.

That, finally, is a very indirect way of putting my point: a true and rounded picture of America cannot be found in contemporary fiction if only because America is everyplace and no place. It is in our goods, and our arts, and our land and people. In Emerson's essays and Charles Saunders Pierce and Norman Vincent Peale; in our courthouses and ranch-houses and churches; in ginmills and cotton mills and General Mills; in Samuel Barber and Joe the barber and John Cameron Swazey; in the Declaration of Independence and Pogo and Peanuts and Little Orphan Annie; in pool halls and dance halls and halls of ivy and Robert Hall's—everywhere and nowhere.

Well, this is approximately and very protractedly what I wrote in a final report to the U.S.I.S., composed on my bed of pain, concerning my experience in India. "The idea that serious modern American literature is an accurate and valuable reflection of the country that produced it needs careful reexamination": my very, professorial words, as I recall them. But although I do know that a good many Indian universities now offer work in American literature where only one did when several others and I were promoting the cause, I don't know that anyone ever did really read that report. And so, frustrated for an audience, I have submitted you to my sentiments. It is nice that *someone* had to listen and I thank you for doing so.

1963

The Essential Philip Young

Books

Ernest Hemingway (New York: Rinehart & Co., 1952).
Ernest Hemingway: A Reconsideration (University Park: The Pennsylvania State University Press, 1966).
The Hemingway Manuscripts: An Inventory, with Charles W. Mann (University Park: The Pennsylvania State University Press, 1969).
Three Bags Full: Essays in American Fiction (New York: Harcourt Brace Jovanovich, 1972).
Revolutionary Ladies (New York: Alfred A. Knopf, 1977).
Hawthorne's Secret: An Un-Told Tale (Boston: David R. Godine, 1984).
The Private Melville (University Park: The Pennsylvania State University Press, 1993).

Introductions

The House of the Seven Gables by Nathaniel Hawthorne (New York: Rinehart and Co., 1957). Reprinted as "Hawthorne's *Gables* unGarbled" in *Three Bags Full.*
Typee by Herman Melville (London: Cassell & Co., 1967). Reprinted as "Melville's Eden, or *Typee* Recharted" in *Three Bags Full.*
By-Line: Ernest Hemingway (London: William Collins Sons, 1968).
The Nick Adams Stories by Ernest Hemingway (New York: Charles Scribner's Sons, 1972).

Pamphlet

Ernest Hemingway (Minneapolis: University of Minnesota Press, 1959).

Essays

"The Earlier Psychologists and Poe," *American Literature* 22 (January 1951), 442-54.
"Scott Fitzgerald's *Waste Land,*" *Kansas Magazine* (1956), 73-77.
"A New England Hagiography," *Sewanee Review* 65 (Spring 1957), 326-31.
"American Poetry in the Twentieth Century," *Indian Literature* 1 (Fall 1957), 36-52.
"Fallen From Time: The Mythic Rip Van Winkle," *Kenyon Review* 22 (Autumn 1960), 547-73. Reprinted in *Three Bags Full.*
"The Dungeon of the Novel," *Kenyon Review* 24 (Winter 1962), 177-83.

"The Mother of Us All: Pocahontas Reconsidered," *Kenyon Review* 24 (Summer 1962), 391-415. Reprinted in *Three Bags Full.*

"The Assumptions of Literature," *College English* 24 (February 1963), 352-57.

"American Fiction and American Life," *Journal of General Education* 15 (July 1963), 109-23. Reprinted in *Three Bags Full.*

"The End of Compendium Reviewing," *Kenyon Review* 26 (Fall 1964), 676-97. Reprinted in *Three Bags Full.*

"Hawthorne and a Hundred Years: A Report from the Academy," *Kenyon Review* 27 (Spring 1965), 215-32. Reprinted as "Centennial, or The Hawthorne Caper" in *Three Bags Full.*

"Hemingway and Me: A Rather Long Story," *Kenyon Review* 28 (January 1966), 15-37. Reprinted in *Ernest Hemingway: A Reconsideration* and *Three Bags Full.*

"On Dismembering Hemingway," *Atlantic Monthly* 218 (August 1966), 45-49. Reprinted as "I Dismember Papa" in *Three Bags Full.*

"Comment [Re-Appraisal as Agony, or the Dungeon Aflame]," *Kenyon Review* 28 (September 1966), 567-73.

"To Have Not: Tough Luck," *Tough Guy Writers of the Thirties,* ed. David Madden (Carbondale: Southern Illinois Press, 1968), 42-50.

"In the Vault with Hemingway," *New York Times Book Review,* 29 September 1968, 2, 28. Reprinted as "Locked in the Vault" in *Three Bags Full.*

"Fitzgerald's *Sun Also Rises:* Notes and Comment," with Charles W. Mann, *Fitzgerald/Hemingway Annual* (1970), 1-13.

"Big World Out There: The Nick Adams Stories," *Novel: A Forum on Fiction* 6 (Fall 1972), 5-19.

"For Malcolm Cowley: Critic, Poet, 1898-," *Southern Review* 9 (Autumn 1973), 778-96.

"The Story of the Missing Man," in *Directions in Literary Criticism,* ed. Stanley Weintraub and Philip Young (University Park: The Pennsylvania State University Press, 1973), 143-59.

"Hemingway's Manuscripts: The Vault Reconsidered," *Studies in American Fiction* 2 (Spring 1974), 3-11.

"Posthumous Hemingway, and Nicholas Adams," in *Hemingway In Our Time,* ed. R. Astro and J. Benson (Corvallis: Oregon State University Press, 1974), 13-25.

"In Search of a Lost Generation," *Kansas Quarterly* 7 (Fall 1975), 127-33.

"Iowa City, and After," *Teacher and Critic: Essays By and About Austin Warren,* ed. Myron Simons and Harvey Gross (Los Angeles: Plantin Press, 1976), 93-97.

"Hemingway Papers, Occasional Thoughts," *College Literature* 7 (Fall 1980), 310-18.

"Born Decadent: The American Novel and Charles Brockden Brown," *The Southern Review* 17 (Summer 1981), 501-19.

"Hemingway: the Writer in Decline," *Hemingway: A Revaluation,* ed. Donald R. Noble (Troy, NY: Whitson Publishing Co., 1983), 225-40.

" 'First American Novel': *The Power of Sympathy,* In Place," *College Literature* 11 (May 1984), 115-24.

"One Man's Apple," State College *Town & Gown* 20 (November 1985), 26-34.

"Small World: Emerson, Longfellow, and Melville's Secret Sister," *The New England Quarterly* 60 (September 1987), 382-402. Reprinted as "History of a Secret Sister" in *The Private Melville.*

"Melville's Last Good-Bye: 'Daniel Orme,' " *Studies in American Fiction* 16.1 (Spring 1988), 1-11. Reprinted in *The Private Melville.*

"Melville in the Berkshire Bishopric: 'The Lightning-Rod Man,' " *College Literature* XVI, 3 (Fall 1989), 201-10. Reprinted as "Intentional Grounding: 'The Lightning-Rod' " in *The Private Melville.*

"These Be Thy Gods, O Ahab!" *Studies in the American Renaissance: 1990,* ed. Joel Myerson (Charlottesville: University Press of Virginia, 1990), 329-40. Reprinted in *The Private Melville.*

"Experimental Melville: 'Cockeye-Doodle-Dee!' " *American Transcendental Quarterly* IV, 4 (December 1990), 343-51. Reprinted in *The Private Melville.*

Acknowledgments

"Fallen from Time: The Mythic Rip Van Winkle"
First published in *The Kenyon Review,* Autumn 1960, OS, vol. 22.4. Copyright *The Kenyon Review.*

"The Mother of Us All: Pocahontas"
First published in *The Kenyon Review,* Summer 1962, OS, vol. 24.3. Copyright *The Kenyon Review.*

"The Story of the Missing Man"
First published in *Directions in Literary Criticism,* ed., Stanley Weintraub and Philip Young (The Pennsylvania State University Press, 1973), 143–59.

"Hemingway and Me: A Rather Long Story"
First published in *The Kenyon Review,* January 1966, OS, vol. 28.1. Copyright *The Kenyon Review.*

"To Have Not: Tough Luck"
First published in *Tough Guy Writers of the Thirties,* ed. David Madden (Carbondale and Edwardsville: Southern Illinois University Press, 1968), 42–50. © 1968 by Southern Illinois University Press.

"Big World Out There: The Nick Adams Stories"
First published in *NOVEL: A Forum on Fiction,* vol. 6, no. 1, Fall 1972. Copyright NOVEL Corp. © 1972. Reprinted with permission.

"Hemingway's Manuscripts: The Vault Reconsidered"
First published in *Studies in American Fiction* 2 (Spring 1974).

"Hemingway Papers, Occasional Thoughts"
First published in *College Literature* 7 (Fall 1980).

"Hemingway: The Writer in Decline"
First published in *Hemingway: A Reevaluation,* ed. Donald R. Noble (Troy, N.Y.: Whitston Publishing Co., 1983), 225–40.

"The Assumptions of Literature"
First published in *College English* 24 (February 1963).

"The Earlier Psychologists and Poe"
First published in *American Literature* 22, no. 4 (January 1951), 442–54. Copyright 1951, Duke University Press. All rights reserved. Reprinted with permission.

Acknowledgments

"Hawthorne's Secret: Fathers and Sons and Lovers"
First published in *Hawthorne's Secret: An Un-Told Tale* (Boston: David R. Godine, 1984), 89-147.

"In Search of a Lost Generation"
First published in *Kansas Quarterly* 7 (Fall 1975).

"The Lost Generation and Yours"
(previously unpublished)

"Scott Fitzgerald's Wasteland"
First published in *Kansas Magazine,* 1956.

"Iowa City, and After"
First published in *Teacher and Critic: Essays By and About Austin Warren,* ed. Myron Simon and Harvey Gross (Los Angeles: Plantin Press, 1976), 93-97.

"American Poetry in the Twentieth Century"
First published in *Indian Literature* 1 (Fall 1957).

"One Man's Apple"

"American Fiction, American Life"
First published in *Journal of General Education* 15 (July 1963).

Index

Index

Index